THREE MEN
OF BOSTON

Also by John R. Galvin

THE MINUTE MEN: The First Fight:
Myths and Realities of the American Revolution

THREE MEN OF BOSTON

John R. Galvin

BRASSEY'S

Washington • London

First trade paperback edition 1997

Brassey's Editorial Offices: Brassey's Order Department:
22883 Quicksilver Drive   P.O. Box 960
Dulles, Virginia 20166   Herndon, Virginia 20172

Brassey's books are available at special discounts for bulk purchases for sales promotions, premiums, fund-raising, or educational use.

Library of Congress Cataloging-in-Publication Data

Galvin, John R., 1929–
      Three men of Boston : leadership and conflict at the start of
      the American Revolution / John R. Galvin — 1st ed.
           p.   cm.
      Originally published: New York: T.Y. Crowell, 1976.
      Includes bibliographical references and index.
      ISBN 1-57488-111-6 (alk. paper)
           1. Hutchinson, Thomas, 1711–1780. 2. Otis, James,
1725–1783. 3. Adams, Samuel, 1722–1803. 4. United States—History—
Revolution, 1775–1783—Causes.   I. Title.
E302.5.G34   1997
973.3'11'0922—dc20   96-34180
                                                  CIP

10 9 8 7 6 5 4 3 2 1

for
Jo and Jo
who never knew each other
but who (kind gods) are
so much alike

ACKNOWLEDGMENTS

There is a temptation to provide a rollcall of helpful individuals and institutions, but I will avoid it and hope instead that the quality of research will meet the expectations of the friends I have made in the last six years of immersion in the Boston scene of 1760–1775. Some thanks, however, must go on record. Dean Edmund Gullion gave me a place to work at the Fletcher School. Bernard Bailyn of Harvard provided more encouragement than he knows, generously discussing his own ongoing work on Hutchinson. Leo Flaherty of the Massachusetts State House proved again to be the most responsive of all archivists. Bill Ward and Paul Fargis took me in at Crowell, and Cynthia Vartan, my editor, showed her patience and good sense. I owe most to the counsel and assistance of my father, John J. Galvin, who understands not only the pulse of history but also that of the human heart.

 # An AUSA Institute of Land Warfare Book

The Association of the United States Army, or AUSA, was founded in 1950 as a nonprofit organization dedicated to education concerning the role of the U.S. Army, to providing material for military professional development, and to the promotion of proper recognition and appreciation of the profession of arms. Its constituencies include those who serve in the Army today, including Army National Guard, Army Reserve, and Army civilians, the retirees and veterans who have served in the past, and all their families. A large number of public-minded citizens and business leaders are also an important constituency. The Association seeks to educate the public, elected and appointed officials, and leaders of the defense industry on crucial issues involving the adequacy of our national defense, particularly those issues affecting land warfare.

In 1988, AUSA established within its existing organization a new entity known as the Institute of Land Warfare. ILW's mission is to extend the educational work of AUSA by sponsoring a wide range of publications, to include books, monographs, and essays on key defense issues, as well as workshops, symposia, and since 1992, a television series. Among the volumes chosen as "An AUSA Institute of Land Warfare Book" are both new texts and reprints of titles of enduring value. Topics include history, policy issues, strategy, and tactics. Publication as an AUSA Book does not indicate that the Association of the United States Army and the publisher agree with everything in the book but does suggest that AUSA and the publisher believe the book will stimulate the thinking of AUSA members and others concerned about important defense-related issues.

CONTENTS

Contents

FOREWORD

Of all the learned disciplines, history is unique in the intellectual demands that it makes of its practitioners. It requires the rigor of science and the refinement of art. When it is done well, historical thinking is both an exercise in logic and an effort of imagination.

At the same time, the study of history also engages another and very special form of intelligence that English-speaking people call judgement. The French have a happier phrase for this faculty of thought. They call it *bon sens*. The German words are less graceful but more exact: *Urteilskraft, Beurteilungskraft, Verstand, Weisheit*. These Teutonic terms bring out four components of judgment: discernment, critical skills, understanding, and wisdom.

Whatever we call it, judgment is a cerebral process that differs very much from other kinds of thinking. Some people have excellent judgment but are not very good at reasoning or imagining. Others are highly creative and strong in the manipulation of abstraction but have weak powers of judgment—as the minutes of any college faculty will attest.

Good judgment is difficult to define, but many of us know it when we see it. It is impossible to teach judgment by rote or rule, but most of us learn more about it every day. A lucky few are born with the gift of judgment, but nearly everyone gains it the hard way—by trial and error, by the slow acquisition of knowledge, and especially by the painful test of experience.

There is a major problem here for the practice of history and also an opportunity for scholars such as John Galvin. Today most professional historians follow the same narrow career path. They begin with an undergraduate major in history. Then they advance to graduate training in history. Finally, they proceed to a faculty appointment in history and hold it until their retirement.

In this process, much has been gained by the rigor of professional preparation, but something important has been lost. As historians have become more academic, they have become more narrow in their range of experience. As a consequence, academic historians are better at reasoning than they used to be, but they are not so good at judging, partly because their range of personal experience is limited.

All of this gives a special importance to the scholarship of John Galvin. He has come to the study of history by a different route and brings with him a wealth of experience about the world.

John Galvin is a soldier. He graduated from West Point in 1954. He commanded a company of paratroopers in the 101st Airborne Division, served as a Ranger advisor to the Colombian army, returned to West Point as a teacher of English, and took a master's degree in history at Columbia University in 1962. Later he served in Vietnam and won many personal decorations, among them the Silver Star, Legion of Merit, Distinguished Flying Cross, Bronze Star, Soldier's Medal, and the Combat Infantryman's Badge. After command and staff jobs, he rose to the command of the 24th Infantry Division and then of the VII Corps in Germany. In 1987 he was promoted to full general and became Supreme Allied Commander in Europe. Since his retirement from the army he has taken on a new job as dean of the Fletcher School of Law and Diplomacy at Tufts University.

Along the way, John Galvin has also pursued another career as an historian. He has published three works on the American Revolution. In all of them, he made important contributions by engaging qualities of judgement that were strengthened by his breadth of experience.

The first major work was *The Minute Men*, originally published in 1967. Mostly it is a history of the day of Lexington and Concord; twenty of its twenty-nine chapters are about the fighting on April 19, 1775. His history of Lexington and Concord is still in print and selling well, thirty years after it first appeared. Its continuing strength is in large part a function of John Galvin's experience and judgment. Many other historians have read the documents with close attention. John Galvin did that and something more. In the expression of Field Marshal Bernard Montgomery, he also read the battle itself, with a soldier's eye. His knowledge of military organization, his training in tactics, his sensitivity to terrain, and his experience of command informed his judgment and have enlarged our understanding of what happened at Lexington and Concord.

Before John Galvin's book appeared, most histories of Lexington and Concord centered on individual American militia companies. John Galvin was the first historian to contribute a larger understanding of the regimental command-structure of the militia, and to recognize the role of field-grade officers. He understood more clearly than most that the American resistance on April 19 was not merely a spontaneous rising of individual farmers but a conflict between military units, in which command decisions were important, and individual commanders, who repeatedly made careful and conscious use of terrain and topography in unit engagements. He brought out the role of leadership in the American brigadier William Heath and other officers. All of this transformed our historical understanding of what happened on April 19. It did so by the exercise of judgment, based upon experience.

In 1976, John Galvin published *Three Men of Boston*, a study of the coming of the American Revolution, centered mainly on Thomas Hutchinson, James Otis, and Samuel Adams. These three protagonists all emerge from the pages of John Galvin's work as deeply interesting in the eighteenth-century sense. All were internally riven by cross purposes of high complexity. The Loyalist leader Thomas Hutchinson appears as a man of high courage, a jurist who was deeply sympathetic to the poor defendants who appeared in his court, and a governor who was driven both by loyalty to the Crown and by an abiding love of his native Massachusetts.

The portrait of James Otis is even more complex—a man possessed by a radical belief in liberty and at the same time by "a fanatically conservative love of order, harmony, and organizational power." Otis dedicated his life to the rule of reason. At the same time he was consumed by passions and even his rages.

The third protagonist, Samuel Adams, is yet more complex. John Galvin interprets him as a man of both the past and the future, a child of the early Puritans and a father of the modern republic; a religious visionary with a sense of humor and irony; a rigid idealist and a highly skilled political tactician.

The book gives much attention to the character of these three men, but it is not merely a set of separate portraits. The work centers on the interplay of personality, principle, and what the author calls

the "cross-exchange of thought." It is about how three men of the
world dealt with one another and the play of contingency in those
relationships. *Three Men of Boston* might be thought of as a braided
narrative, with three tightly interwoven strands.

In John Galvin's reading of these men and events, one finds a quality of judgment that comes from broad experience. The author's
understanding of how leaders behave has derived from his own experience of leadership. His respect for the importance of individual
leaders, particular events, and specific choices is informed by his own
participation in events.

As such, *Three Men of Boston* is very different from much academic
historiography that came off the press at the same time. It is interesting to compare John Galvin's work with an academic monograph on
a closely related topic, published at about the same time, John
Waters's *The Otis Family* (1968, 1975). Both are very good books, but
they are good in different ways. Waters gives us a social history of the
Otis family in the context of their community. The result is strong on
cultural inheritance and social structure. John Galvin's work has a different strength. While not neglecting the social context, *Three Men of
Boston* is strong on the interplay of individual character, thought,
action, and contingency.

When this book first appeared, the new social history was flourish-
ing in academic monographs such as those of John Waters. Today,
historical scholarship is developing in a different direction. It is moving toward the integration of social and political history, toward a
linkage of structure and event, toward a reunion of process and contingency. As we try to link these two historical genres, John Galvin's
work becomes important not only for what it tells us about the
American Revolution but also for what it teaches us about history
itself. It is a pleasure to welcome it into print again. I hope that others will read it with understanding and reflect on the importance of
judgment and experience in the world.

DAVID HACKETT FISCHER

INTRODUCTION

What do we mean by the Revolution? The war? That was no
part of the Revolution. It was only an effect and consequence
of it. The Revolution was in the minds of the people, and this
was effected, from 1760 to 1775, in the course of fifteen years
before a drop of blood was drawn at Lexington.

JOHN ADAMS TO THOMAS JEFFERSON, 1815

This book might be thought to stand alone, but it has a companion. My first writing of any length was *The Minute Men*, a book that
contested a number of myths and misconceptions surrounding the
battles of Lexington and Concord, that extraordinary, evocative, and
so much misunderstood event that opened the great era of the
Revolution and subsequent rise of the United States of America. It
was during my research for that book in the archives of Massachusetts
towns that I found, over and over again in the old records, the labored
writing of unlettered clerks recording what had been said at town
meetings, the first signs of the answer to a question that had fascinat-
ed me for some time: why did the American Revolution begin n
Massachusetts rather than in bustling and very political New York, or
in fiery Patrick Henry's Virginia, or in Pennsylvania, or in any of the
other colonies along the east coast of North America? I began to see
not just the clash of ideas and personalities, the partisan infighting
between the American extensions of London's Tory and Whig factions, the disgruntlement of hard-pressed merchants over questions of
trade and taxes, and the sensing of the burgeoning strength in these
colonies that were outgrowing the mother country. There was something more. In the minds of common people, the ideals and values
that have come to be the guiding principles of a giant nation were
being recognized, articulated, and presented as a challenge to the old

order. Nowhere was this challenge pressed harder than in Massachusetts, where three individuals stand out in history as more responsible than all the others for the chain of events that led to war. They were: Thomas Hutchinson, one of the most accomplished sons of Massachusetts, gentleman, merchant, historian, and consummate politician, whose ambition to govern Massachusetts in the service of the Crown would make him an exile; James Otis, writer, political theorist, and member of the Boston bar, who will always be in the first handful of great American lawyers, whose strange personal mix of ingredients eventually would destroy him; and Samuel Adams, failed merchant, failed tax collector, obscure local politician, who became the most proficient political writer and successful political manipulator of the American Revolution.

Thomas Hutchinson was two months short of twelve years old when he went to Harvard, where one of his "deepest impressions" occurred the day he very uncharacteristically slipped a pony of Greek into a Latin book which he was supposed to translate in class. His instructor noted his cheating and said simply, "*A te non expectave*"[1]—"I did not expect that of you"—punishment enough for a young man who had an extraordinary respect for authority. Hutchinson's most salient characteristic—unmistakable—was his intellectual and physical courage: he could not be intimidated by an opposing idea or an angry mob, a point that he confirmed many times in the later hectic years. Though autocratic, he was also a humanitarian with strong sympathies for the poor and unfortunate whom he dealt with as a judge. He was an elitist; politics to him was a struggle to keep power in the hands of men who were bred to it by class, education, and inclination, men who could be depended on to fend off the attempts of the mob and its leaders to push at the pillars of a carefully built political structure.

Thomas Hutchinson's great mistake was to give battle against James Otis and Samuel Adams in the newspapers. In addition to his heavy schedule in the positions of political leadership that he constantly occupied during this period, Hutchinson was writing what would become a comprehensive, three-volume *History of the Colony and Province of Massachusetts-Bay*. He was proud of his skills as an historian and he felt that his years of research had given him a special and perhaps unique understanding of the saga of his native colony. Smarting at the challenge of Otis and Adams, he took to the pages of the Boston press himself, encouraging his friends to do the same. The newspaper war, beginning in 1763 and continuing into the Revolution more than a decade later, brought a new focus on the rights of the colonists and greatly heightened the efforts of Otis and Adams to sustain a running argument against the supporters of strong British control and in favor of those who wanted to take steps in the direction of independence.

Samuel's cousin John Adams emphatically insisted that Otis was in fact the essential figure in leading the colonies toward independence, the creator of the monumental tracts that supported not only the Adamses but Thomas Paine and a long list of other American political activists. Nonetheless, Otis unfortunately remains shadowy, wraithlike, in history; he cannot be adequately comprehended, it seems, without Sam Adams by his side, and much of this book is an attempt to understand why this is so. James Otis was not a single personality but rather two tragically irreconcilable men. One side of him yearned for a political existence in which the rules were simple, where even the King had to bend to the undeniable force of reason. This side of Otis could resign his lucrative and prestigious government post and later sacrifice his law practice and his health in an effort to stop political activities he saw as unconstitutional, or could challenge Parliament with his own personal view of the correctness of a law and then fail dramatically to understand why he should be called a radical. The other side of Otis possessed a fanatically conservative love of order, harmony, and organizational power, sublimated in the symbol of Britannia. This Otis wrote a book on Latin and another on Greek prosody, praised Parliament as supreme, constantly professed undying allegiance to the King (and was nearly killed in a brawl when someone questioned his loyalty). An opponent of Otis thought him "designed by nature for a genius, but it seemed as if by the impetuosity of his passions he had wrested himself out of her hands before she had completed her work, for his life seemed to be all eccentricity."[2]

If Otis was misunderstood, Samuel Adams was a visitor from another epoch, an antique man with a primal vision unblemished and undaunted by the modern world. Stiff, idealistic, unyielding, he was seen as closer to Cato the Elder than to men of his own time. Aiming at first for the ministry, he changed his mind at Harvard when political history absorbed his interest, but he never lost a deep religious vision of a bleak puritanism that often made him seem emotionless in his political writings and even in his personal letters (in fact, he possessed an exquisite ironic wit that, fortunately for us, he could not keep below the surface of his serious work). Once discovered for what it is, his stiff and wry humor, deeply intellectual and complex, enlivens and sharpens the sting of the political repartee which made him famous on both sides of the Atlantic—so much so that, when John Adams first went to his ambassadorial post in France, he was forced to explain that he was not *the* Adams.[3]Hutchinson correctly named him as the "first who asserted the independency of the colonies," and it is interesting that the earliest writing that can be attributed with certainty to Adams, the 1764 instructions to Boston's four representatives to the provincial assembly, contains a call for a united front in America to challenge Parliament on the new tax laws.

Otis and Sam Adams, an unlikely pair, accomplished together what neither could have done alone. Otis was initially too ambivalent and later too disorganized to have carried the banner of revolution without Adams. On the other hand, Samuel Adams depended on Otis and derived his own conceptual political thought from him, but gradually controlled the actions that led to the first armed conflict of the American Revolution. Otis has had no "definitive" biographer since 1823, Adams is still best presented by the nineteenth-century volumes of his grandson William Wells, and only Bernard Bailyn has tried to resurrect Hutchinson. The lives of these three men of Boston are so uniquely intertwined that each, by himself, is only part of the story of those crucial fifteen years.

PART I

The British Apply Pressure

In the mid-eighteenth century the relentless centrifugal forces that were pulling at the burgeoning British Empire opened a small but dangerous crack: the American port town of Boston became progressively alienated and unwilling to play its part in a world picture created by the empire's administration in London. From the beginning it was clear to thinking men on both sides of the Atlantic that the widening crack might be the sign, the warning, of an unprecedented upheaval.

Perhaps the flow of events was inevitable; it was only a matter of time before some new political arrangement would have to develop from the American colonial organization. Populations were climbing on the seacoast and the colonists were pushing westward, opening the vast potentialities that lay inland. Great questions were answered, unfortunately, by men in London who saw a global problem through the eyes of a local politician, who determinedly maintained that Massachusetts Bay was no more than another borough.

The most effective and constant force pushing the American colonies along the road to revolution after 1760 was a short-sighted and turbulent British Parliament that turned over its leadership eight times in the nine years between 1761 and 1770. In general, mercantile interests ruled the day and left little room for statesmanship. Still, the inevitable shifting of power could have taken many forms. Why it became an early, violent, and permanent separation of America from the empire rather than any of the other possible adjustments is in great part a question that can be answered only in a biographical vignette involving the men who found themselves precisely at the spot where the crack appeared. And though men are not able to influence the course of events as much as they sometimes think they can, nevertheless it is often a certain few of them who bear the pressures, who make the decisions, who articulate the theories, and who try to persuade or force their fellow beings into particular choices among the unknown paths ahead.

1

The New Chief Justice

August 1760–January 1761

> The Lieutenant Governor is nowhere expressly charged by me with acting dishonorably, as he seems to suppose. My whole argument will as incontestably follow upon his Honor's state of facts as from mine. 'Tis but this, namely, that *a seat, or imagined cause of offense given my father, might not to be considered as the sole spring and motive of all my public conduct.*
>
> JAMES OTIS, 1763

IN THE HEART OF BOSTON, around the skirts of Beacon Hill, a hundred structures built before the Revolution still stand, some gaunt and gnarled and hardy, some frail and fast-dissolving. The old relics are surrounded by asphalt now and shadowed by tall concrete structures, for the landscape has changed drastically—even the hills of Boston have disappeared, nibbled away in a million dumpcart loads and deposited to build new land on the mud flats east and west of the city's old peninsular neck. Though most of ancient Boston is gone, one can still feel the old town in momentary vignettes that harken back to earlier days. The docks are farther out now, but the taps and knocks and creakings of ships at anchor recall the old harbor, where the fogs and the salty chill of the Atlantic easterlies are ever the same. The same streets still wind up from the water to the hustle of the market at Faneuil Hall and on to Beacon Hill, conjurers of spirits long gone, of people who stood in the archways on gray days and watched the rain in the cobblestoned streets or strolled the slanted sweep of the Common on bright mornings.

Called Shawmut by the Indians and Blackstone's Neck[1] by the first settlers, Boston in 1760 was still almost an island, with little room for its 1,600 houses. The streets were narrow and winding, with front doorsteps jutting into the flow of traffic. Openings for cellar stairways were a hazard; a stranger walking at night was "in continual danger of falling into a victualling cellar or gin shop, perhaps with a broken limb." As the principal port of the New England coast, Boston was a seafaring, shipbuilding town, with its mechanics and tradesmen facing to the sea—shipwrights, ropewalkers, sail lofters, lumbermen, wagoners, fishermen. It was also a merchant's town. Very little merchandise was made there, because the British colonial laws did not permit it, but much passed through. It was a slave-trading town, a rum-making town, a sailor's town. There have been times in history when a place, for countless reasons, became the matrix, the incubator, however imperfect, for social or political or artistic creation, as Dublin may have been for Joyce or as Elizabethan London was for Jonson and Shakespeare. These places have to be small enough for all the members of a group to be constantly forced to interact, but also large enough to sustain the goals, the obstacles, and the sustenance for the movement. Boston was such a place. It provided a mixing place for the cosmopolitanism and social diversity of a busy ocean port, the political factionism of a colonial capital city, and, with Harvard across the river, the intellectual energy of a university town. It had several well-established newspapers and a score of taverns and coffeehouses which served as informal offices and conference rooms for businessmen and politicians. In a heyday of clubs, guilds, societies, and sodalities, the town spawned more than its share of special-interest organizations, among them the Sons of Liberty, the Loyal Nine, the Merchants' Society, and the Caucus Club, all of which had the capability to influence the march of events. In Boston in 1760 a man could convince himself that he knew everyone worth knowing in town.

The port was booming and busy, even after the end of the

Seven Years' War and the loss of many government contracts. The waterfront was lined with scores of fat warehouses. Trade with the West Indies provided molasses for 60 Massachusetts rum distilleries. Lumber and fish paid for the molasses, while the rum went to England for manufactured goods (with a substantial proportion siphoned off for use in the slave trade). Evasion of customs was a simple matter, and smuggling was rampant. The British government had not been willing to create the extensive administrative system needed to police the ports and sea lanes; instead, the port was run by a token force of minor officials who often looked the other way simply to keep from being overwhelmed by the volume of illicit trade. For this laxity many of them received due compensation from shipmasters and traders. In this manner business flourished, and every year 500 square-rigged ships sailed from Boston docks for Europe or the West Indies, while uncounted numbers of small coastal schooners transshipped cargoes throughout New England and to the southward. In addition, 130 whalers operated in the North and South Atlantic out of Boston and the other New England ports.

In contrast to crowded Boston, the rest of the province westward over the low, rolling hills and into the Connecticut Valley was a scattering of small farming settlements, self-sustaining and self-centered. By 1760 their fields had been worked for three, four, or even five generations, and the thousands of miles of low stone walls attested to the clearing and organizing that was now nearly complete. Talk at town meetings was of road repair and field surveys and schoolmasters' salaries; the town records of that era, in the labored handwriting of unlettered farmer-clerks, show the prototypical rural orderliness, stability, and exclusive interest in affairs within the bounds of the community. The province of Massachusetts Bay was prosperous; with 210,000 people in 200 towns, it was second only to Virginia with its population of a half million. These were halcyon days not only for Massachusetts Bay but for all the American colonies as economic prosperity continued unabated into the postwar years.

Seen from the other side of the ocean, the colonies were an entirely different picture to William Pitt and the Parliament of dying King George II. Staggered by the Seven Years' War, the British government faced a heavy national debt which had grown during the war years from 72 to 123 million pounds and was continuing its relentless climb. Much of this expense had gone to the fighting in North America, and from a London point of view the Americans were enjoying great advantages. Relieved of the threat of the French and protected by a string of military outposts running for 1,500 miles from the West Indies up the Mississippi and Ohio Valleys to the Great Lakes and on to Newfoundland, the colonies now reaped a fruitful postwar trade that paid practically nothing into the coffers of the Crown. The Lords of Trade, who by the logic of the times were in charge of colonial affairs, still saw the American colonies as, in essence, a string of trading posts. Pitt urged that the Americans be required to contribute at least some fraction of the cost of the war. After all, the colonies were enterprises originally founded with the idea that they would not only pay their own way but also would reimburse the home country for the many efforts expended on them.

Pitt emphasized that he called for no new taxes; this, he said, would not be necessary. He intended only to close the chinks in older tax laws which had not been enforced. In August 1760 he sent a letter to all of the governors in the American colonies, ordering them to "be aiding and assisting to the collectors and other officers of our admiralty and customs."[2] In other words, to put a stop to all smuggling and to make examples of those who were caught at it. Pitt's letter was the harbinger of a new attempt to increase Parliamentary control over the colonies, the first step on a long, hard road in which there would be no turning back. The force behind it—the force of empire—asserted itself in the simplistic commercial view of the colonies as controlled markets and sources of raw materials rather than as partners in trade. Parliament, ever more sensitive to American economic assertiveness, remained in virtual ignorance of what actually was going on across the Atlantic. London half-listened to a jumble of outdated, biased, and misinformed reports of the state of the colonies. The members pondered new ways to express their authority and to maintain the subservience of the colonies, blind to the obvious realities of their expansion and growth. After his letter to the governors, Pitt, sensing the void, ordered all customs officials to occupy in person their posts in America. Until this time most of them had stayed at home, accepted their salaries, and hired deputies to maintain a presence in the colonies. Headquarters for the revitalized customs operation was to be in the port of Boston. Serenely unaware of the impact that these changes would make, Parliament resolved to make America pay for itself.

Governor Thomas Pownall of Massachusetts was recalled,[3] and in his place came the bumbling and uncomprehending Francis Bernard, ex-governor of New Jersey, looking for a slightly better financial situation and some chance to assure comfortable sinecures for his sons. Bernard arrived in Boston in the summer of 1760. He was well aware of the town's reputation for smuggling, and he hoped that such activities would soon provide him the opportunity to receive his allotted one-third of all monies resulting from seizures of contraband. Incongruously enough, he assured London that there would be a long period of peace and quiet in Massachusetts, since he intended to base his administration on a solid bottom of unity and agreement between the main political elements.

Bernard had somehow achieved a reputation as a sensitive man with a scholarly cast of mind. He could, he used to say, recite all of Shakespeare by heart; he could write elegies in Latin and Greek.[4] Whatever scholarly or artistic abilities he possessed failed to show themselves in his extensive letters, which are those of a self-aggrandizing, heavy-handed, virtually characterless man whose major contribution to the history of the times is the comic relief which his writings and doings almost invariably provide.

In Boston, one young lawyer was unusually sensitive to indications of a change in customs procedures, although he did not fully understand the erosion of British authority in America. The thirty-five-year-old advocate general of the Vice-Admiralty Court in Boston was the Crown official most deeply involved in prosecuting customs violations. Already disgusted with the corruption he saw in the customs procedures and with the general incompetence that characterized Crown appointees, he found himself siding more and more often with the local traders, to whom he was naturally drawn as a member himself of a prominent merchant family. This was James Otis, whose father, Colonel James Otis, had long been a leader in the political and mercantile world of Massachusetts.

The younger man was now just coming into his own as a figure to be reckoned with in the province. Few individuals have captured more conflicting elements in a single body and mind, but this was to become apparent only with time. In physical appearrance James Otis passed for a provincial farmer, with a roundish face set on a short, thick neck and powerful shoulders. His bright eyes made his narrow smile appear friendly enough, but he had also the reserved, unyielding look that characterized the New England country yeoman. Behind his steady gaze there was a hint of tension; his movements were quick and catlike, as if his reflexes were too highly tuned. He always seemed to be waiting for something to happen. When his mind was at work, his body burned excess energy, muscles twitching in constant motor activity. Although his friends were kind enough to be careful of the way they said it, several of them had noticed already that Otis was a man who could not control himself well, either physically or mentally. There was some kind of strange inner fire: his masterful, restless mind ranged impatiently, punctuating his brilliant talk with occasional incoherences.[5]

He was a man of many interests. He had just published a linguistic study, *A Dissertation on Letters and the Principles of Harmony in Poetic and Prosaic Composition,* a critical analysis of style concerned not with English composition, but with Latin. The book, a derivative compilation, was praised by John Adams as an "exciting discovery of the laws of philology." Otis also had read the Greek poets and concluded they could not be fully enjoyed without a thorough knowledge of Greek prosody. He therefore wrote a companion book on Greek poetry and prose, "a work of profound learning and great labor," which remained unpublished for lack of proper typesetting, although it was circulated in manuscript.[6]

His attraction to political philosophy did not stop with his graduation from Harvard in 1743; he continued to read widely in the whole range of classic sources. These studies were not diminished by the hard work of a varied law practice; he was a leader in a field of active, competitive lawyers that included Benjamin Pratt, Edmund Trowbridge, Oxenbridge Thacher, and his own mentor, Jeremiah Gridley. As an apprentice to Gridley, he had quickly gained a reputation for voracious reading and an extraordinary retention of details of the law. In addition to his skills at the bar, his good humor and accessibility made him much admired and emulated by rising young lawyers such as Josiah Quincy and John Adams. Among his clients he could number the most influential merchant families in Boston—the Hancocks, the Vassals, the Hulls. His private practice had taken him as far afield as the Admiralty Court at Halifax, Nova Scotia, where he successfully defended merchants accused of piracy, receiving the highest fee paid to a Massachusetts lawyer up to that time.[7] Yet a few years earlier he had been forced to take in his shingle and close his small office in the town of Plymouth for lack of business, while other lawyers in the vicinity—including his father—prospered. There may have been something of the misanthrope in Otis at this period, or at least a greater liking for books than for people. At any rate, he found himself unwilling to suffer the tedious daily round of a country lawyer's life—the litigation for trespass, the paternity suits, the attachments of estates for nonpayment of small debts. Bored and stagnated by the lack of intellectual challenge, he decided to move to Boston to attack the more arcane problems of mercantile and Admiralty law.

His family's involvement[8] in the business world of the province kept him almost as occupied in Boston with trade as with the law. Colonel Otis had inherited a prosperous general store and trading post in Barnstable which he built into a wide-ranging enterprise, shipping and marketing goods as various as oysters, shingles, rum, wheat, and pork. Half a dozen ships were under his contract on voyages to the West Indies with white-oak lumber and fish to trade for molasses, salt, and money. Colonel Otis was also a subcontractor in the transatlantic trade, dealing in cloth, whalebone, rice, oils, flour, and fish. He kept no agent in Boston, relying instead on his son. Young James kept his father well informed of timely business opportunities, made trades and purchases for him, and generally supervised his Boston interests. As a consequence, he became part of the circle of merchants and traders, even though as an Admiralty attorney he was duty-bound to prosecute those who failed to obey the laws of trade. Socially James Otis had reinforced his ties to the Boston business world with his marriage to Ruth Cunningham, daughter of an important merchant. She was an intelligent and very pretty woman, heiress to a substantial fortune and possessing a mind of her own with a strongly conservative cast.

In Boston Otis also became involved in the business of town meetings and found it much to his liking. Within a few months he was a member of committees that brought him into working relationships with the ordinary people of the town, where his willingness to contribute his legal knowledge was much appreciated and where he found a greater interest in the doings of his fellow townsmen and a desire to serve them that had not been a part of his experience in Plymouth. Actually he was becoming a politician; more and more of his time went to town activities.

Otis' turn toward politics was almost unavoidable. His father had been a member of the Massachusetts House of Representatives for the past 15 years and was now Speaker of the House. Colonel Otis was also the head of the popular party, a loose alliance of rural agricultural interests in the province. The colonel had seen to it that Governor Pownall appointed his son justice of the peace for Suffolk County (which included Boston), and young Otis was as often his father's political assistant as he was his Boston business agent.

It was his role as political assistant to his father that turned James Otis toward the Town House one day in the second week of September 1760. He carried a letter from the colonel to the lieutenant governor, Thomas Hutchinson, asking a favor. The death of Stephen Sewall had left an opening on the Superior Court, and the colonel wanted to be the man who filled the empty seat. Only the day before, however, young Otis had heard that Hutchinson himself coveted the position.[9] At the Town House, Otis found the lieutenant governor at his desk.

Hutchinson was physically opposite to Otis. At forty-nine, he was slim and regal, with prominent nose and quiet, dark eyes that gave him a look of reserved aloofness. If Otis was compulsive and volatile, Hutchinson's deliberate composure, fixed expression, and quiet hands gave him an air of watchfulness.

Colonel Otis ruled the popular party, but Thomas Hutchinson was the other political boss of the colony. Governors had come and gone while Hutchinson consolidated the court party, the relatively small group of politicians who consistently supported the governor and the Crown, and who occupied all the important civil and military positions in the province. It had been suggested many times that a cure for the political ills of the colonies would be the establishment of an American nobility, and to a degree the elitist members of the court party, particularly Thomas Hutchinson, saw themselves as a rough parallel to the English House of Lords.

On that day Hutchinson had guessed the purpose of Otis' visit, but he was nonetheless surprised when Otis bluntly asked him if the rumor that he desired the justiceship was true.

Hutchinson was taken aback at this directness and gave "a general answer of . . . uncertain nature." Otis, encouraged, expanded on the reasons his father should have the position. Hutchinson listened although he already knew the story well.

Colonel Otis had been a strong supporter of Governor William Shirley's war policy, and in gratitude Shirley had promised to move him up to a seat on the Superior Court as soon as an opening appeared. This was nothing out of the ordinary. Otis was a well-known lawyer, which was considered a prerequisite as a matter of course. Although judges customarily were chosen from among members or ex-members of the council, this was not a formal requirement. Unfortunately for the colonel, when the death of Chief Justice Sewall provided a space on the bench, Shirley was no longer governor. Pownall, his successor, had renewed the promise to Otis, but he too was now gone, replaced by Bernard. It was the colonel's understanding, James Otis said, that the new governor would accept these previous arrangements concerning the justiceship now open—that the senior justice would now move up to replace Sewall, creating a vacant spot on the bench which could be filled by Colonel Otis.

There were, Hutchinson knew, many reasons why Colonel Otis might expect his help on this occasion. He and the colonel had served on Shirley's Committee of War as early as 1745, and they had worked together on a delegation to Casco Bay to make a settlement on territorial rights with the Maine Indians. Their "friendship of convenience" continued for years, and Hutchinson profited by it. When in 1747 he wrote and presented to the House a brilliant paper advocating the establishment of a "hard-money" economy in the province, Colonel Otis was his chief supporter, driving the legislation through the House and personally delivering it to the council. And it was the elder Otis who stopped a countermove in the paper-money lobby of Tyng and Allen in 1751, preserving the success Hutchinson had achieved. Over the next decade, Colonel Otis, often for his own reasons to be sure, was continually on Hutchinson's side of the fence.

In Hutchinson's mind, however, Colonel Otis was a peripheral figure who merited no special loyalty; he was a shrewd, canny, powerful, and unprincipled political manipulator. Hutchinson actually had little respect for Otis and three years earlier had moved to block him from a seat on the governor's council, commenting (in words that got back to the senior Otis) that the colonel "never did carry things while in the court by any merit but only by doing little low dirty things for Governor Shirley such as persons of worth refused to meddle with."[10]

Otis may have thought that a comradeship existed, but to Hutchinson the relationship was tempered by an overall concept of the realities of politics in the province and in the world: the most highly skilled and worthy men of the land pitted themselves in constant battle against the forces of decay, decline, sloth, corruption, and self-interest. Hutchinson's deepest conviction was that power and control belonged to an elite that by achieving excellence deserved the positions of trust. In that world Otis was an outsider.

Governors came from England one after the other. For 15 of his potentially most productive years, Hutchinson had served three as a deputy. He was convinced he knew the possibilities of the land and people better than any of them. But he also knew that a native of the colonies had little chance to receive the nomination to a governorship, although there had been a few instances in which men of the highest caliber had overcome the prejudice

of custom and precedence, in competition with London gentlemen of rank close to the Crown. Now in middle age, he wondered
whether his merits would ever be enough to place him in contention among the political maneuverers in London. He felt that
as an American he would be thought deserving of such consideration only on the basis of a very obvious series of successes in lesser
positions. His ambition to best his competitors by sheer hard
work and excellence gave him a determination that to his political opponents seemed a desire for power. Bostonians seized on
this pretentiousness and sobriquetted him "Summa Potestatis"[11]
—the "supreme power." Shortened to "Summa," the name stuck;
it fitted Hutchinson only too well.

Hutchinson did not see himself as the opportunist that he perceived Colonel Otis to be; in his mind the colonel was a man up
from the ranks, a self-taught lawyer who lacked education and
finesse and who stood ready to compromise with principle for
profit. In his answer to James Otis, therefore, Hutchinson was
able to sublimate his desire for the justiceship with his overall
political philosophy. Still, he found it very difficult to be direct in
this case:

> I told Mr. Otis the proposal to me was new and what I had not
> time to consider of, and expressed my doubts of my ability to
> give the country satisfaction. I said many civil things of his
> father, as I had done before and have since, and of the friendship
> there had been between us; but I must deny that I gave him any
> reason to suppose that I was determined to refuse the place, or
> that I promised to use my interest with the Governor that his
> father should be appointed.[12]

This was a careful answer, intended to hedge against the disappointment that Hutchinson knew would come, for he was certain
that, whatever the final decision, Governor Bernard would not
give the justiceship to Colonel Otis. In all the discussion—the
charges and countercharges—that followed this meeting, the pre-
cise wording of question and answer is forever lost. But the most
important part—the nature of the misunderstanding—is quite
clear: Otis believed Hutchinson had agreed to help his father.
As Otis said,

he assured me that he had no thought nor desire of the office, told me that some of his friends had indeed mentioned such a thing to him, but he had already engagement enough upon his hands; expressly declar'd he tho't Col. Otis had the best pretensions to be judge of that court, promised me his interest.[13]

As far as Otis was concerned, Hutchinson was his ally and would support Colonel Otis for the justiceship. As far as Hutchinson was concerned, he had been politely noncommittal. Thus Otis left his father's letter in Hutchinson's hands and departed on the most friendly terms with the lieutenant governor, convinced that he had succeeded in his mission and that only formalities now separated his father from the position he had coveted for 20 years.

Otis then went to see Andrew Oliver, the secretary of the province, with a letter from his father almost identical to the one he gave Hutchinson. Oliver, too, was encouraging. He would do his best to help. He suggested that Otis also speak to Charles Paxton, surveyor of customs. At Paxton's, Otis met the same good will and was advised to see the governor himself, since Paxton felt Bernard would not appoint a candidate who did not make personal application. Later in the day, Otis set out on horseback for Roxbury to see Bernard. On the way over the narrow causeway connecting Boston with the mainland, he was surprised to see Hutchinson and Paxton in a carriage returning to Boston. Later, at Bernard's home, he found a cool reception and no desire on the part of the governor to commit himself.

Ever since Justice Sewall's death, Governor Bernard had been deliberating on a replacement, and he would continue to do so for several weeks. His newness to Massachusetts politics did not blind him to the fact that there were two major candidates for the justiceship, representing factions he would have to deal with throughout his time as governor. As the leader and chief spokesman for a group united by the desire to see less Crown influence in the colony, especially with relation to trade, Otis loomed large among the possible obstacles to a peaceful reign. Hutchinson, on the other hand, strongly supported the prerogative and the court party, and was probably the only unofficial political leader more powerful than Otis. What decided Bernard, however, was not a comparison of the relative weights of the factions. He knew that his first significant act as governor would have to be the strengthening and execution of the dormant Molasses Act of 1733, in accordance with his orders from Pitt. He was aware that to a great extent his future rested on the outcome of this endeavor. The Lords of Trade and, in fact, all of Parliament watched Massachusetts, he thought, waiting to see what he as the new governor would be able to accomplish.

Bernard's ability to control trade through customs activities depended on the power of peremptory search warrants called "writs of assistance," giving customs officials the right to search for contraband items with or without permission of the owner. These writs had not constituted an aggravation in the past because they were not much used, but now they were sure to see greater service. Already he had heard murmurings that the writs would not go unchallenged and he had discussed the matter of enforcement with the Admiralty prosecutors, including young James Otis, who, Bernard thought, seemed more interested in the rights of smugglers than he was in the effective prosecution of Crown policy. Bernard had told him that he wanted to see a harder line of action against illegal trade and a greater effort to seize contraband and to convict smugglers. Since the new governor was a man who did not take lightly the monetary aspects of his office, he was quite aware there was much to be gained if only a portion of the goods illegally entering and leaving the province were confiscated—his salary of £1,000 per year could be substantially augmented. His share, he wrote, "if the authority of the customs house is maintained, would be worth reckoning." Under the present conditions, however, he had little hope of profit.[14]

The climate of the Superior Court with respect to the enforcement of customs laws—especially as related to searches and seizures—became one of Bernard's prime concerns. None of the present judges, in his opinion, combined respect for Crown policy with a determination to see it carried out. None of them had the personal prestige that would enable them to take strong action against the entrenched trading interests. Only one man of stature and power in Boston filled these requirements and had given evidence that he was convinced of the legality of writs of assistance and favored their extensive use to stop smuggling. That individual was Thomas Hutchinson. Judge Sewall, before his death, had "expressed great doubts" on the legality of the writs. It was important, Bernard convinced himself, to get someone who was not troubled by such doubts.

On November 13, after two months of deliberation, Governor Bernard announced his decision.[15] There could be no balancing, he said, between the two major candidates for the office. Instead of moving the senior member of the bench, Benjamin Lynde, to chief justice and nominating a new man to become the junior member, Bernard chose to appoint Thomas Hutchinson as chief justice of the Superior Court. When Bernard informed his deputy of the appointment, Hutchinson offered to step aside for Colonel Otis if Bernard felt it would save trouble, but he knew as well as anyone that this was only talk. Hutchinson in his quiet way had forced Bernard to a choice: either the court party's assistance in carrying out the new customs legislation, or the popular party's opposition and an unpredictable future. Bernard chose to adopt the quarrels of Hutchinson, and he would live to regret the day.[16]

Even with all their experience in political maneuvering, the Otises were stunned. They had been watching Bernard carefully, cultivating his support, since his arrival—and now he had moved away from them. Hutchinson's duplicity was quite clear: he promised to look after their request in order to forestall their efforts to attain the appointment, then he moved quickly to block the choice of Otis and to consolidate another powerful position within the confines of his own clan. He could now add this appointment to his list of offices: lieutenant governor, president of the council of the General Court, judge of probate in two different counties, and commander of Castle William, the fort controlling Boston harbor. Although the Otises continually sought additional political offices for family members and popular-party associates, no one in the province approached the scale at which Hutchinson had succeeded in garnering important positions to himself and his relatives.

The Otises also were astute enough to see the purpose behind the choice of Hutchinson—a strengthening of the attack against customs violations, which seemed to them prompted by an alliance of two evils: the desire of British Parliament and unscrupulous men within Massachusetts to dominate the colony and take away charter rights, and the greed of a petty and venal governor who saw profit in seizures of trading vessels. This was to them the first clear example of a turn of events that included the removal of the previous governor, Pownall (whose last act had been the approval of Colonel Otis as Speaker of the House, to offset the growing influence of Thomas Hutchinson). The province of Massachusetts and, for that matter, the rest of the American colonies were suffering persecution by a small group of influential men in the Crown government who sought to consolidate a tyrannical power, and Thomas Hutchinson now became the chief symbol of an evil plot. This was not an idiosyncratic thought, nor was James Otis alone in thinking it. John Adams, as a young bystander, said later that "every observing and thinking man knew that this appointment was made for the direct purpose of deciding this question [writs] in favor of the Crown."

Even in his own time there were differences of opinion about the forces that drew James Otis into the fiery furnace of Boston politics. Otis' enemies circulated a quotation, denied by him, that he had sworn "if his father was not appointed a Justice of the Superior Court he would set the province in a flame if he perished in the attempt." Bernard six years later said that James Otis had threatened him before the decision was made, stating that both the governor and lieutenant governor would "repent of it" if Colonel Otis did not get the appointment. The gossip of history has its grain of truth, and it is correct that James Otis never forgot this "betrayal."[17] Revenge was not the driving motive, however; the reality was that party lines now were drawn along matters of colonial policy. The court party was in support of new parliamentary restrictions on the colonies, and the popular party was opposed to them.

2

The Writs of Assistance

January–May 1761

> I will to my dying day oppose, with all the powers
> and faculties God has given me, all such instruments
> of slavery on the one hand and villainy on the other as
> this writ of assistance is. It appears to me (may it please
> your Honours) the worst instrument of arbitrary
> power, the most destructive of English liberty and the
> fundamental principles of the constitution that ever
> was found in an English law-book.
>
> JAMES OTIS before the Massachusetts Bay
> Superior Court, 1761

THOMAS HUTCHINSON ACCEPTED the post of chief justice of the
Superior Court on November 13, 1760, and James Otis immediately resigned as acting advocate general of the Admiralty Court.
For both men, these were decisions of deep significance. Hutchinson committed himself finally and unalterably to the support
of Crown policy, and Otis rejected any association with the
Crown. Although these were long-term, far-reaching moves, they
were made in the light of an immediate threat of cutting the lifeline of the colony—the triangular trade patterns that connected
Massachusetts with the West Indies and with Europe. The Boston merchants were demoralized by the harsh application of the
old, hitherto dormant Molasses Act. Four ships, including Boston

merchant and politician John Erving's brigantine, the *Sarah,* had been seized for customs violations and sold at auction, the first such seizures in 16 years. The penalties—loss of full cargo and ship—seemed harsh and unjust, and the practice of paying informers up to one-third of the value of the seizure created a network of spies and an atmosphere of intrigue. Hutchinson himself agreed that a realistic tax on molasses—one that would not damage the trade—would have to be less than three pence per gallon. The inordinately high rate of nine pence accounted for the long history of illegal trade, winked at by local officials and accepted by all under the age-old philosophy of ignoring unrealistic laws. Now the sudden enforcement of this twenty-year-old regulation threatened to close all the rum distilleries operating in Massachusetts. Molasses would be priced out of the market, and the cycle of trade that included many of the other businesses in the province would come to a halt.

In this mounting crisis some of the merchants turned to Otis. After all, who understood the legal aspects of the Boston business world better than he? As an insider, a member of a trading family, he knew the mind of the entrepreneur and the small shopkeeper, and as an informal commercial agent for his father as well as a leader in the Admiralty Court with ten years' experience at the bar he knew how to exercise the art of the possible. Otis had what the Boston merchants needed, and it was at their urging that he took the first tentative steps on the road to political leadership.

From his Admiralty experience, Otis knew that the newly enforced customs arrangement was already corrupt. The money resulting from sales of seized cargoes and ships was supposed to be split three ways—a third for the king (for use in the province), a third for the governor, and a third for the customs officials involved in the seizure. The king's share, however, was not going into the province coffers. It was being used to pay informers who assisted the customs men, although no authority for this expenditure existed in the laws. As Hutchinson later noted, "Mr. Otis, bred to the law, and at that time a practitioner in the courts, took the advantage of this irregularity." Otis saw that this was not only a chance for the merchants to discredit the customs men by proving they were acting illegally, but also an opportunity to cut down the amount of money going to the commissioners and the informers by forcing them to draw their pay from a single share. Most important, he could embarrass the Crown and the administration by haling the customs men into court and suing them for large sums of money—which is what he now proceeded to do.[1]

Acting on behalf of several merchants, Otis on December 17, 1760, petitioned the House of Representatives to authorize Treasurer Harrison Gray to sue the customs men for recovery of nearly £500 that had been paid to informers. Bernard attempted to block legal action by insisting that the province share belonged officially to the king and that he could not be sued except by the attorney general of Great Britain. The House, however, agreed with Otis and approved an action against the customs officials, but Otis still had the council to convince—and Hutchinson, as lieutenant governor, was a member of the council.

Hutchinson argued that the Admiralty Court had acted within its powers in allotting the money from seizures, but Otis insisted that the question could be resolved only by a trial. This argument prevailed, and Treasurer Gray went ahead with the province suit to recover £357 from Customs Commissioner Paxton as the part for which Paxton was responsible. There were months of legal maneuvers on both sides, in which the Inferior Court twice decided in favor of the province only to be reversed both times by the Superior Court, Hutchinson presiding. Otis lost his case, but in doing so he emerged as a champion of Boston business interests.

There were other gains. Otis publicly and emphatically had pointed out a case of government corruption and had given the governor no alternative but to defend the improper conduct by resorting to technicalities. Hutchinson in his role as Superior Court justice had ruled in favor of the governor and, in effect, condoned the corruption. It pleased Otis and the merchants immensely to succeed in blocking, at least temporarily, Bernard's attempts to squeeze more money out of the customs process. The fact that Otis lost the case against Paxton was, as everyone in town realized, immaterial.

Once committed against the customs organization, Otis was

determined to attack from every possible approach. While the action continued on the Paxton case, he turned to help John Erving, who by this time had paid £500 to regain possession of his brigantine, seized for running the customs. Otis convinced the merchant that the next step was to sue the customs men for trespass. Such a suit, he said, would take place in the inferior courts, where neither Hutchinson nor the Admiralty lawyers had any say. As Otis predicted, the courts found in favor of Erving, but the customs officials appealed to the Superior Court, where once again Otis saw his move frustrated by Hutchinson. Still, the victory for Hutchinson and the administration was a hollow one, since Otis had shown Boston that the Admiralty Court was at odds with the rest of the provincial legal system. By maneuvering the court into unpopular decisions, Otis helped create the general opinion that there was little justice to be gained at the hands of Admiralty law, which was politically influenced. In the minds of Bostonians he had associated the chief justice so closely with the Crown that every appeal he lost before Hutchinson's bench gained Otis new friends in town.[2]

These cases became, in effect, preliminary skirmishes before the main battle, in which Otis impressed the Boston merchants with his broad knowledge of Admiralty law and his willingness to challenge the administration. Then the event occurred which thrust him into the mainstream of American political action. King George II died on October 25, 1760; the news of his death reached Boston on December 27. The passing of the king meant that within six months all commissions and all official papers bearing his personal seal would have to be renewed under the new king, George III. In accordance with this law, the surveyor general of customs in North America, Thomas Lechmere of Boston, asked for a renewal of the writs of assistance, which were his authority to search for contraband.

These writs, of course, had been the principal source of trouble for the merchants, who had long contended they were being misused by the customs commissioners. The originals, issued under Charles II, permitted search and seizure of contraband only under specific strictures. The customs man had to present information under oath to show a high probability of smuggling before he could obtain the writ—and if he used it to search for goods, he had to be right; if he failed to turn up the contraband, he could be sued for trespass. These original writs, issued for a particular search and good for only one month, later were broadened to become licenses for searching any property, although Parliament never passed a law permitting this. Also, sheriffs could be called on to assist the customs men if necessary. In Massachusetts the writs were issued by the Superior Court, although, as in the case of the payment of money to informers, no specific legislation existed to authorize it.

Lechmere's request to renew the writs gave the Boston merchants the opening that they needed, and the leaders of the Merchants' Society decided to take the customs men back to court again. They did not at first choose Otis as their lawyer, even though he had been their most active defender; they wanted the brilliant Benjamin Pratt, an iron-willed man who lived in intense and continual pain from the crushed nerves of his amputated right leg. But Pratt, for his own reasons, declined to represent them, and the merchants then turned to Otis and to Oxenbridge Thacher. Both immediately accepted and worked as partners.

Otis and Thacher drew up a petition which was then signed by several of the leading merchants, insisting that the writs as issued in the past were unconstitutional. Thomas Lechmere, caught off guard, quickly responded with a counter request to the Superior Court that the writs of assistance be granted as usual. Thus the battle lines were drawn.

On a blustery November day, the court opened for its midwinter session in the council chamber of the Town House. Opposing Otis and Thacher was Jeremiah Gridley, the aging dean of Boston lawyers. Sensing the importance of the case as precedent for many other legal actions, most of the city's other lawyers were present. Dressed in black robes and carrying ink bottles, papers, and quill pens, they filled the center part of the small, plain room with its balconied window facing eastward where wide, cobblestoned King Street led down to the harbor. The seats at the tables were filled by the justices and participating lawyers; most of the onlookers were forced to stand along the walls. Pratt hobbled into a corner "hanging by the shoulders on two crutches, covered with a great cloth coat."[3]

The court rose, and Hutchinson and the four other justices took their places at the front of the room. Wearing white wigs and dressed in the scarlet robes of their office, they sat at a table in front of a crackling fire, flanked by gold-framed portraits of Charles II and James II.

Hutchinson's life was rarely free of ironies. Ten years earlier he had fought against these same arbitrary search powers. At one point he had defended his brother Foster's warehouse against a crew of customs men who were determined to break in and look for illegally imported ironware, warning the inspector that the search warrant signed by Governor Shirley was illegal and "of no value." (Shirley later withdrew these warrants and ordered that they be issued henceforth by the Superior Court.)

This was Hutchinson's debut—his first major case—and he was far more conscious of his shortcomings than his appearance indicated. He knew that no scarlet robes, no immense wig, no long table and formal atmosphere would supply him with what he personally had admitted many times he lacked: a judicial background, a formal foundation in the ramifications of British law, a depth of understanding and experience that would place him on equal footing with lawyers such as Gridley and Otis. He was also aware that nearly all the lawyers in the room were convinced the Crown's case was unassailable and had come to witness a battle that was bound to be more political than legal. The real matter at hand was a testing of power. Was it possible to oppose the thrust of Crown policy? Was there enough political strength in the province to make itself felt in London on specific issues?

Gridley opened for the Crown. He was reserved, aloof, "majestic," a man of unchallengeable authority, the teacher not only of Otis but also of Thacher, Samuel Quincy, and many of the other lawyers in the room. He began in a stiff and businesslike tone, detailing the laws which applied to the case, laws which had been signed into being by Charles II. John Adams, listening to Gridley, wrote, "His words seem to pierce and search, have something quick and animating. He is a great reasoner, and has a very vivid imagination."[4] Gridley emphasized the need for customs officials to get on with their work so that the port of Boston could be run as efficiently as possible. As for the particular writs in question, he insisted that this was an old and settled issue; certain restrictions of individual liberties were necessary in any society. Taxes and tariffs had to be honored and collected or the province would fall apart. The writs of assistance, which had worked successfully in the past, should continue, even though he admitted that public opinion was overwhelmingly against them; a finding to the contrary would disrupt the whole economic structure of government.

Oxenbridge Thacher was the first to speak for the opposition. Gaunt, always tired, always brilliant, Thacher at forty-one was fighting the tuberculosis that would end his life four years later. He began by asking exactly what this writ would look like, forcing Hutchinson to acknowledge that there was no standard example of the form. He then insisted that power to establish and enforce writs of assistance had not been officially delegated to any court in the colony. In addition, he said, there was a serious question as to whether the Superior Court could consider itself a mirror of the British Exchequer, where writs of assistance were issued in England. There, the conduct of customs was easily supervised; in Boston there was no such control to keep the customs officials from overstepping their authority to detain and search. Like Gridley, Thacher spoke briefly and adhered to the legal and administrative aspects of the writs.

When Otis took his turn, however, the atmosphere changed. He was not brief, nor did he confine himself to specific details of the immediate question. He knew what the real issues were, and why all the lawyers of the city and the neighboring towns were present. His argument ranged through the world of law, literature, and history. He began on a personal note, reminding the court that he had recently resigned a Crown position because it had become clear to him that certain laws which he was being paid to enforce were unconstitutional. The Admiralty Court, he said, had asked him much earlier to study the legality of the writs when he had been advocate general, and this he had undertaken. Thus his presence, he insisted with sardonic humor, was not as much in opposition to the court as in continuation of his assigned duties. For this reason he was sure the court was anxious to know the results of his research into the writs question. He mentioned in passing that he did not intend to accept a fee for his services, because his own principles required him to speak out. The rights of man were at stake, and nothing less—man's uncontestable right to "his life, his liberty . . . his property."

From the rights of man Otis took the court through the history of the navigation acts of the century past. He called them "narrow, contracted, selfish" and drew visions of the possibilities inherent in these acts, had they been executed with the energy intended: raids into homes to search out pieces of foreign linen, families wakened in the night. Turning to the writs, he separated special writs (in which informers and specific infractions were named) from the general "blank check" writs. He agreed that the special writs, long in use, were valid, but he rejected the general writs. They supported arbitrary and abusive practices. Any excess was possible with a general writ. "If this commission be legal," he said, "a tyrant in a legal manner also may control, imprison, or murder anyone within the realm." The possibility of misuse had to be considered in the analysis of any legal power. He cited as an example the well-known case of the customs man arrested and punished for cursing, who then obtained a writ and searched the house of the constable who had arrested him and the judge who had convicted him.

But it was not simply because of the dangers involved that the writs of assistance should be rejected. Quoting Sir Edward Coke and the Swiss authority Emmerich von Vattel, Otis assured the court that the greatest legal minds had supported the assertion that any act contrary to the unwritten British constitution was void. British law was based on the Magna Charta and the undeniable rights of man. Parliament, as a part of the scheme of this constitution, had to act with reason and justice and could not be arbitrary. It had the power to create laws but had to frame its legislation within the bounds of equity and reason set by the constitution and natural law. It was therefore simple enough for any man to see: if the writs violated the natural law, the basis of the British constitution, no amount of approvals, imprimatures, or precedents could make them legal. "I oppose that kind of power," he said, "the exercise of which in former periods of English history cost one king of England his head and another his throne."

For four hours he continued, while lawyers scribbled in their notebooks the phrases that would help establish the literature of the revolution. Spellbound in the courtroom, John Adams later in life tried to remember the emotion-charged atmosphere in which he had written his notes. Otis to him was "a flame of fire,"

> with a promptitude of classical allusions, a depth of research, a rapid summary of historical events and dates, a profusion of legal authorities, and a torrent of impetuous eloquence, he hurried away everything before him. American independence was then and there born. . . . Every man of a crowded audience appeared to me to go away, as I did, ready to take arms against writs of assistance. Then and there was the first scene of the first act of opposition to the arbitrary claims of Great Britain.[5]

When Otis finished, it was Hutchinson's turn to make his first important decision as chief justice. Facing the mass of black-robed lawyers, every one of whom had more legal experience than he, he sifted quickly through the possible options. Assert the obvious Crown position and summarily overrule the Otis-Thacher objections? This would force him to be as arbitrary as Otis said he was. Concede that Otis had made a unique point of law that did, in fact, change the situation? Even if Hutchinson believed this to be true—which he most assuredly did not—such a concession would be a resounding defeat for the Crown, opening the door to chaos. With the experience of two decades of Massachusetts Bay politics, his political sensitivity, rather than his legal expertise, told him what to do: postpone a decision pending advice from home. He announced that it would be necessary to send to England for more details. The court would recess. Since it was Otis who insisted that execution of the writs was a misreading of the present state of affairs in England, he could not very well object to an attempt to clarify the home government's point of view, although in this way it was sure to be many weeks before the answer could be known.[6]

Although Thomas Hutchinson could gain by postponing a decision on the writs case, Otis knew they had achieved a most important victory, placing the administration on the defensive and opening an opportunity for new initiatives by the popular party. With Bernard and Hutchinson firmly in the spotlight as oppressors of the merchants, and with the customs inspectors momentarily set back by a challenge to their authority, James Otis had become almost overnight the most popular man in Boston. Not only had he resigned a lucrative post in the Admiralty rather than carry out Bernard's strict measures against illegal trade, but now he had stood up to Hutchinson and the whole Admiralty system of searches and seizures, establishing a doubt as to their constitutionality. Previously, the townspeople tended to see the popular party as exclusive representative of the agricultural interests of the province, and thus often opposed to the views of the traders, merchants, fishermen, shipbuilders, and city folk in general who made up the population of the port. Now Colonel Otis had become, as Hutchinson said, a strong advocate for the town who "drew much of the country interest after him,"[7] while the performance of his son against Hutchinson in Superior Court captured the attention and sympathies of the same voters. The result was that the Otises, who as representatives of popular party interests had been "obnoxious" in Boston, became the town's heroes.

For young James Otis the die was cast. His connections with the Merchants' Society and the Caucus Club members, which to this time had been primarily in business and law, became definitely and strongly political; a new dimension would be added to his town-meeting activities, and in embracing this "Boston faction" he was drawn to the center of the circle that contained the chief personalities behind the stage of Boston politics. Since every barrister for miles around had been present in the room, his words were prime news in Boston and the province for days. He had detailed the drift away from charter rights, constitutional principles, and most of all from the former respect for individual rights. He had illuminated, for all to see, the movement of arbitrary power away from the traditional democratic bases of British government.

In these aspects Otis was not at all revolutionary; in fact, he was calling for a reestablishment of ancient liberties under common law and saying that power was dangerous when it became arbitrary, overtopping the bounds of the constitution. Although his arguments during the writs case often had appeared anachronistic and out of place in assigning such great weight to the unwritten British constitution and to natural law, it was soon clear to perceptive political thinkers that he had seized on theories that could match the power of parliamentary decrees. No single arbitrary act, he said, could stand against the constitutional history of the country or against the rights of free men. It was for Otis the first of his influential statements of political philosophy.

A month after these courtroom scenes James Otis was elected to the House of Representatives. As Peter Oliver later said, "Through his opposition to government, he was elected a representative for *Boston*. And in this lower house of Assembly he could rail, swear, lie, and talk treason *impunite,* and here he never failed to take advantage of his privilege, so that the Assembly, in his time, was more like a *Bedlam* than a session of senators." But at the time of his election, when the news reached Worcester, the astute Timothy Ruggles told dinner guests that the younger Otis would be nothing but trouble in the future. "Out of this election will arise a damned faction," he predicted, "which will shake this province to its foundation."

3

Otis in the House

May 1761–May 1762

Perhaps I should not have troubled . . . the public
with any thoughts of mine had not His Honour, the
Lieutenant Governor, have condescended to give me a
personal challenge. This is an honor that I never had
vanity enough to aspire after and [I] shall ever respect
Mr. Hutchinson for it, so long as I live, as he certainly
consulted my reputation more than his own when he
bestowed it. A General Officer in the Army would be
thought very condescending to accept from, much
more to give a challenge to a Subaltern.

JAMES OTIS, writing on the currency question
in the *Boston Gazette*, 1762

AT THE END OF MAY 1761, Governor Bernard opened the spring
session of the General Court with the usual speech to the House.
As he was to do so often, he misread the situation in the province
and the mood of the representatives. He assured them that the
squabbles of party and faction had ceased to exist, having been
resolved into loyalty. "Whig and Tory, court and country, all are
swallowed up in the name of Briton," he said, and England is
enjoying the contentment of a great civilization and empire.
"Can we look on this happiness and not desire to partake of it?"
He cautioned the representatives to pay no attention to the cur-

rent "declamations" that the charter rights of the province were in danger; it simply was not so.

His words fell flat. The House of Representatives responded the next day with a polite but firm rejection of the bright picture Bernard had painted. As for his assurances that their rights were not threatened, they said, "It is our intention to see for ourselves." This bold refutation was one of the early signs that control of a large bloc of representatives already had passed to Otis. Part of this Otis owed to his father's influence with the popular party, and part was his own recent popularity as a result of the writs case. His immediate strength, however, came in the growing unity between political power in Boston and in the countryside. Assisting in creating this union were the Boston merchants, with their newfound faith in Otis. There were also other forces providing support to Otis, and these can be traced to the influence of Samuel Adams, who after years of hard, grass-roots effort was beginning to gain a hold on Boston's workingman vote and an ability to direct it.

Adams had known Otis for a decade, since Harvard days when they overlapped a year. Adams had been sent to Harvard to study for the ministry, but had shifted quickly first to law and then to political history. His seven years at the college left him unprepared and unsuited for his first job, a clerkship in a mercantile house. He soon left his accountant's desk in search of something more congenial to his nature and in the process let slip through his fingers £1,000 which his father had given him to start a career. He then returned to the family brewery business, but unlike the senior Adams, he could not balance out his work as a maltster with his political endeavors. After his father died in 1748 he allowed the brewery to fall into bankruptcy, barely saving the house.

At this period Adams was far more interested in his political writings, published in the *Independent Advertiser*, a newspaper in which he held a part interest with several other young men. He was also making it a point to meet and know hundreds upon hundreds of the citizens of his home town—on the docks, in the taverns, at market, and at work in the ropewalks, shipyards, shops, stables, streets, and squares of the town. Since he needed a job that would pay him a salary, he was happy to accept the assignment in 1758 as one of the four tax collectors for Boston.

Throughout the decade of the 1750s, while Otis learned his law, Samuel Adams wrote and spoke in opposition to the Crown administration of Governor Shirley, insisting that too much political power was concentrated in the hands of the Crown and too little was allowed to the province. With John Locke's writings and especially the principle of the sovereignty of the people as his guide, he argued that the citizens of Massachusetts were surrendering, bit by bit, their right to govern themselves, that it was right and proper to criticize abuses of power, adding that anyone who disagreed was himself a rebel; this point, that the tyrant is in fact the traitor, was one that he would use at critical times much later. He invoked the charter, talked of the rights of man, and criticized the immorality of the administration, all in vain. The Indian troubles, followed by the long war beginning in 1756, kept up a spirit of unity with England in the face of danger and allowed very little room for criticism of government policy. But the days of Adams' hard apprenticeship were not wasted. When the war ended and the impact of a much stricter economic policy began to be felt in Boston, Adams had laid the foundation of a political career. If he did not control the Caucus Club by this time, he certainly was one of the major figures. He had become the link between the Caucus Club, the Merchants' Society, and the hundreds of mechanics and workmen who carried out the minor tasks (and who had begun to vote as they were told).

Otis, on the other hand, was tied more closely to the merchants, but both men were gaining a broadening base of political support —Otis through his town-meeting work was beginning to know Bostonians from all walks of life; Adams through his control of Boston's workingmen was becoming important to the merchants. The two men, already close friends, were moving toward a partnership that would change the future of Massachusetts Bay and the continent.

The popular party now could claim one-third of the seats in the House,[1] and Otis was determined to use this base to attack anything he perceived as an abuse of governmental power, but from the beginning he was bent on reform, not revolution. The true interests of America and Great Britain were "mutual," he wrote for the press, "and what God in his providence has united, let no man dare attempt to pull asunder." Nevertheless, he wanted all Superior Court justices out of the legislature and he wanted new writs of assistance in which the informer, if any, had to be named. Calling on Montesquieu and the doctrine of separation of legislative and executive powers, he introduced a motion into the legislature to prohibit all Superior Court justices from sitting in the General Court, whether in the House or the council. This, of course, would oust Hutchinson from the General Court and also would severely weaken the court party, since the other justices tended to be allied politically to the governor and the Crown and most of them had seats on the council. After much debate, the motion failed to carry, missing by a scant seven votes. As usual, however, in the process of losing his point, Otis won another: the debates placed on public view the plural office-holding within the administration, embarrassing Hutchinson, who remained the key offender in terms of the number of offices held by one man. Both the governor and Hutchinson were shaken by the close vote, which showed the growing strength of the popular party. Another resolution, which did pass, called for "restraining the Superior Court from issuing writs of assistance except upon special information to a custom house officer oath being first made, the informer mentioned, and the person supposed to own the goods and place where they were suspected to be concealed." This would have nullified the power of the writs by exposing all informers. Needless to say, the resolution was vetoed by Bernard. Of the newfound strength of the Otises, Hutchinson could only say, "Two lawyers of the same name carry all before them in the House," and Bernard complained, "Mr. Otis Junr. is at the head of the confederacy. If you are acquainted with the natural violence of his temper, suppose it to be augmented beyond all bounds of common decency."[2]

With the House out of session, Otis found he could transfer his energies to law work and still keep up his attack on Crown policy. Acting for the merchants, he brought five new lawsuits against the customs men, forcing each case to a successful verdict in which the commissioners were ordered to repay the money used to buy information.

Then Hutchinson struck back. When the Superior Court convened in Boston in November, he was in possession of a copy of the kind of writ then in use in London, which had been sent to him by William Bollan, the province agent ("lobbyist" for the province in London). With this new support, Jeremiah Gridley returned to defend the same ground covered in the earlier sessions, this time with Robert Auchmuty as his assistant. The choice was an unfortunate one, since Auchmuty was James Otis' replacement as advocate general of the Admiralty Court and the opposition of the two men symbolized for Bostonians the fight of Massachusetts against oppressive Crown policy. Gridley began by emphasizing the control the writs provided. Since the writs called for a sheriff to accompany the customs inspector, the owner of the goods was protected against any illegal activity. The writs were thus of great benefit to the citizens and to the preservation of law and order. Gridley also anticipated the kind of argument Otis would provide the court. "Quoting history is not speaking like a lawyer," he said. "If it is law in England, it is law here."[3]

Oxenbridge Thacher held his ground as before, insisting that no law authorized the writs in their present form and that it was illogical to attempt to draw legal parallels between the Exchequer in London and the Superior Court of Boston. He foresaw abuses of the rights of citizens by overzealous customs men with too much power—and with ambitions spurred by visions of a share in the confiscated property. "It can't be in the power of any judge," he said, "at discretion to determine that I shall have my house broken open or not."

The courtroom was dark when Otis again spoke, for the argument was continuing into evening. Disregarding Gridley's admonition to stay away from history, he went to the source of the writs. If Parliament sanctioned these regulations in England, he said, then Parliament had made a mistake. The writs were contrary to the British constitution. They were also contrary to the Massachusetts Bay charter, which was issued long before the law regarding writs came into being, and therefore they were illegal on the day they were first created. "Let a warrant come from where it will improperly, it is to be refused," he said, "and the higher the power granting it, the more dangerous."[4]

The *Boston Gazette,* in a column that may have been written by Adams, reported that Otis and Thacher argued "with such strength of reason as did great honor the gentlemen concerned, and nothing could have induced one to believe they were not conclusive, but the judgment of the court [was] *immediately* given in favor of the petition." The presence of a bona fide writ as a sample of the usage in London was a powerful argument. This evidence, coupled with the determination of Hutchinson and the other justices to support Crown policy, made it a foregone conclusion that the writs would continue as before. They were approved for issue, and Paxton received his renewal from Hutchinson about a month later. The argument did not end there, however; opposition to the writs continued for five years until Otis and Thacher were proved to be right: when the Superior Court of Connecticut in 1766 asked for legal advice from London as to whether or not it had the same power as the Exchequer for issuing writs of assistance, the attorney general of England, William de Grey, in an official, written opinion, said he could find no legal basis for the colonies to issue these writs.

Hutchinson took great personal pride in the return of Massachusetts Bay to a silver-currency economy. For decades in the first half of the eighteenth century the province, like all the rest of the American colonies, produced its own paper money as legal tender. Since notes issued at various times came to have different values when compared to the pound sterling, purchases and payment of debts became almost as complicated as the bartering system which money was supposed to replace. Pressed by the appearance of a large amount of counterfeit money, the province was faced with calling in all paper money and redeeming it with silver, the only legal tender. Because of the shortage of silver, there was a great deal of pressure to make gold also legal tender, and the House passed a note making it so "at the rate it passes."[5] Hutchinson, however, with his long-standing and keen interest in economics, saw clearly that if both metals were stabilized, the result would be an artificially high value on gold. People would use the gold to buy silver, which they would hoard, knowing it would eventually be worth more. The gold would depreciate and the province would be back where it started and the economy strangled. Hutchinson's interest, as always, lay with the "home" view of the problem. The major creditors were British businessmen or their representatives in the colonies, and they were concerned with getting the most value—in silver—for the pound. "I stood in the front of the opposition," he said, "and it was with great difficulty the council was kept from concurring."[6]

The debate was carried into the newspapers, where Hutchinson argued the currency question and Otis argued politics, personalities, and separation of powers, emphasizing Hutchinson's conservative—and unpopular—position on the whole issue of hard currency and concluding, "I know it is the maxim of some, that the common people in this town and country live too well; however, I am of quite different opinion, I do not think they live half well enough." Hutchinson could not afford to remain silent, and as he had been preparing a history of the currency of Massachusetts, he now published it in the *Boston Evening Post,* hoping to show the evils of paper money and the impossibility of maintaining both gold and silver at a static level. But his opponents realized better than he that the newspaper readers would not heed his involved logic. Oxenbridge Thacher and Otis produced a long pamphlet ostensibly on the gold-versus-silver question but actually attacking Hutchinson as a man who did not have the interests of the province at heart, and who favored creditors over debtors.[7]

The disagreement over the bill for making gold legal tender resulted in a conference in which Hutchinson led the delegates from the council and Otis opposed him as the head of the committee from the House. Neither man would yield, and with deadlocked committees the bill went back to the House for reconsideration. Again it passed, making both silver and gold legal, and this time the council would not stop it. Bernard delayed until March 6, but then signed the bill. Otis had won, and in one of the many ironies that follow the twists and turns of Hutchinson's life, the price of silver in England fell to the point where gold and silver were just about equal in value. Bernard, only a few months later, wrote the Lords of Trade that it was "a very timely prudence to change the tenor of the bills and make them payable in gold and silver indiscriminately."[8]

In the continuing session of the House after the new year opened, Otis organized his popular-party members behind the siege of the court party while he tried to drive a wedge between Hutchinson and the governor. He saw an opportunity when several towns in the area between the Kennebec and St. Croix Rivers (now in Maine but then still part of Massachusetts) applied for incorporation. In close proximity to these towns was a large island, Mount Desert, which had not been granted to any developer. Bernard's interest in improving his own financial situation during his tenure as governor was quite obvious to his associates, and Otis concluded that Bernard might be brought over to the side of the popular party or at least neutralized if the House were to make him a grant of land. Such a grant would occupy a part of his time and might also divert his interest from the seizure of cargoes and from other customs activities. Otis therefore went ahead, and, much to the surprise of the court party, advanced the idea of the grant of Mount Desert island to Governor Bernard in appreciation of his services. With the co-operation of both parties, the resolution passed quickly, and Bernard found himself in possession of an immense tract of land, almost beyond his capability to manage. He fastened on his new interest with the singleness of purpose that Otis had predicted. He spent a month in the fall of each year on a voyage (in the province sloop) to see his land, and from 1762 to 1771 he constantly endeavored to pull strings at court in London to get official approval from the king, laboring over scores of letters on the subject. ("I need not urge to your Lordships the expediency of encouraging, by all proper means, the cultivation of the wastes of North America.")[9]

If Otis was willing to hold out a carrot for Bernard in terms of Mount Desert, he also was quite ready with the stick. The House, responding to a request from Hutchinson's close friend, Israel Williams, granted a charter for opening a new college in Hampshire County. This was voted down in the council after Harvard administrators indicated it might provide too much competition, but Bernard decided to go ahead on his own and issue the charter. To Otis this was another case of arbitrary and illegal action. With the help of Samuel Adams and Oxenbridge Thacher, he engineered a petition accusing Bernard of yet another infraction of the constitution and calling on him to delay any further action on the college. A list of objections to the new charter was being drawn up when Bernard gave in and withdrew it.[10]

Hutchinson knew it was futile and dangerous to try to deal with the Otises. "The Governor," he wrote, "flattered himself that he should be able to reconcile to him both father and son." At the same time, Hutchinson saw his own influence diminishing as a result of the confrontations. His positions on the writs case, the Paxton trial, and the currency issue had cost him "a number of friends," and the angered House, influenced by Otis, had not provided for his pay as chief justice.[11]

As the session came to a close, Otis could look back on a very successful first year. His legal brilliance, articulateness, and restless energy had given him command of the popular party, enabling him through his father's old coalition to exercise a power that had been dormant for years. He had united the popular party and the Boston merchants because he seemed to present an alternative that was reasonable, moderate, and above all legal and legitimate. It was through the exercise of existing legal appeal that the merchants hoped to return to an earlier and more liberal trade arrangement. It was through legitimate negotiation that the province as a whole hoped to keep its charter rights. Otis was obviously a fighter, willing to confront the administration, and perhaps through him the colony could obtain a better economic arrangement allowing manufacturing and providing other advantages that would eventually put the province in the black.

Part of his appeal to the conservative agriculture-based backcountry towns was his loyalty to the Crown and his continually expressed adherence to the ultimate vision of a great British empire. He could not have catalyzed a new, strong popular party without his obvious essential conservatism: neither the merchants nor the small towns would have approved of him in those years.

Adams, on the other hand, demonstrated no such conservatism and mentioned loyalty to the king only when it was tactically productive to do so—and then usually as an afterthought. His talk of tyrants and of the people's abdication of power made Boston merchants uneasy. Although his control of Boston's workingmen grew ever stronger and although he was obviously quite ready to follow his father in politics, the town did not look to him when it came time to elect its representatives to the General Court, nor in fact was he given any significant duties at the town meeting. He remained a fire warden and one of the four tax collectors.

4

The Vindication

May 1762–January 1763

Look over the declaration of rights and wrongs issued by Congress in 1774. Look into the declaration of independence in 1776. Look into the writings of Dr. Price and Dr. Priestley. Look into all the French constitutions of government; and, to cap the climax, look into Mr. Thomas Paine's *Common Sense, Crisis,* and *Rights of Man.* What can you find that is not to be found in this "Vindication of the House of Representatives"?

JOHN ADAMS to WILLIAM TUDOR, 1818

THE FORTUNES of the Otis family were on the rise. Colonel Otis, at the opening of the summer session of the House, was elected speaker but turned down the job with the comment that his living at a distance made his constant attendance "uncertain."[1] Actually, he was hoping to be elected to the council, and on the same afternoon he achieved his wishes, being nominated to the board by 112 votes, "the largest number perhaps that any person that was new almost ever had so I hope that matter is now settled."[2] The matter was the question whether the colonel had "carried things" in the court because he was Governor Shirley's flunky or whether he had the power to succeed on his own.

45

Fiercely loyal Brigadier Timothy Ruggles, the popular veteran of the French and Indian War, was elected speaker in place of Colonel Otis—over the objections of James Otis. Thus the father refused the position of speaker and the son tried to block the next choice of the House—a combination of moves that infuriated the conservative members. In objecting, however, James Otis was running true to form. He could not accept the idea of Ruggles, who was also a judge, sitting in the legislative branch, since it was clear that the governmental powers were meant to be separated. And now he was in a position to back up his convictions with political strength. The Otises, working together, then directed an attack on Hutchinson's friend, William Bollan, and were successful in obtaining a motion for his dismissal. Hutchinson countered with a recommendation that another of his friends, Richard Jackson, be made agent. This was defeated when the Otises led the popular party in a strong drive that succeeded in placing Jasper Mauduit, a liberal who sided with the Boston members of the popular party, in the London agency. Throughout the spring session of the General Court, Otis carried on his campaign in the *Gazette* against Hutchinson's attempt to balance the currency, using a combination of facts and insinuations to paint the lieutenant governor as a heartless oppressor of the lower classes.

By July, Hutchinson was happy to escape the political pressures of Boston and turn to his judicial duties on the "eastern circuit" to the towns of Portsmouth and York. While he was away and the council out of session, Bernard was presented with what seemed a minor problem. The towns of Salem and Marblehead petitioned him for protection of their fishing fleets against marauding French privateers, which rumor placed off Nova Scotia near the Grand Banks. Normally Bernard needed House approval for any unplanned expenditure of funds, but he considered this an emergency. Besides, since the armed province sloop *Massachusetts* was available, it would be a simple and inexpensive matter to augment her crew from a skeleton six to 24 and send her off. An advertised bounty of $10 per man quickly filled out the crew, and the sloop sailed to the northeast on a patrol that turned out to be quiet and uneventful.[3]

Not so the response of the House to a depletion of the treasury by an act of the governor. To Otis, the unauthorized use of funds, whatever the reason, was another step toward arbitrary autocratic rule. It was time to stop this misuse of power. The General Court convened on September 8. In Bernard's usual message to the House, he informed the representatives of his action at the request of Salem and Marblehead and asked reimbursement for the province fund. Otis moved very deliberately. First he isolated the issue of the sloop by ignoring it while the House voted a generous response to Bernard's request for troops for the frontier and cleared the table of other business. Bernard, fretting at the silence concerning the sloop, sent a new request for after-the-fact authorization. Otis was then voted chairman of the committee charged with preparing an answer.

The committee's draft response was ready almost immediately, and when it was read to the House, some of the representatives found it most objectionable. Otis had said that, in drawing out province money, the governor had usurped the most important privilege of the legislature, which was the levying of taxes and the disbursal of tax monies. If the king could allow his administration to take over control of the money in the province, then he would be as arbitrary as his contemporary, Louis XIV of France. "It would be of little consequence to the people," Otis said, "whether they were a subject to George or Lewis, the King of Great Britain or the French King, if both were arbitrary as both would be if both could levy taxes without Parliament."[4] Timothy Paine and other conservatives saw the wording as an affront to the king himself, but Paine's cries of "Treason, treason!" were smothered by a large majority that voted to pass the remonstrance up to the governor, with the words standing as Otis wrote them. Not surprisingly, Otis found himself on the committee appointed to present the paper to Bernard.

Bernard received the House committee but made no immediate answer, saying only that he would have to study their document before he could reply. Later in the day he sent an informal letter back to the House speaker, enclosing the remonstrance with a black line drawn under the "George or Lewis" remark, which he considered disparaging to the king. He recommended the phrase be stricken from the letter and from the minutes of the House, adding that, if the message were allowed to stand, the representatives would "again and again wish some parts of it were expunged." On the floor of the House, Otis defended his comments as appropriate to the occasion, especially since they were not addressed directly to the king, and suggested that a qualifying phrase such as "with due reverence to his Majesty's sacred person" might be added to assuage the governor. The moderates prevailed, however, and with friends to government crying, "Erase them—erase them!" Otis reluctantly consented to remove the objectionable passage.

Bernard accepted the revised message and sent back his answer, admitting that the House and not the governor controlled the treasury, but insisting that his actions in the affair of the sloop were logical and lawful and not without precedent in other provinces. He then prorogued the General Court before it could continue the exchange, hoping that this would end the trouble, but what he intended as the "final" message turned out to be only the beginning. Muzzled by the closing of the court, Otis chose to answer in another way. Within a few days he put together a 53-page pamphlet that he titled *Vindication of the Conduct of the House of Representatives of the Province of Massachusetts-Bay,* an essay which was to become one of the most widely read early statements of the fundamental principles of American revolutionary theory.[5]

Otis once again assumed the role of the objective and rational critic who acts only out of a desire to improve a system he loves and respects. It was his duty, he said, to attempt "a modest and humble endeavor, by calm reason and argument, to convince mankind of their mistakes when they happen to be guilty of any." He then published the series of messages that had passed between Bernard and the House since the opening of the General Court a month earlier, which he insisted were evidence of the governor's lack of understanding of the province. Bernard, announcing a new request for troops from General Jeffrey Amherst, had asked the House to respond with a levy. His schoolmasterish tone, unfortunately, insinuated that Massachusetts had to be coaxed into providing troops for his majesty's service.

Otis took up this matter first. There should be little reason, he said, to believe that the Massachusetts legislature needed additional encouragement to support the Crown. Since 1754 the province had sent 30,000 soldiers to the frontier in the service of his majesty. Whether in money or in blood, Massachusetts stood ready to support the king—but at the same time, the province would not stand idly by while portions of tax money, however small, were misused. In the case of the province sloop, it was "high time to remonstrate." He then provided the exchange of documents between the House and the governor. In justification of the "George or Lewis" passage, Otis laid down ten premises which he called his "data." The premises restated the heart of his argument, which was that all men—including the king—were equal and subject to the same laws. He declared without reservation his loyalty to the king and the British constitution, but insisted that "kings were (and plantation governors should be) made for the good of the people, and not the people for them."

In his earlier naming of the two kings, Otis said, he was attempting to emphasize that the difference between these leaders lay not in their Christian names but in their use of power. There were rules that governed power, he said, and the House of Representatives ought to be able to speak of these rules in plain English to the governor, without the need for repenting "again and again." Like the king, the governor could not make arbitrary use of his position; he had to remain within the specific parameters of province law, which derived from the charter. Using long quotations from Locke, Otis bore down hard on the constitutional limits of executive power and the undeniable rights of the legislature: the House had the right of remonstrance and would make itself heard, and when the governor and council hear the truth, then with their goodness and wisdom they will follow it.

Otis then moved from the specifics of the sloop incident to the greater question of might versus right. "It is by no means a good inference in politics," he said, "any more than in private life, or even in the state of nature, that a man has a right to do everything in his natural power to do." Bernard had excused the expense of the sloop as an "insignificant amount," used for warding off imminent danger. The province charter and laws made it quite clear, however, that Bernard could not take a shilling out of the treasury for any reason without approval of the House. But, said Otis, what if he does? The House then has no way to call him to account, except by a remonstrance—first to the governor himself, and, if that is not successful, to the king. And after that, what then? "The Parliament of Great Britain have as a last resort been known to appeal to Heaven, and the longest sword; but God forbid that there should ever be occasion for anything of that kind again."

In his conclusion, Otis called for the proper balance between the legislative and executive branches. If Bernard's arbitrary practices continued, he warned, the House of Representatives "would become, as some desire to have it, a very insignificant, unimportant part of the constitution." And while the present governor may be a just and kindly man, some in the past have been "as absolute as Turkish Bashaws," ready to seize all power. The related powers of taxation and appropriation belong only to the House, said Otis, and the governor, in the case at hand, acted wrongly. He deserved a remonstrance, and there was nothing insolent or presumptuous about the action of the House. The governor should reflect on the rights and privileges of the colonists, which are the same as those of any British citizen. Had he "time or room," Otis said, foreseeing his future writings, he might show precisely the rights of British colonists as set forth in the common law and the colonial charters.

5

The Acts of Trade

January–May 1763

Bluster, however, can by no means be charged with
want of zeal and industry in the business in which he
has so *solemnly* engaged. He has exerted the utmost efforts of his genius and employed every art of calumny
and detraction. Nothing that envy and spite, sharpened by the rage of disappointment, could do has been
left undone; and had his ability been equal to his
malice we should probably before now have been involved in a horrid scene of tumult and confusion. But
kind Providence that planteth the antidote not far
from the poison seems to have ordered the weakness of
his head as a balance to the wickedness of his heart,
and has taken care that the mischievous devices of the
one should be checked & defeated by the imbecility of
the other.

Boston Evening Post, 28 March 1763

IN EARLY 1763 Hutchinson changed direction in a way that for a
man of fifty was significant. He turned over the major part of his
mercantile interests to his sons, Thomas and Elisha, and began a
dedicated effort to produce a history of Massachusetts. His personal collection of documents already amounted to the most extensive unofficial archives in the province and his duties gave him

access to all the other manuscripts that remained from the earliest days. Knowing of his interest in these papers, many Bostonians—including even James Otis—had encouraged him to write a history,[1] and at this point he decided that he would make whatever sacrifices necessary to provide a comprehensive view of the past. Such a history, he hoped, would serve as a balancing perspective for an understanding of the problems of the day. In January he put the first words to paper, beginning with an expansion of some of his own reports of the investigations which Bernard had commissioned him to do.

As he wrote, the first heavy blizzards of the New England winter howled over the harbor islands and through the frigid streets of Boston. The shivering townsfolk piled wood into their fires, and on January 16 a faulty chimney on Newbury Street poured hot sparks into an attic. Soon the volunteers were out with their fire buckets, struggling through high snowdrifts in answer to the clamor of bells from church and meetinghouse. But even the salted water froze to slush and six wooden houses burned to the ground before brick walls slowed the spread of the flames. It was a minor fire; Boston had seen much worse.

In midwinter Boston was full of rumors that the preliminaries to a peace treaty had been worked out and agreed upon in Paris and that the state of war with France would soon be over, leaving Great Britain in possession of Canada. The general feeling of euphoria that comes with the end of a war, the conviction that good times lie ahead and that the government has done well, made it extremely difficult for the popular party to sustain a strong opposition to Bernard's administration or to Crown policy. It was the beginning of a period of frustration for the Otises, when they could not muster the strength in the House to establish control, and when the patronage of Bernard and the careful political maneuvering of Hutchinson were enough to cancel every move they made. Nevertheless, even under these conditions, they were able to accomplish much to consolidate the strength of the party and prepare for the future.

Another test of strength came when Jasper Mauduit, the new province agent, complained that he was not well and asked the General Court to nominate his brother, Israel, as his assistant, to take his place if that became necessary. Soon after the House opened in January, before some of the delegates from distant— and normally more conservative—counties had arrived, Otis brought out Mauduit's request and succeeded in gaining its acceptance. When the full House assembled, however, this was promptly reversed. Otis was furious, convinced that Hutchinson had played the major role in the reversal so that later he could secure the position as agent for himself or for one of his friends.

Waiting for a Saturday when only 45 House members, most of them his own supporters, were in attendance, Otis called for approval of a letter to Jasper Mauduit to inform him that his brother could not be made his assistant because the province did not want to vote the extra expense, thereby avoiding the true reason, the inability of the weakened popular party to push through the measure. Once again his motion passed, only to be repudiated by a fuller House the following week. To a demand that the letter be put before the House for reconsideration, Otis replied too quickly that he had already sent it to England, missing the obvious fact that no ship had left Boston over the weekend. He would not produce the letter, however, and his stubbornness touched off a violent debate in the House. A motion was begun to censure Otis if he refused to tell what he had done with the letter, but was fought down. Bernard called Otis "a gentleman of great warmth of temper and much indiscretion." Otis had lost twice on the same case. "Damn the letter, and damn Mr. Mauduit," the opposition reported him as saying. "I don't care a farthing for either, but I hate the Lieutenant Governor should prevail in anything." His feelings were more accurately stated in his own personal letter to Mauduit, in which he bemoaned the inability of the popular party to keep Hutchinson from his control of key positions in the province. If Hutchinson could be held to "any one or two great posts, as chief justice or anything but governor-in-chief, we might do well enough," he said, but that was not to happen.[2]

Thomas Hutchinson prepared a paper on the Mauduit case for the press, highly critical of Mauduit, which he gave to Thomas Fleet, editor of the *Evening Post*. He asked that it be used without attribution, but Fleet let Otis, Adams, and a few others read it.

James Otis responded in the *Gazette* of January 31 with a harsh personal attack, saying that he knew the identity of the author who left a paper signed "A.Z." at Fleet's establishment. That man, whom Otis said he would not name at this time, was a tall, slender, fair-complexioned, fair-spoken gentleman whose "beauty has captivated half the pretty ladies, and finess [sic] more than half the pretty gentlemen of the Province."[3] But under this beauty, Otis warned, is a man who has brought to perfection the arts of hypocrisy and chicanery—and worse, one who was born to a love of power. "The nourishment of a perpetual dictator flowed from his mother's breasts" and this tyrant's maxim was *"I'll have everything or nothing."* This attack struck home harder than Otis knew: Hutchinson admitted to a friend that he was out of humor for two weeks after reading that issue of the *Gazette,* adding that there was no remedy but patience.[4]

But Hutchinson was doing more than simply being patient. He was quietly enlisting the help of his friends to write articles against Otis. Among these friends was one staunch supporter who would never desert him and who had the necessary ability with the pen—Peter Oliver, a brilliant man with a searching mind, a rollicking, energetic sense of humor, and an unbreakable devotion to the Crown. He and Hutchinson had been friends since childhood.

Peter Oliver's first article of a series in the *Evening Post* stated flatly that Otis was "mad." His habit of stuttering when excited and his disdainful carelessness of style were pointed out as symptoms. Early instances of apparent instability, which had been considered by his friends as a nervous characteristic, were now seen by his enemies as sure signs of insanity. After all, who but a lunatic would attack Thomas Hutchinson? "The more common opinion," said Oliver, "was that a frenzy had seized the unhappy author," who was known around town as "the crazy man." This was "Bluster," the man of ungoverned passions, disappointed ambitions, implacable malice, and envy of superior merit. The name "Bluster," Oliver's invention, fitted perfectly into the plan to make Otis appear as the frustrated and maddened petty politician.

Otis later said the name was more a help to him than a hindrance, but in fact it stung hard, and he responded in kind with a volley of invective in the *Gazette*. Alluding to Hutchinson's lack of legal training, Otis said that the "great luminary of the law" was a tyrant who gloried in the "pomp and puff"[5] of his robes, but those who looked closely could see a cloven hoof peeping out from under the flowing black and the gorgeous scarlet. Hutchinson's friends had said that "Bluster" was a key member of a dark cabal. The real junto, Otis said, were the men he called "the Benefactors," who aimed at destroying the liberty of the province and establishing absolute control for their own benefit. Oliver, in his earlier writing, masqueraded as a country squire who received his news from his friend, the parson, and the parson had predicted that Otis would come to no good end. Otis enjoyed that. "Go on, then," he said with derision, *"Evening Posts*, pimps, parasites, sycophants, predicting parsons and pedagogues, I am ready for ye all." When all other attempts fail, he told them, represent me as a madman. But Bluster, or whoever is meant by that name, "shall never seek or accept or any office during life but shall devote all his leisure to . . . detecting and exposing state-rooks and robbers."[6]

The following two issues of the *Post* were full of responses to Otis' latest rally, and included Samuel Adams as a target of attack, revealing the concern that Adams' articles were causing in the ranks of the court party.[7] Bluster, said Peter Oliver, "had under him a journeyman scribbler" who could best be described in the words of Hudibras:

> A paltry wretch he had, *half-starved*
> That him in place of *zany* served
> Whose business was to *pump* and *wheedle*
> And men with their own keys unriddle
> To *fetch* and carry *intelligence*
> Of *whom*, and *what*, and *where*, and *whence*
> And all *discoveries* disperse
> 'Mong the whole *pack* of *conjurers*.

Adams was much worse, because he, possessing judgment, gained his daily bread from a madman. The battle was not confined to writings alone. Samuel Otis reported that James was threatened with a beating by "six Yanky officers," who, he asserted, were kept from striking his brother only by their knowledge that it "would have caused them a drubbing from the people of the town."[8]

What assistance Adams was giving Otis in 1762 will never be completely known, but the reaction of Hutchinson's writers makes it clear that he was doing at least two things—writing damaging articles against the administration and providing information which Otis was able to use in combating the resurgent court party. There were anonymous columns in the *Gazette* that concentrated on the misuse of power—Otis' main theme at this time —and it may be that the collaboration began on this point of attack, one that would prove to be a lifelong obsession for both men.

The *Post* on March 21 topped its front page with mocking lines that all would recognize as the stutter of an angry James Otis: "So! Jemmy—So! So! Jemmy—well—well—why aye Jemmy— Very well—so—so—so, Jemmy—so." On the inside pages a long dialogue set to verse ridiculed Otis and Adams in a burlesque of Swift's "Traulus":

> TOM: Whence come these inconsistent fits?
> ROB: Why, Tom, the man has lost his wits.
>
> X X X X
>
> Tom, you mistake the matter quite,
> Your barking curs will seldom bite
> And Tho' you hear him stut-tut-tut-ter
> He barks as fast as he can utter.
> He prates in spite of all impediment
> While none believe that what he said he meant.
>
> X X X X
>
> What e'er he speaks for madness goes
> With no effect on friends or foes.[9]

Another column that day attacked the Caucus Club as a cabal where political bosses of the town met to decide ahead of time who would win and lose in the voting at town meetings.

In the flashes and thunder of this political storm John Adams sailed serene, contributing to the *Post* a column of pastoral philosophy signed "Humphrey Ploughjogger." These occasional pieces talked of husbandry and of making hemp, noting blandly that "it is a pleasant thing to see one's words in print," and took no sides. Although John Adams attended some of the key events of these days and wrote much about them later in life, he was not himself one of the important movers in 1763. He was young, ambitious, interested in many things, and searching for himself, but he was as yet uncommitted and of little consequence to either side in Boston.

At this point in the battle of the presses, Otis printed in both the *Gazette* and the *Post* a speech he had made at a town meeting, a glowing tribute to King George III, and to the British constitution.[10]

There was one point in his speech that struck the court-party writers as particularly incongruous. To them it was high comedy to find Otis talking of kings and constitutions, dominions and powers, liberties and rights, and the future of the British Empire to a motley group of "wardens and hemp-surveyors, firewards, assessors and tax-gatherers, board-surveyors, fence-viewers and stave-cullers, haywards and constables, leather-sealers and market clerks, scavengers, town clerk and hogreeves." It was hard for them to visualize without laughter these rustics as the recipients of a lofty address that began, "Fathers, Friends, Fellow-citizens and Countrymen." To their own amusement Hutchinson's writers juxtaposed the visions of simple tradesmen and clouds of political oratory, but their brilliant comic thrusts reveal their tragic misunderstanding of the powerful, irreversible changes already under way in these town meetings, in the small towns of the province as well as in Boston. Peter Oliver produced a burlesque of the speech in verse, a masterpiece in the genre of political lampoons:

> We are here to exercise one of our *privileges most dear;*
> Namely to *choose officers* for the ensuing year.
> Let us keep the public good in sight;
> And *choose such,* and such *only,* as we *pitched* upon last night.[11]

The writers concluded that they were lucky: the wickedness of Otis' heart was balanced by the weakness of his head.

A few days later, Otis announced he had three books "prepared and preparing for the press." He would publish an "impartial history" of the past session of the House, an account of the background behind the grant of Mount Desert to Bernard, and an analysis of the political situation in Massachusetts Bay. The history of the House was probably an expansion of the *Vindication;* although it was never published, it served as a basis for several later writings. The story of Mount Desert never appeared anywhere, unfortunately, and may have been among the papers he burned in July of that year. His comments on the rights of the colonists would be delayed a year, indicating the amount of time he used in researching the legal precedents and also the time he spent in the newspaper battles of that spring and summer. At the end of his announcement of works in progress, Otis placed a few lines of poetry after Virgil, to be descriptive of himself:

> Nor vulgar fame nor charms of earthly crowns,
> Nor purpled tyrants with their angry frowns,
> Nor faithless brothers sowing seeds of hate,
> Nor all the terrors in the powers of Fate
> Can turn him from the pleasing paths of right
> His guide's the father of eternal light.[12]

At least one point of those lines had to have been true; those he saw as tyrants surely must have purpled on reading the *Gazette* that day.

In England, now that the expenses and sacrifices of a great war were over and another large territory had become a part of the British Empire, statesmen, merchants, and ordinary London citizens were asking just what significance could be attached to this victory. Certainly it would mean increased political responsibility and trade. The western-hemisphere possessions, new and old, would have to be guarded by greater sea and land forces, and Britons would have to pay the heavy expenditures involved. Beyond this, Englishmen asked themselves, "What have we profited?" The context of the question was purely material, and in an age of rapidly growing mercantile interests, the answer had to be phrased in terms of the pound sterling.

And it was. In England the Acts of Trade were signed in April, although they did not reach Boston until mid-September. The news was followed closely by speculation that more trade laws were coming and that the molasses tax of nine pence per gallon would be even more strictly enforced. Boston merchants, struggling to renew trade connections in the postwar depression and harassed by the customs officials with their writs of assistance, were not ready to welcome any new tax burden. By April their disgruntlement had served to create The Society for Encouraging Trade and Commerce, a union of 147 merchants in opposition to any change in trade policy, customs procedures, or taxes. It was the duty of a watchdog committee of 15 merchants to call a full meeting whenever infringements of current trade practices made it necessary.[13]

The main function of the association was to serve as what would now be called a lobby, protecting the interests of local merchants. The society exchanged correspondence with the Massachusetts General Court and even with members of Parliament, explaining the complex trading cycle that sent fish, lumber, horses, and provisions to the West Indies in exchange for molasses, which went out again as rum to the southern colonies (for grain and naval stores) and to Africa (for slaves, which were sold in the West Indies) and to Europe. The hard money that Boston traders siphoned off this system was used to pay for manufactured goods from England. They insisted that the trading arrangement was a delicate balance that could be destroyed by an unthinking application of new tax pressures, and they threatened that England, in the end, would suffer most from a collapse of colonial trade. The society made sense to other merchants, and soon the ports of Salem, Marblehead, and Plymouth formed their own lobbies. The idea spread to Newport, New York, and Philadelphia in the following year.

The fighting between the Court party and the popular party continued throughout May and June, but without the fire and brimstone of earlier weeks. Otis during this time concentrated on the plural officeholding of Hutchinson and the principle of separation of powers. In the throes of this exchange, Hutchinson was surprised to find that Otis sought his company and treated him with a friendliness that went beyond mere civility. This led him to believe that his attempts to conciliate Otis were working, but what Otis said about him in the press proved him wrong. He could not understand Otis, he wrote to Israel Williams. "He professes to have buried the hatchet every three of four months. As soon as ever anybody affronts him, be it who it will, he wreaks all his malice and revenge upon me."

Hutchinson continued to work on his history, and when writing later on the subject of his research to fellow historian Ezra Stiles, he added, "I threaten Mr. Otis sometimes that I will be revenged of him after I am dead."[14]

6

The Rights of the British Colonies

May 1763–July 1764

There has been a most profound and I think shameful silence, till it seems almost too late to assert our indisputable rights as men and citizens. What must posterity think of us. The trade of the whole continent taxed by Parliament, stamps and other internal duties and taxes, as they are called, talked of, and not one petition to the King and Parliament for relief.

JAMES OTIS, *Rights of the British Colonies Asserted and Proved*, 1764

THE GENERAL COURT OPENED in May 1763 with Timothy Ruggles as speaker and Roland Cotton as clerk. Colonel Otis was re-elected to the council, but there he found himself facing Hutchinson, the two Olivers, William Brattle, and Hutchinson's close friend, Israel Williams. The popular party was becalmed in a quiet province, and John Adams echoed the feeling of political placidity in his "Humphrey Ploughjogger" essays in the *Post*, calling for less "writing pollyticks, breaking heads, boxing ears, ringing noses, and kicking breeches."[1]

Governor Bernard's opening speech expressed his satisfaction with the end of the war with France and provided to the Boston merchants the unnecessary warning that war profits would be drying up and that new commercial enterprises would have to be found. "Your fortunes are now in your own hands," he said, speaking to men who perceived ironies in those words even if he did not, "and on yourselves will greatly depend the future welfare of your country." Otis was a member of the committee appointed to reply to the governor, but his party's fortunes were so low that he could not prevent an obsequious answer ("We hope your Excellency will have the honor to be distinguished in England for your attachment to our interest"). Earlier in the day Otis had made a motion to pay Bernard his salary, "which was considered as an overture of reconciliation and occasioned some mirth in which he joined."[2] Now, however, he found himself unable to stomach the sugary language of the draft reply, which he could not prevent. The court party prevailed in every action, and hostilities ran high. Edes and Gill, printers of the House journal, lost the contract because they had also printed articles by Otis, Adams, and other popular-party writers in their *Gazette*. Even the chaplain of the General Court was replaced by another man of God more friendly to the Crown.

On the third day of the session Otis reached the boiling point and walked out, swearing he would resign and not return. His friends prevailed on the House to delay acceptance of his resignation and that night urged him to recognize the futility of his gesture. He did, and on the following day "desired leave to resume his seat, which was granted not without some humiliation."[3] Bernard thought that under the circumstances Otis would be more quiet. "However," he said, "care must be taken to prevent his rallying which I doubt not he will be ready to do upon the first opportunity."

That opportunity lay not far away. It was said that Parliament was drawing up new acts of trade that would give much stronger powers to his majesty's naval forces in North America, allowing officers to seize violators of customs laws and prosecute them in Admiralty Courts. This meant to New Englanders that the British men-of-war would become, like the pirates and the French privateers, ships to avoid at all cost. The benevolent picture of the protective forces of the Crown was fading, to be replaced by an image of arbitrary power and suppression. Letters from knowledgeable men in London warned that there would soon be a new and stiffer tax law, affecting primarily the molasses trade. Molasses was always an inviting target. A Parliament indifferent to other aspects of colonial life paid a great deal of attention to the possibility of competition from Massachusetts and the other provinces; governors were obliged to write the home ministry at frequent intervals, describing any new effort, no matter how small, to manufacture any product. Raw molasses from the West Indies went into American distilleries and came out as rum, the only significant "manufactured" product among all the items— fish, lumber, grain—shipped by American colonies. It was thus a potential competitor and therefore fair game in the scheme that made "external taxes" double as tariffs.

Angered by what he saw as the complicity of the province administration in the arbitrary attitude of Parliament, James Otis challenged Peter Oliver to "undertake a ramble" in another series of debates—but by the time this challenge was published Otis had entered his first serious slide into gloom and despondence. In the grip of these forces, beset by what doubts, pressures, fears, and evils no one knows, he took all his papers out into his back garden and burned them, consigning to the flames his manuscript on the granting of Mount Desert Island to Bernard, his legal papers, and probably many other notes and drafts, including the manuscript on Greek prosody. Word of his act spread through the town and his enemies were quick to capitalize on it. A week later the *Post* asked the question, Was the writer who said he had a book dedicated to the king "raving mad" when he *wrote* his piece, or when he *burned* it? Other irregularities, such as his quitting his seat in the House, were called up as evidences of insanity.[4]

August 15 was set aside for celebration of the Treaty of Paris.[5] At one o'clock, standing on the narrow balcony outside his window at the Town House, Governor Bernard read the proclamation of the king announcing a new era of peace, while the cannons at Castle William fired a 21-gun salute. The militia paraded through the town and in the evening the governor hosted an elegant dinner for 200 guests at Faneuil Hall. This era of good feeling, however, was doomed to be short-lived. Hutchinson had already looked ahead, following in his mind the inevitable results of the new pressure on the molasses trade, and he feared the problems that were sure to follow. "Do they see the consequences?" he asked a friend in London. Taxes on molasses would bring a call for revenue from other sectors of trade. Would this, he asked, be consistent with "the so much esteemed privilege of English subjects, the being taxed by their own representatives?"[6] There was certain to be trouble.

Bostonians did not like to pay local taxes either, and for this reason Samuel Adams was very popular as one of the tax collectors who was not terribly conscientious. There had been a long line of benevolent tax men, who by no coincidence were also members of the Caucus Club and potential political figures in the town. The general philosophy was that Boston had suffered more than most towns, with its devastating fires, its decimating plagues, and the requirements to support a long war with men and money. So, like many other cities then and now, Boston postponed its tax problems whenever possible, and one way to do this was to be lenient with the collectors, who in turn did not press overly hard upon those who could not or would not pay.

Adams was only one of several collectors who found it impossible to balance the books. In 1758, when Adams was first voted a tax collector, tax official Thomas Downe, Jr., was found in arrears by "considerable sums" for the years 1751 to 1755. In Downe's behalf it was pointed out that "there were many persons in some of the above years taxed, so extremely poor that said Downe could not get one farthing of them, nor are they yet able to pay any part; many others have been dead for some time and left nothing."[7] Each of the four Boston collectors had responsibility for three wards of the town and each collector was pledged to turn in the sum of money assessed against his list of citizens, from which he was paid a commission of nine pence on the pound. The collector, however, had very little leverage in seeking his money. By law, he could seize the estate of a person who did not pay. He then had to retain the seized goods in his own control for four days, after which he could sell them at auction to recover the money. This was a cumbersome and harsh procedure, and for this reason collectors often simply brought suit against the debtor, although there was no specific provision in the law authorizing such legal action.

By September of 1763 Samuel Adams had fallen so far behind in his tax collections that the situation was becoming hopeless. Hutchinson saw an opportunity to make his position more difficult and possibly to show up his "defalcations" against the town. He ruled in Superior Court to enforce an old province law which made it illegal for tax collectors to bring citizens to court and sue for back taxes, making the only recourse the seizure of the goods of the debtor and their sale at auction. Adams and the three other Boston tax collectors appealed to the General Court with a petition to remove the old law and allow common suits. The House then, after some strong objections, passed a temporary bill making it legal for Boston collectors to sue for taxes,[8] frustrating Hutchinson's attempt to put pressure on Adams.

As the province began to realize that the ministry in London was determined to push through new taxes, the power of the popular party was increased by the return of many merchants to its ranks. The reason was clear. In 1763, 15,000 hogsheads of molasses were imported into Boston, all but 500 from non-British ports, representing £100,000 sterling. To buy the molasses, the province had to export a large amount of fish and lumber. A heavy duty on molasses would stop the trade and dry up the sources in the West Indies. It would also cut British profits by £100,000. "Would it not be the case," Bernard asked, "of the man whose curiosity (or expectation of extraordinary present gain) killed the goose who laid the golden eggs?"[9]

But it was soon apparent that no effort on the American side of the Atlantic could stop Parliament from voting a new tax, and in this extremity the Massachusetts General Court turned to the man who had solved the toughest problems in the past—their delegate to the Albany Congress, the several border disputes with New Hampshire, New York, and Connecticut, the conference with the Indians at Casco on the rights of settlement above the Kennebec. The House of Representatives requested that Hutchinson, the recognized master of negotiation, be sent to London as a special agent to explain the Massachusetts position in Parliament and to stop the new tax measures before they became law. The call for Hutchinson was almost unanimous—the council gave him all its votes and the House tally was 80 to 8, with four of the negatives coming from Otis and the Boston bloc.

As was obvious from the session a year earlier, Hutchinson had long coveted the position as agent for Massachusetts, hoping that close contact with Crown policy makers in England might help him to secure the governorship when an opening came. It was therefore extremely difficult for him now to weigh the advantages of the assignment as special agent against the problems that would accrue if he left the colony. To go to London he would need the complete support of Bernard, or else it would appear that he had been too quick to leave his responsibilities as lieutenant governor to seize this opportunity. Bernard, however, would not give his blessing. He needed Hutchinson's help in the running of province administration, but also he foresaw his lieutenant gaining a position too close to the Crown. He knew Hutchinson's ambitions, and he knew that Hutchinson, and not himself, actually controlled the court party and would make further gains if his mission to London were successful. Also, if Bernard approved Hutchinson's going, he might be acting contrary to the wishes of the Crown; there were no instructions on this point, and Bernard did not like to act without instructions. After all, he had been appointed to carry out the policy of the Crown, which in this case meant enforcement of tariff regulations, not objections to them. He therefore neither approved nor disapproved the idea, but he let Hutchinson know of his unofficial reservations. He would consent, he said, to Hutchinson's going, but this should not be taken to mean he had given leave of absence.

Bernard's hesitation was enough to convince Hutchinson that he would risk too much by agreeing to make the journey. Even without this element, the thought of leaving his family disturbed him; there had been sickness in the household; he still wanted to be able to help his son Thomas with the inevitable problems of taking over the family trading interests. Also, leaving Boston meant risking the loss of his political posts. The *Gazette* was openly speculating that "the various offices his Honor now sustains will become vacant." Hutchinson decided not to accept. He wrote to Secretary Andrew Oliver requesting the General Court "either wholly to excuse me from this service or to admit of my engaging in it when the present obstructions can be removed."[10]

The motion that Hutchinson be "wholly excused" passed in the House by a vote of 41 to 32, but the council refused to change its earlier vote. The question became deadlocked and was carried over to the next session. Bernard, obviously pleased, commented that this was "the best that could have happened." Hutchinson's opportunity was lost, although he continued to hope for another chance in the May session, writing to Halifax and to the Lords of Trade for permission to go to England if the next vote should be in his favor.[11]

Before the General Court session closed on February 4, Bernard found that he had yet another decision to make concerning the Otis family. Since the previous September, when Sylvanus Bourne died, Bernard had demurred in filling the vacant position of chief justice of the Court of Common Pleas in Barnstable. He knew that Colonel Otis thirsted for the job and that it would be a direct insult to give the position to someone else. Still, Bernard did not like to give up one of his few patronage appointments to Colonel Otis without receiving in return a profession of loyalty to the province administration. He lingered over the selection, trying to force Otis into line, and finally professed to have exacted a promise from the colonel that his nomination as justice would "wipe away all the ill humor which his former disappointment had occasioned," the loss of the Superior Court justiceship four years earlier. Even John Adams came to believe that the Otises had sold out to Bernard for the price of a Barnstable office and that there would be a new cooperation with Hutchinson in support of Crown policy. Many years later he confessed that he had condemned James Otis as "a mastiff that will bark and roar like a lion one hour, and the next, if a sop is thrown his way, will creep like a spaniel."[12]

The creation of the Lords of Trade and the establishment of a secretary of state for North America had done little to improve the British ministry's lack of knowledge of affairs in the colonies. There were now a few more minor Crown officials in the ports and capitals along the western side of the Atlantic, but Parliament on the whole, in exercising "control" of this vast area, depended for its information on the gossip and speculation and bias of letters arriving in London after a two-month journey. Governors wrote, businessmen wrote, friends wrote. Parliament read and listened to the vague and sporadic news of the American possessions and their doings.

This nearly complete lack of communication was more psychological than it was geographic. The men of London felt they were missing nothing; they knew the people of America and the temper there only too well. There was very little to be learned. Resolute action would solve the few problems that did exist, problems that, in the eyes of the ministry, were caused by an inadequate revenue from America. The immediate solution, putting theories to practical expression, was a new tax law.

The old Molasses Act of 1733 had been instituted for a 30-year period and was due to expire; George Grenville, chancellor of the Exchequer, therefore seized this opportunity to renew the essentials of the act, to provide it with a stronger enforcement, and to expand its coverage. He presented to Parliament on March 9, 1764, an act that would place a tax on certain items by the requirement to purchase stamps. The act, he insisted, was equitable, logical, and even beneficial to the colonies. Duties would be laid on the correspondence associated with business activities across a broad range, thus falling fairly and evenly on the whole population. This legislation, soon to be called the Sugar Act, set a tax of three pence on imported molasses. The cost of smuggling, Grenville figured, ran to about 1½ pence per gallon. Since the tax was only twice as much, it would be simpler all around for the merchants to pay it, especially since it was only one-third of the old (and entirely evaded) tax of nine pence. Trade might be reduced under the three-pence tax, he calculated, but not by very much. If Parliament and the king were willing to drop the tax to one penny per gallon, trade would continue at present rates, but of course there would be less revenue.[13]

There were a few sections of the Sugar Act that favored Americans, including a prohibition against importing into England all rum except that produced in the colonies, but the fundamental purpose of the act was to provide revenues that would offset the "operating costs" of the colonies and would also reimburse the home country for at least one-third of the expenditures of the war in North America. In brief, in addition to reestablishing and reinforcing the old Molasses Act, it gave more authority to customs men (who were made immune from damage suits) and to the Admiralty Courts; it increased the list of American raw materials such as iron and lumber, destined for European ports, which had to be offloaded and reshipped from England; and it put heavier duties on "foreign" (non-English) goods such as wine and coffee. The main weight, of course, fell on the molasses trade.

There was relatively little opposition in Parliament to this new legislation. Grenville believed that mutual good faith between England and America would make the new act work; his argument was helped by the absence of an alternative. The act passed Commons on February 27, Lords on March 8, and was signed for the king by his commissioners (George III being ill) on March 22. Nothing remained but to publish it in the American colonies. The effective date for implementing the tax would be September 29, 1764. Massachusetts at this time produced 2,700,000 gallons of rum annually in its 60 distilleries. The British West Indies, at full production, could supply only 25 percent of the molasses needed to keep the provincial distilleries running; the rest came from the other islands in the West Indies. The new law, however, allowed import only from the British Islands. The merchants had a choice: they could violate the law or close the plants.

For James Otis the tightening of restrictions on trade and the warning of more to come was a powerful stimulant, providing him with a focal point he had been unable to find in months past. He began to make notes for a new essay,[14] one that would begin with the forces that formed the origins of government. There were several ways that governments could be created, he wrote— through brute force, through negotiation of a compact, or on the rights to property. None of these, however, had the force of natural law, where absolute power rests with God alone. The unwritten law of British constitution, he said, represented the best arrangement of political power on earth. This was an ideal framework of law and custom in which every man's rights were recognized. The lesson of history, however, taught that even the British Parliament could be "subverted," and therefore the people had to be wary and to cherish their right to the ultimate power in the kingdom. Parliament had authority to make laws, but there was a limit to all power. Parliament could not "make two and two five," and it could not levy taxes without representation, because men would be forced to obey a law to which they had not consented.

If Parliament, "deceived . . . misinformed . . . or misrepresented," makes an erroneous law, Otis wrote, British subjects must obey it until it can be repealed. In its collective wisdom, however, Parliament would soon perceive the unwise legislation and change it. If Parliament did not recognize its errors, the people would bring them to light, for "if our hands are tied by the passing of an act of Parliament, our mouths are not stopped." It was the right of every man to seek redress from any wrongful law, and since Parliament was an objective, rational body, it would always change the law when it recognized its own error. Americans must make Parliament see the error, in this case, of the unconstitutional Sugar Act.

As for ideas of independence, the American colonies would never move in that direction unless "driven to it" by ministerial oppression; however, "one single act of Parliament . . . has set people a thinking, in six months, more than they had done in their whole lives before." The essay, titled *Rights of the British Colonies Asserted and Proved,* is a strong plea for reconciliation, based on a vision of the future British Empire as the greatest political power of all time. Otis insists that a clear-thinking Parliament, understanding its limitations, can move toward this goal by allowing American representation in London. Perhaps the central weakness of the work is his idealistic description of an enlightened and objective Parliament, capable of self-analysis, self-restraint, and self-correction. It was what he desperately wanted to believe.

While Otis was working on *Rights,* Samuel Adams also was

writing. He had been appointed to draw up Boston's annual instructions to its representatives in the General Court, and he presented his draft at a town meeting on May 24. He, too, considered the actions that should be taken in response to the new laws. If trade may be taxed, he said, why not land? And if land, "why not the produce of our lands and everything we possess or make use of? This we apprehend annihilates our Charter Right to govern and tax ourselves." To Adams, acceptance of the taxes as legal would turn Americans into "tributary slaves." The most significant comment in the instructions were the final words, in which Adams called for a united approach by all Americans:

> As his Majesty's other North American colonies are embarked with us in this most important bottom, we further desire you to use your endeavors that their weight may be added to that of this province; that by the united applications of all who are aggrieved, all may obtain redress.[15]

The instructions were approved by the town on Thursday, May 24, and published in the Boston newspapers on the following Monday. When the House of Representatives met for the new session, it approved Otis' *Rights* as the sentiments of Massachusetts and immediately appointed a committee (including Otis, Thacher, and Cushing) to correspond with the other provincial assemblies on the subject of joint petitions to the Crown concerning the rights of the colonists—in other words, to fight the Sugar Act.

Bernard sensed from the beginning that this move would cause trouble. He wrote the Lords of Trade that the "union" which the Massachusetts House had in mind "may seem at first sight only an occasional measure for a particular purpose," but he himself was convinced that "the purposes it is to serve are deeper than they now appear." Otis, he said, intended to divide the General Court and lay the groundwork for an organization of the American colonial assemblies to oppose Parliamentary legislation that might run contrary to their ideas. "Perhaps I may be too suspicious," Bernard concluded. "A little time will show whether I am or not."[16] The House dispatched Otis' *Rights* to London and to all the other colonial assemblies. Hutchinson and Bernard tried to force the House to reconsider, withdraw *Rights*, and work with the council toward a joint statement of policy, and when the House refused, the governor prorogued the General Court. He then also sent several copies of *Rights* to England, noting that "as the writer is by nature violent and vehement in his principles, this piece appears to us more temperate and decent than was at first expected, however indecent and intemperate it may show on your side the water."[17]

Thomas Hutchinson was not so charitable as Bernard. He told Jackson that Otis' *Rights* was "a loose, unconnected performance," not worth sending to London except that the House had made reference to it in its letter to the agent Bollan. More of the same kind of thing could be expected in the future, he said; it was unfortunate that the home government did not understand the inflammatory effect of its recent acts. He supported this point of view with a surprisingly strong essay of his own, written during the same weeks that Otis worked on his *Rights*. Hutchinson sent both papers to Jackson—but at the last moment he drew back, requesting that his authorship be kept secret. In fact, he asked Jackson to doctor the writing enough to make it appear that it had been composed in England. Perhaps he recognized that his arguments were surprisingly close to those of Otis. Parliament was supreme, he wrote, but there was a need and a definite place for the colonial legislatures as part of the system of government. The rights of the colonists were the same as those of any Englishman, regardless of geographical location, and it was obvious that Americans were not represented in Parliament, no matter how representation was defined or qualified. Those simple facts, he said, should be evident to all.[18]

History might have been different if Thomas Hutchinson had signed his name and had given his weight to that pamphlet, but he could not bring himself to say anything that might be contrary to Crown policy. Because of his loyalty, Hutchinson's political ideas, which were as hard-hitting and pertinent as Otis', were never given the stature that his reputation would have provided. As one consequence, the widespread belief that he favored the new taxes was never dispelled. Ironically, his own words and ideas in this essay, distributed to many London politicians by Bollan, became the rallying cry for British Whigs, making Barré and Conway the toast of the colonies.

With writings by Otis, Thacher, and Hutchinson circulating in London at the same time, there was no lack of explanation of the Boston position. Even Bernard was busy writing, and he, too, insisted that the new taxes would cause far more trouble than the administration needed at the moment.

7

Jemmibullero

July 1764–April 1765

And Jemmy is a sorry jade,—ah! Jemmy hasn't mettle,
And Jemmy pleads his bloody nose when quarrels he shou'd settle!
And Jemmy is as great a puff as Jemmy's a poltroon,
—'Tis Jemmy blusters all the morn, to slink away at noon.

Boston Evening Post, May 13, 1765

THERE WAS NOTHING that Otis, Hutchinson, or anyone else could do to stop the Sugar Act, which would go into effect on September 29, 1764. Bernard had intended to call the next session of the General Court on September 5, but he knew feelings would run high since the date for implementation of the act would then be only three weeks away. Rather than face a House in session when the new taxes went into effect, he delayed the opening, but this tactic proved of little help. When the House finally assembled on October 18, James Otis was ready with a new draft petition to be sent to the king. The subject: taxation without representation.[1]

Otis' petition was approved in the House but summarily rejected by the council. As a conciliatory measure, a joint committee was then formed to rewrite it. Among the 21 members were Otis, Thacher, Bourne, and Cushing from the House, and Hutchinson, Trowbridge, and Colonel Otis from the council. Hutchinson did not want to see the loss of the colony's rights and privileges, but he believed that the American colonial charters, designed for little trading and farming settlements, inevitably had to disappear as the burgeoning colonies became more and more a significant part of the empire. Like Otis, he revered the greatness of Britannia, but he stressed more than Otis the strength that grew out of uniformity in government. Roughly phrased and insulting petitions to the king and Parliament, he argued, would only hasten the demise of the charters. For ten days and several drafts the committee struggled with the rewording of Otis' original petition, with Hutchinson, unmatched as a negotiator, pointing out line by line the parts that would give offense in London. After what Hutchinson called "a fortnight in altercations,"[2] the committee reached an impasse—Otis would concede no further changes, and a majority of the members would not sign the draft. Hutchinson then submitted his own version, calling on Parliament to allow the "privileges of British citizens," and requesting relief from the Sugar Act as an indulgence rather than a recognition of the rights of American colonists. Otis disagreed violently, but he was in a weak position, since his own draft had failed. The popular-party members were able to effect a few minor substitutions and word changes, after which Hutchinson's draft carried the day.[3]

The victory, however, was costly for Hutchinson. The word went out in Boston that the responsibility for the change in tone of the petition was to be laid at Hutchinson's feet—Harbottle Dorr scribbled on his copy of the *Evening Post*'s report of the petition, "by the management of Gov. Hutchinson the above spiritless thing sent."[4] After the fighting was over and Hutchinson had won the field, he began to have second thoughts. Weak as the petition was, it nonetheless objected to the king's law, and Hutchinson was now himself associated with this "folly and madness." He sank into one of the gloomy moods that visited him with increasing frequency, and wished himself elsewhere: "If I was in the beginning of life I should be tempted to go back to Lincolnshire from where my great grandfather came but it is too late in the day."[5]

Massachusetts was not the only colony to feel the impact of the Sugar Act. In Rhode Island, Governor Stephen Hopkins had written an essay explaining the fragile interrelationships of his colony's trade. Warning that the new restrictions would upset the economic structure, he urged all the colonies to unite in providing Parliament with a better idea of the effects of these disastrous new laws. This stirred the Rhode Island loyalists, who were anxious to discredit Hopkins. Then in another pamphlet, *The Rights of the Colonies Examined,* published in December 1764, Hopkins expanded his view to ask whether the American colonists were to be allowed all the rights of British subjects or whether these were to be taken away by an arbitrary Parliament. He concluded, as had Otis, that power had its limits, a fact that Parliament should understand. Hopkins was immediately challenged in the press by the loyalist Martin Howard, who—much to the distaste of Otis—earlier had advocated doing away with Rhode Island's charter and establishing a nobility in America. Otis then entered the controversy in support of Hopkins with a new essay, entitled *A Vindication of the British Colonies.*

Vindication is a work that has affected readers—then and now —in different ways. Those who favored the stand Otis had taken against autocratic and arbitrary rule and who believed that Parliamentary legislation of that time had more bad than good in it were ready to see this latest essay as a very appropriate and successful response—powerful, pointed, and full of excellent wit. Those who saw Otis as a dangerous and unpredictable politician of the masses were appalled by his crudities and were quick to assert that the piece was riddled by inconsistencies and shallow reasoning.

With his informal style Otis had by this time published enough of his writing to constitute a profitable target for those who wished to prove him inconsistent. In his earlier work Otis had said that Parliament had the *power* to make legislation, but not necessarily the *right* to do so. Now he varied his phraseology slightly: Parliament had the *right* to tax the colonies, but *fairness* would dictate that it should not do so. Colonial representation in Parliament, he said, exists "by law" but not "in fact."

There was no question in his mind, however, of the jurisdiction of Parliament, and he quoted passages from *Rights* to show he continued to admit the subordination of the colonies. The empire, he reasoned, was a civilizing power of the greatest importance in the world, bringing good to mankind. Its driving force was the British constitution, which was based on and complementary to natural law. The king, as the head of this political organization and Parliament, as its arbitrator and legislator, represented the supreme earthly power. It was Otis' view that professing allegiance and respect for the king and Parliament was simply stating one's faith in the most effective political organization on earth. That much said, Otis insisted that it was the responsibility of every citizen (and especially those in the legal profession) to criticize any discrepancy in the law and thus improve the empire. Again as in the past he emphasized that the members of Parliament were human and could err, but they were objective and rational and would rectify their errors whenever these were pointed out. In expressing support for Howard, Otis signaled the loyalists that he was ready for another battle, and many a pen was put to paper in the months ahead in the preparation of heavier assaults on Otis than he had ever before received.

It was a cold winter that year, and a heavy blanket of snow added to the problems of the many unemployed mechanics and laborers. The West Indian trade had dropped off to practically nothing. It was in this New England winter that the farmers as well as the merchants began to believe that Otis was right—the policies of Parliament, which the court party so strongly supported, were destroying the commerce of the province. Rum distilleries were closed, shipbuilding stopped, and money became scarce. Otis, who was convinced that the "middling more necessitous and laboring people" would bear the brunt of the new restrictions, wrote his father, "The time has come which we have long foreseen. I blame the people in England not half as much as I do our own." Thomas Hutchinson and the court party, he felt, would have to bear the responsibility for the demise of prosperity. "If we will be slaves I am only sorry 'tis to a pack of villains among ourselves."[6]

By January the full force of the depression fell on Boston as the ice-locked port suffered under temperatures that were "the coldest of any for 12 years." Several of the best-known merchants were forced to declare bankruptcy, including first-rate business-men such as Nathaniel Wheelwright, John Scollay, Peter Bourne, and William Hasking.[7] There were shuttered and barred stores on streets that had been bustling for decades, and Otis wrote that the townspeople were filled with "pale horror and dread."

Throughout the summer and fall Hutchinson had been hard at work on his history. He was chagrined that the pressure of his affairs had kept him from devoting to the book the necessary re-flection, so that his chapters were more an amassing of facts than a well-developed historical approach, and he also mourned his lack of capability as a writer. The first volume, however, was an immediate popular success. Published in December, it sold out and was widely read throughout New England.

If he was dissatisfied with his writing, Hutchinson also was well aware of his shortcomings as a judge. He continued to read in the law, but his shallow background forced him to rely on his politi-cal and mercantile experience and his own common sense to make the decisions required of him. In one case that occurred at this time, a woman was forced to sell most of her clothing in or-der to help pay her husband's debts. Hutchinson deeply regretted that the lawyers in this instance had so little legal erudition in their arguments. He had wanted "more authorities cited, in a matter of so great consequence," in order to obtain some basis for a ruling. His comments reveal his sympathy for the woman and his distress at his own lack of contribution to the case.[8]

The first problem for the January session of the General Court was to agree on a replacement for Jasper Mauduit, who had asked to be relieved of his duties as agent because of ill health. Bernard wanted Jackson as a replacement, while the popular party again supported Israel Mauduit, Jasper's brother. In the end it was Otis who surprised his fellow Boston members by siding with Bernard. Jackson won easily when it was clear that Otis favored him. Otis further surprised the popular party when he voted to compensate Hutchinson with a bonus of £40 for extra work be-yond the requirements of his position. This motion passed by one vote. Many saw the conciliatory action by Otis as an effort to in-fluence fellow representatives of the General Court, which was then considering his own petition for compensation for a six-mile square of land the Otis family had lost because of a change in the boundary line between Massachusetts and New Hampshire. Although Bernard responded to Otis' cooperation by approving his election as speaker pro tempore in the House, he did not support the Otis petition on the land, which passed in the House but was rejected by the council. Otis never received any compensation for his lost land.[9]

The troubles of the port town and the province were just beginning. In London, George Grenville, still the most powerful man in the king's ministry, struggled against the onslaught of domestic problems that ranged from a heavy national debt to an extraordinarily corrupt Parliament, and at the same time tried to come to grips with the financial difficulties created by the American colonies. The large customs establishment and the standing army in America were taking far more out of the treasury than the colonies supplied annually to England in tax payments. Grenville thought the Sugar Act was a continuing success and a good indicator of the direction to take in gathering in more money for the depleted treasury.

In Boston, Otis was still confident that the pamphlet version of Rights, which had been sent off to London, would awaken Parliament to the American problems. Encouraged by its reception in the Massachusetts House, he imagined Rights being welcomed in England as a carefully reasoned analysis; he saw Parliament accepting his views and acting to correct the mistakes of the past and to improve relationships with the colonies. In fact, the opposite was true. When members of the Board of Trade read Rights, Otis' words only infuriated them and hastened the drafting of harsher legislation. Fighting down the challenge of Barré and other defenders of the colonies, Grenville was able to push through Parliament a new act requiring American taxes in the form of the purchase of stamps for practically every piece of paper that moved—from newspapers to court documents, from mortgages to college diplomas, from contracts to playing cards. This new act passed the House of Commons on February 27 and cleared the House of Lords a week later. For two more weeks, until March 22, the ministers waited to see if the king might recover enough to sign the act. He did not, and the commissioners signed for him. Thus the Stamp Act, in 117 sections, passed into law and was dispatched on its winter sea voyage to the colonies. As a prelude to the arrival of the act, a violent and destructive northeaster swept across Boston harbor all night and all day on March 24, hurling wind and wave against the docks, smashing shipping, flooding warehouses, and leaving the city in watery chaos, with one large ship driven from its anchorage and sunk in the harbor. Boston's merchants sorted out their ruined goods and tallied heavy losses.

In the spring Otis' defense of Hopkins with the *Vindication* opened him to new assaults by Howard. Using Otis' own words, Howard accused him of reversing his earlier stand, deserting the radicals, betraying his party, and toadying to Parliament out of fear of punishment. An enraged Otis joined battle once again, and this time there were no holds barred. Otis' reply, titled *Brief Remarks on the Defense of the Halifax Libel,* survives as one of the best examples of a genre of the times—the partisan, invective-filled personal attack, bursting with uncontrolled self-righteous anger and aimed at unsettling the opponent while allowing one's followers to read along with vicarious enjoyment. Otis lambasted Howard with a barrage of insulting and provocative emotionalism.

> Am I a man, and must not speak? Tears relieve me a moment! Thank God there is no law, human, or divine, against treating a Halifax letter-writer as he deserves.

He characterized Howard and his Newport political associates as a "dirty, drinking, drabbing, contaminated knot of thieves, beggars and transports . . . made up of Turks, Jews, and other infidels, with a few renegado Christians & Catholics."

The scurrilous brickbats fly throughout the essay, but by far the major portion of its 40 pages is a carefully reasoned response to Howard's accusations of "betrayal." Professing absolute loyalty to the Crown, Otis apologizes for anything offensive in *Rights* and *Vindication* and asks pardon for "the least iota" that may have displeased his "superiors." He announces his admiration for a recent pamphlet by Grenville, entitled *Regulations Lately Made Concerning the Colonies,* a conservative view which strongly emphasized the binding authority of Parliamentary legislation on the colonies. Noting the "traces of genius in every sentence," he agrees with Grenville that Parliament is the supreme authority, but again stresses his point that even Parliament can be wrong and can be made to see and rectify its errors. He has never questioned the jurisdiction of Parliament, he says, and he admits that Americans are *legally* represented there. He has, however, two points to make.

First, Parliamentary supremacy does not mean it is above criticism; power always carried the responsibility to be equitable and just. The exercise of Parliament's jurisdiction, even though it is presumed always to be aimed at the good of the people, is open to valid inquiry and criticism. Without "modest and humble enquiries after truth and reason," there would be no human progress. At this point, however, Otis hedges as he has never done before. He adds that critical analysis of legislation must take place while a bill is pending and before it becomes law; after that, there must be humble acquiescence in the decision of Parliament. This rule he urges all men to follow.

Otis' second point concerned American representation in Parliament. The colonies, he says, have *legal* but not *actual* membership, which he called "the essence of a perfect Parliament." Again, his attachment to the ideal of an all-encompassing British Empire is evident in his argument for American representation:

> Upon the reasonableness of an actual American representation I placed my foot and built my only hope and desire, and that not for myself nor for the Americans only, but because I thought it would be for the interest of the whole empire, and be one means of answering some very great purposes, and among others, that of most perfectly conciliating the obedience and reverence of every individual in the empire.

Otis insists that his position on the authority of Parliament has not changed. His opponents, he says, are magnifying out of context some of his minor differences in phraseology. He is a loyal subject, using his abilities in the best and most constructive manner to insure the equity of the king's laws and thus the happiness of the people and the strength of the British Empire.

But in fact Otis had done some backsliding. His concession

that laws, once in effect, ought not be criticized was a major weakening of his earlier position, as was his admission that Americans were legally represented. Under the first restriction he would not have been able to argue against the validity of writs of assistance, at least not from the point he had used to advantage, which was that an act against the constitution and natural law was void as soon as it was made.

Brief Remarks appeared in print in the first week of May, just before elections, adding to the annual storm of abuse then in full force in the newspapers of both sides. To the Boston merchants, the position of Otis seemed to be one of acquiescence to the new legislation. He was saying that the law had to be accepted, that it was beyond argument. Harbottle Dorr opined that the reelection of Otis looked doubtful, and John Adams later recalled, and perhaps overstated, that "the rage against [Otis] in the town of Boston seemed to be without bounds."[10] At this time, fortunately for Otis, his reputation continued to rest on his main work, *Rights*, which was going into its fourth printing in Boston. In it he had taken a much stronger position, declaring that Parliament was fallible and could be challenged by reasoned arguments on the validity of any law. Otis himself must have felt that he had lost ground in the exchange with Howard, because he was in print with a defense of his politics on the same day that *Vindication* was first published. Referring to past sacrifices for the good of the community, he said in a *Gazette* column that he had lost peace quiet, and dear friends in the course of protecting the welfare of fellow Bostonians. His heart, he said, was ready to burst:

> At this instant, I have reason to believe many of you are pouring forth the most severe and undeserved censures of a man, who has risked his life, his family, his all, in your service, more than once . . . so far have I been from giving up one of your rights and privileges, that I have contended for them . . . as for the last and best drop of your and my heart's blood.[11]

As it was, Otis received last-minute help from an unexpected source. Samuel Waterhouse, a minor customs official with a reputation for heavy drinking, gave the *Evening Post* several doggerel-verse stanzas intended to be sung to the tune of "Lillibullero," which was itself a bantering song of ridicule originally aimed at the Irish Catholics during the revolution of 1688. Published in the *Evening Post* on the day before elections, it was calculated to attract attention to a summing-up of Otis' faults:

> And Jemmy is a silly dog, and Jemmy is a tool,
> And Jemmy is a stupid cur, and Jemmy is a fool,
> And Jemmy is a madman, and Jemmy is an ass,
> And Jemmy has a leaden head, & forehead spread with brass.
>
> And Jemmy wrote of government, & Jemmy made a bounce,
> Yet Jemmy's found a scraping pedant—Jemmy is a dunce.
> And Jemmy wrote the Letter too, and Jemmy's now afraid,
> But Jemmy needn't scare himself,—they know
>   what's Jemmy's trade.

The effect of the poem turned out to be the reverse of what Waterhouse intended. Widely read on Monday night and Tuesday, election day, the attack against Otis convinced the Boston townsmen that he was, after all, on their side. If Otis had gone over to the Tories, they said, why would he still be their prime target? The frivolous hyperbole of the Waterhouse stanzas in the *Post* suffered by contrast with the pleas of Otis in the *Gazette* of the same day, asking for consideration of his past efforts on behalf of the Bostonians. As John Adams said, the poem was conclusive evidence that Otis "had not committed the unpardonable sin against them."[12] Otis was reelected at the bottom of the list of the Boston representatives; Thacher, Cushing, and Gray all received more votes than he. His own comment was, "The song of the drunkard saved me."

PART II

Boston Objects With Violence

As A RESULT of his battle with Martin Howard, Otis came to realize that he was, indeed, dependent on the support of his Boston constituents, and in an extraordinary self-adaptation, the man who earlier in life had a greater fulfillment in theoretical studies than in his relationships with other human beings now sought to identify himself with his Boston contemporaries in all walks of life. As he drew closer to his fellow townsmen, the mechanics, laborers, and storekeepers of Boston, he also became more accessible and receptive to the philosophy of Samuel Adams, a man he already knew very well, and thus began a friendship, a working partnership that is one of the most interesting in American history.

Otis was a man whose life was a constant intellectual development and broadening. The element of tragedy in his maturation was the erosion of his personal control; as he reached the point where his knowledge of the law, his experience in the House, and his popularity as a political figure provided him with an unlimited future, he had already begun to show the hints of emotional deterioration that would eventually close off his career. It is interesting to think what might have happened if Hutchinson had been able to communicate with Otis, but this was impossible. For Hutchinson, Otis was unfathomable, a man of quirks and eccentricities, "the great incendiary" whose strength lay in the Boston mobs, while in Otis' eyes Hutchinson was the power-greedy and unprincipled plotter who detested the man in the street and cared nothing for the province itself. Otis was by instinct the perfect opponent to Hutchinson, and Bostonians such as Samuel Adams were quick to see it.

Adams, completely self-effacing, the original anonymous man, was content to support Otis as the leader and symbol of the radical movement. It was only later, when he saw that Otis' days were numbered, that he stepped into the breach himself.

8

The Arrival of the Stamp Act

May–July 1765

America, in fact or eventually, consumes one half the manufactures of Britain. The time is hastening when this fair daughter will be able, if well treated, to purchase and pay for all the manufactures her mother will be able to supply. . . . The Sun rises and sets every day in the sight of five millions of his majesty's American subjects, white, brown and black. . . . The period is not very remote when these may be increased to an hundred millions. Five millions of as true and loyal subjects as ever existed, with their good affections to the best civil constitution in the world, descending to unborn miriads, is no small object. God grant it may be well attended to!

JAMES OTIS, *Considerations*, 1765

THE MASSACHUSETTS political organizations were altering. The House of Representatives, always jealous of provincial rights and its own prerogatives, more than ever before began to divide into two warring groups—the supporters of the king, with Hutchinson as leader, and those who opposed the Crown administration's new policies and who looked to Otis as their chief. The

Boston town meetings were changing, too, and again Otis was the key figure in the move to broaden attendance and convert the meetings into a forum for discussion of province-wide problems. Already these gatherings had become a kind of miniature legislature in which debate ranged over the same subjects that were covered in the House, aided and abetted by the unofficial but powerful lobbies—the Caucus Club, the Merchants' Society, and the Sons of Liberty.

As the political organizations changed, a new radical literature grew up after the example of Otis, who broke trail for Oxenbridge Thacher and Samuel Adams—and benefited by their essays in support of his views. Against these three, a diffident and cautious Hutchinson lost ground by choosing not to attach his name and prestige to the writings he sent to England and refusing to emphasize his disagreement with the heavy-handed strategies of Parliament. Like Otis, he was arguing that Parliament as the supreme power had to consider and protect the rights of British subjects and was refusing to accept the idea that Americans were represented in Parliament. Both men were aiming strong criticism at the administration, but Hutchinson's words were anonymous. It is interesting, in retrospect, to see how close were the political positions of the two. Each said that a breaking away from the empire would be disastrous, but that taxation without representation was contrary to the charter rights and the privileges of Englishmen. Each saw the problems and dangers created by the series of impositions from London—the taxes that would hurt trade, the imposition of Admiralty Courts to replace local judiciaries. They even agreed that the relationship of the growing colonies to the mother country inevitably would have to change, though neither could foresee what the change would be and both hoped the empire would be the better for it.

The essential difference between the two men in 1765 was that Hutchinson was willing to be expedient, to watch in silence the inroads of what he considered a misguided and obtuse effort by London to manage the colonies—first, because he believed so strongly in the politicosocial system of which he was a part, and second, because he realized that he could not rock the boat of crown policy and still keep himself in line for the governship, or even stay in office as lieutenant governor. Otis, on the other hand, sensed the expediency of Hutchinson and attacked it as an indication that the lieutenant governor was, indeed, the leader of a group of plotters who were ready to sacrifice the province for their own ends.

The metamorphoses of Massachusetts political organizations were partly a result of the influence of Otis, Thacher, Adams, and other radicals and partly a reflection of the changing views in the province. At the same time that more and more political figures in London voiced sympathy for the colonies, Americans were becoming increasingly aware of the depth of corruption that characterized British politics. This awareness and the resulting alienation heightened the unifying effect of the Sugar and Stamp Acts in Massachusetts.

The impending Stamp Act probably contributed more than anything else to the reestablishment of Otis. The speculation was salt to old wounds for Bostonians, who were already suffering the economic effects of earlier legislation. Hutchinson was no exception. He had received a letter from a member of Parliament who warned that these first few taxes would be followed in due course with others "in proportion or degree as it shall be found the colonies will bear," and he replied that the people of Massachusetts already despaired of their liberties and looked upon them as gone. In such a situation, anything could happen.[1]

Then on May 27, 1765, the Stamp Act arrived in Boston, giving the colony six months to prepare for putting it into effect. Beginning in November, stamps would be required for nearly all documents and would have to be paid for in silver, which meant yet another one-way drain of currency out of the colony. Parliament seemed to be trying to provoke resistance; instead of simply increasing existing taxes, it now made certain that every colonist would be subject to daily reminders of his subservience and of the restrictions placed on his life and business. The stamps also would be a harassment to precisely the people most likely to influence public opinion: lawyers, shopkeepers, traders, printers.

Otis had stated that there should be no criticism of acts of Parliament once they had become law; he now disregarded his own advice and devoted himself to a campaign against the Stamp Act.

On a visit to James and Mercy Warren, his brother-in-law and sister, in the summer of 1765, Otis told them he was thinking about the possibilities of an intercolonial conference on ways to fight the act.[2] Encouraged by the enthusiasm of the Warrens, he broached this question to compatriots within the popular party, and when he found support for a move in that direction, he resolved to try it out in the House of Representatives. Bernard had spoken to the assembly at the opening of the session, asking—as always—for a quiet acceptance of the will of government, and the House had not yet made its customary reply. After intense behind-the-scenes maneuvering, Otis mustered enough support to push through a motion calling for a meeting of committees from each of the colonial assemblies to discuss a single united petition to the king requesting repeal of the Stamp Act. The result of his efforts came to be known as the Stamp Act Congress, and not surprisingly he was elected one of the three men to represent Massachusetts.

Bernard and Thomas Hutchinson were unable to stop Otis, but they succeeded in getting a court-party man, Ruggles, elected to head the delegation of three, Oliver Partridge being the other representative. The House dispatched letters to all the other colonial assemblies announcing the congress and requesting attendance. Bernard commented that "nothing will be done in consequence of this intended conference," but he could not hide his preoccupation with yet another step toward the colonial union that he prophesied would come about unless strong measures were taken to stop it.

On June 14, Hutchinson left for the Superior Court circuit to the east, planning to return on July 4 or 5. With the new rise of tension in the colony, he found much of the resentment beginning to focus on him. Though he was himself a merchant, he had strongly supported enforcement of the earlier trade acts throughout the Seven Years' War. He had been the chief stumbling block of the other Massachusetts businessmen, the man they faced every time they tried to evade a trade law. His earlier insistence on a hard-money economy for the province now was recounted as an indication of his lack of concern for the average man, and his stand on the writs of assistance was made to show his unreflective, automatic support for "the prerogative." In addition, Hutchinson himself insured that his name remained linked to the writs by his determination to issue new writs to the commissioners without hesitation whenever they were requested.

Hutchinson's stubborn adherence to Crown policy and his refusal to seek a more popular course—or even to defend himself—now became critical as events took an ominous turn. He began to be cast as a major supporter—even possibly one of the originators —of the Stamp Act, although few men had argued more consistently or more cogently against it. More and more his name became synonymous with the stamps and with repressive legislation in general. When John Adams that summer wrote in the *Gazette* on "*rights* that cannot be repealed or restrained by human laws— *rights* derived from the great legislator of the universe," Harbottle Dorr scribbled in the margin of his copy, "How different this from the opinion of Governor Hutchinson!" Hutchinson knew that "a jealousy prevailed among the people that I was in favor of the duty," but his makeup was such that he would take no action to change this view.[3]

An event that took place far to the south of Massachusetts now contributed new fuel to the fires that raged around Hutchinson. In Virginia, the other great colonial center of revolutionary theory and action, Patrick Henry prepared a set of fiery resolves to be presented to the House of Burgesses. These were somewhat watered down by conservative elements over Henry's objections, but when the list was sent to the newspapers, the original wording was reinserted. Thus the "Virginia Resolves" traveled quickly up the seaboard as a much stronger version than the set approved by the Virginians themselves. When these powerful, bold statements were published in Massachusetts on July 2, radical Bostonians were chagrined at their own comparatively submissive letter to Parliament.

Otis at first was shocked by the implications of the Virginia Resolves and their repudiation of all Crown authority. He called them "high treason," but it was not long before he realized they expressed the hearts of his own party. Oxenbridge Thacher read the resolves on his deathbed, saying quietly, "These are men, these are men." The newspaper articles praised the Virginians and lamented the poor, weak product of the Massachusetts assembly, raking Hutchinson over the coals as the man who had changed the Massachusetts resolves into a shadow of what they had been, making a great province send to Parliament a slave's reply. The popular party was stung into a fury that surprised even Bernard, who wrote that it was inconceivable how the resolves had roused up the Boston politicians.[4]

Responding to a sophisticated essay by conservative Soame Jenyns in defense of British taxation of the colonies, Otis produced yet another essay, *Considerations on Behalf of the Colonists*,[5] published in sections in the *Gazette* in July and early August. In a turnabout, Otis insisted that Americans were not represented in Parliament and therefore should not be taxed. But he said much more than that and revealed a great deal about himself as he attacked the reasoning of Jenyns and explained his own views of the British political machine. In place of encomiums on the empire, Otis now wrote of the growing strength, prosperity, and prestige of the American colonies, which had made the British Empire "the wonder and envy of the world." Already America consumed one-half of all the goods manufactured in Great Britain, he said, and the time was not far off when she would be able to buy all the goods Britain could make and sell, having far outstripped the British Isles in size and importance. Still, while the colonies might be in the future the main part of the empire, it was the union of all the parts—the empire itself, under the British constitution—that always would be the prime consideration. There was a good possibility that it might someday extend to all the world, but it would have to continue to adapt itself; England could not retain all the power; the world could not be managed by the "occupants of the Cornish bars and alehouses." Otis professed absolute loyalty to the king and the British constitution and recognized the supremacy of Parliament, but emphasized again the role of the dutiful critic who questions the "mode and manner" of legislative procedures and decisions, insisting that only through adaptation to realities could the empire survive. By "realities" he meant the growing strength of America.

Liberty, said Otis, was all the colonists desire—freedom to contribute to the empire in the best manner they could, but as equal partners. No other solution, he predicted, would ever hold the empire together. Heaven had given Britannia every conceivable advantage, but would she have "wisdom and integrity enough to see and embrace an opportunity which once lost can never be regained"? The adaptations he suggested, the "nourishing" needed, were simple in concept: the American colonies, with their virtually independent legislatures, had to be recognized as equal partners. Within the loose union, held together only by a mutual adherence to an unwritten constitution, there could be, for example, no more condescending talk of "our" colonies—especially since it was obvious that the population of those colonies as they expanded through the western hemisphere "may be increased to an hundred millions" in a period not too remote. With remarkable foresight, Otis argued that the key to survival of the empire lay in the recognition of the shift of its power center westward across the Atlantic. The beginning of this move toward this more perfect union, said Otis, should be the repeal of the Stamp Act.

9

Hutchinson as Target

August 1765

I pray God to give me a greater share of fortitude
and discretion . . . than I have ever yet been master
of.

THOMAS HUTCHINSON, August 16, 1765

LACKING A POLICE FORCE and dependent on the sheriff and a few
old men of the night watch, Boston mirrored every other large
town in its vulnerability to violence. Sometimes crowds gathered
for sport, as on Pope's Day, November 5, when the South End
mob marched with their effigy pope against the pontiff of the
North Enders, to battle with fists and brickbats for the glory of
seizing the opposing icon. Usually only cuts and bruises were the
results of this endeavor, although a young boy was killed in the
1764 affray when he fell beneath the wagon carrying the South
End pope. Other riots were more than a friendly gang war, as in
1747 when the town was angered by British impress squads who
seized local sailors and forced them to serve on Royal Navy vessels. In this violence the colonial town reflected the goings-on at
home, where London was dominated on many occasions by
raging mobs that intimidated the city and even attacked members of Parliament.

At daybreak on Wednesday, August 15, those who passed the

"Liberty Tree"—the giant elm on the corner of Essex and Washington Streets—saw a guard of citizens posted to protect two effigies hanging high in the branches.[1] One was a scarecrow figure marked with the letters "A.O." (Andrew Oliver was a stamp commissioner) and the other was a large boot, with the devil crawling out of the top, representing Lord Bute, who was mistakenly hated as the originator of the Stamp Act. The tree displayed its decorations all morning, attracting crowds that included out-of-towners who had received word of the symbolic hanging.

Bernard saw the effigies as an affront to Crown authority and a sign of impending mob activity. He ordered Sheriff Greenleaf to have them cut down and destroyed immediately. Greenleaf, a slow and very cautious man, returned to the Town House empty-handed. There was no need to cut down the figures on the tree, he said. The people there had promised him they would soon take the effigies down and see to it they received a proper burial. They did not need the help of the sheriff. The crowd, he said, meant no trouble. Hutchinson answered that he thought very differently and the governor called a meeting of the council for that same afternoon, to discuss the state of affairs in Boston.

In the late afternoon as the council members took their seats in the meeting room of the Town House, the effigies were being carried over the heads of a mob marching toward King Street. The Town House was soon surrounded by a noisy crowd of 2,000 Boston workers, calling for "liberty and no stamps!" The council could hear crashing and jostling as the images were carried in through the ground floor of the Town House, which at that time was used as an exchange.[2] Bernard and his advisors sat helpless as the tradesmen below "gave three huzzas by the way of defiance and passed on." The cheering mob then surged down King Street to Oliver's Dock, where they surrounded a wood frame building, only a few weeks old, which Andrew Oliver had built to be rented for shops. Assuming it had been put up to provide a place for storing stamps, the mob attacked it and tore it to the ground in a matter of minutes.[3]

Carrying lumber from the destroyed building, the crowd then headed for Fort Hill to build a bonfire. Unfortunately for Oliver, the road to the hill led past his house on Oliver Street, and the temptation was too great. With due ceremony they carried Oliver's effigy into his front yard and there beheaded it. They called for Oliver to come out and, when there was no answer, began to throw stones at the house until they had broken out first the shutters, then the glass, and finally the frames of the windows. Hutchinson, suspecting that Oliver's house might be an object of the crowd's anger, had gone there himself and was inside as the stones bounced through the rooms. When the first attackers broke into the house, Hutchinson and Oliver left by another door and went for help.

Hutchinson sought out Sheriff Greenleaf and demanded that he return to Oliver's house to restore order. The two men made their way back to Oliver Street, where "the cry was god damn their blood, here's the sheriff with the Governor—stand by, my boys, let no man give way!" Hutchinson had to duck a volley of stones and bricks as he headed for the house. As he entered, a frightened boy warned him, "For God's sake, sir, put out the lights or you'll be dead in a moment." After the candles were put out, more cobblestones crashed into the darkened room. Hutchinson debated whether to take cover in the house or to make a run for it. "I chose the latter," he said, "and escaped with a slight stroke in my arm and another in my leg, and soon after it appeared by the hallooing they were dispersing."[4]

The mob left the house a windowless wreck, and soon on the top of Fort Hill a bonfire blazed, fed by pieces of Oliver's shop building and his house. Cheers resounded as Oliver's headless image on top of the fire exploded into flames. The fire was still burning on the hill at eleven o'clock when a large part of the crowd, led by Ebenezer Mackintosh, a shoemaker by trade, returned once more to Oliver's house, smashed his fence, and again went inside to look for him. Threatening his death, they searched nearby homes until neighbors convinced them Oliver had gone to Castle William to spend the night. Hutchinson and Sheriff Greenleaf tried once again to disperse the rioters—and were answered with more flying bricks and cobblestones. Hutchinson then found the colonel of the Boston militia and ordered him to call out his men to restore peace, but the colonel's answer was that, if the alarm were beat, the drummer would be knocked down and no one would respond. The militia, he said, would do nothing. After midnight, the crowd lost its momentum and began to break up. The danger was past for the moment, but Hutchinson knew this was not the end of the trouble.

On the following morning, John Adams drafted a letter for the Boston press on the attack against Oliver: Although he found no evidence that Oliver had ever caused the province any damage or admired the creation of the Stamp Act, he asked, "If there is no proof at all of any such injury done to the people by that gentleman, has not the blind, undistinguishing rage of the rabble done him irreparable injustice?" There were other considerations. There was the plural officeholding that involved Hutchinson and Oliver. There was the watering-down of the letter to the king in response to the Stamp Act. And there was the Massachusetts agent, Jackson, supported most strongly by Oliver and Hutchinson with full knowledge that he had been secretary to Grenville, author of the Stamp Act. Oliver, he concluded, should have tried harder to "remove these jealousies from the minds of the people." He tied Hutchinson and Oliver together, underlining his conviction that they were part of a dangerous cabal.[5]

The council met again on the following day and agreed on a proclamation offering a reward for information on the leaders of the mob, a move which Hutchinson recognized as a mere formality. When the governor asked for military sentinels in the town for that night, the council would agree only to "increase the number of the ordinary town watch"—which in the end was not done. During these discussions several members of the council told Oliver that, as stamp distributor, he was faced with a citizenry unalterably opposed to him, which "would never submit to the execution of the stamp act, let the consequence of an opposition to it be what it would." Someone noted pointedly that the people of Connecticut planned to hang their stamp distributor "on the first tree after he entered that colony."[6] This was more than enough for Andrew Oliver, who then and there announced that he would not spend another night as stamp distributor. He resigned the commission he had not yet received and asked that his resignation be shown about the town immediately. That night the mob was back at Oliver's house and the fire burned again on the top of Fort Hill. This time the ex-distributor was not attacked or threatened; he was offered instead a derisive serenade of thanks for his patriotic actions of the afternoon. The governor had lost one of his best supporters and the Boston rabble had gained a new sense of power. With Secretary Oliver out of the way, Hutchinson was the only loyalist who had spoken out against the Boston mob and the Stamp Act violence and who was still untouched.

Mackintosh was not always able to control the rioters as well as he wished, and this was true especially after he had assembled several thousand people and whetted their appetites for novelty and righteous vengeance. On the afternoon of August 16, part of the mob did not disperse.

After dusk a crowd assembled to march to Hutchinson's beautiful town home on Garden Court Street in the North End. They gathered outside his fence and hallooed for him to come out and speak to them (echoing the catcalls that Oliver had heard a few hours earlier). Hutchinson, inside, could hear the voices debating the next move: "Shall we begin with the coach house or stables?"[7] This was followed by furious knocking at the door. He would not reply, and the mob grew more restive and began to break some of the windows in the front of the house. At that a neighbor, a "grave elderly tradesman" who was friendly to the radicals, threw open his window and "harangued them for some time." Another neighbor called down that he had seen Hutchinson leave for Milton in the afternoon. The crowd in frustration pelted Hutchinson's house with stones, breaking some more of the windows, and then drifted away.

Hutchinson was angered by this attempt to intimidate him and depressed by his own lack of power to do anything about it. But he was not afraid. Bernard, on the other hand, left the Province House to stay at Castle William, although no attempt was ever made against him or his property. In those grim days, when stubborn men tested the wills of equally determined opponents, the figure of Bernard was a contrast: lost in a paroxysm of fear and foreboding, frightened into immobility, and ensconced behind the ten-foot-thick walls of the castle, he looked past his artillery gunners and British warships to the half mile of harbor that separated him from the town and felt himself "entirely at the mercy of the mob" which at any moment might snatch him. "I have no place of safety," he wrote Pownall, "but this fort with a weak garrison," and as for the mob, "how merciless it is I have seen."[8] He still did not dare to ask outright for the support and protection of British regulars, fearing that it would ruin him politically in the province; his letters studiously avoid a specific request while desperately trying to get across the idea that troops were an absolute necessity. He wrote to Agent Jackson: "It is a shocking thing that British troops should be employed against British subjects, but a defection of the colonies is a greater evil."[9]

On Friday night, August 23, a seemingly minor event served as a harbinger of things to come. Three men entered the home of Benjamin Hallowell, comptroller of customs for Boston, in what appeared to be an attempted burglary. Discovered, they escaped, leaving behind the disordered evidence of a hasty search. What were they looking for? The following Sunday, Reverend Jonathan Mayhew, minister of the West Church and a strong supporter of the Boston radicals, gave a sermon intended as a general attack against the Stamp Act. He chose as his title a quotation from Galatians: "I would they were even cut off which trouble you." He was later accused of contributing to the heat of the mob, which was rapidly reaching a fever point. Peter Oliver, never one to balk at exaggeration, said some of Mayhew's listeners "could scarce contain themselves from going out of the assembly and beginning their work," and Mayhew himself later agonized over this exhortation and its possible effect.[10]

Hutchinson spent Sunday at Milton with his family, returning on Monday morning to prepare for the opening of the Superior Court in Suffolk County. Friends who sensed a disturbingly high level of restlessness and rumor in the town warned him of a possible resurgence of violence, although they felt that he would not be a target; talk was that the customs officials would be taught a lesson.

That night, as the lieutenant governor sat down to a quiet supper with his family, the mob had again formed under Mackintosh and another evening of terror and destruction was already in progress. After the customary bonfire and harangue in King Street, the crowd headed for the house in which Charles Paxton, commissioner of customs, who had been active in ship seizures, had rooms. The landlord, after convincing the crowd that Paxton was not at home and was, after all, only renting rooms, announced he would stand all to a barrel of punch at a nearby tavern. This satisfied the rioters, who then continued on to the home of William Story, deputy registrar of the Admiralty Court, who kept many of the court records in an office in his house.

Story fled, unwisely leaving the house at the mercy of its invaders, who smashed the doors and windows, then systematically gathered and burned his records and part of the furnishings. Satisfied with this quick surgery, they moved on at command to Benjamin Hallowell's place.

Hallowell, too, had left his house to the mercy of the mob, but it did not stay empty long. One group of men who entered the house far ahead of the mob were still there when the Mackintosh squadrons arrived. The larger group joined in to finish what the first intruders had begun. They smashed windows and furniture and burned all Hallowell's papers—including, of course, the customs records. In his cellar they found wine and rum, which fortified them for the further efforts of that night. Once again at a signal they left the house and marched the streets to the sound of riot music—the bell and horn and drawn-out war whoop that struck fear in the hearts of stay-at-home citizens, who listened in their shuttered rooms.

Hutchinson heard them coming. He rose from his dinner table and quietly told his four children to leave the house by the back garden and go to the nearby home of Reverend Samuel Mather, his dead wife's brother-in-law. Hutchinson was then ready for whatever might come. At the last minute two of his children, Sarah and Tommy, hurried back to the house to appeal to him to leave. When he refused, Sarah replied, "Then I'll stay with you. I'll not leave unless you come away, too." She was a girl much like her father, and he knew she meant to stay. He took her hand and they hurried together through the garden toward the Mather house as the crowd surged through his front gate. Twenty-five-year-old Tommy lingered behind his father. Hutchinson wrote of what happened in his diary:

The hellish crew fell upon my house with the rage of devils and in a moment with axes split down the door and entered. My son being in the great entry heard them cry, "Damn him, he is upstairs, we'll have him!" Some ran immediately as high as the top of the house, others filled the rooms below and cellars, and others remained without the house to be employed there. . . .

Not contented with tearing off all the wainscot and hangings and splitting the doors to pieces, they beat down the cupola or lanthorn and they began to take off the slate and boards from the roof and were prevented only by the approaching daylight from a total demolition of the building. My garden fence was laid flat and all my trees etc. broke down to the ground. Such ruins were never seen in America. Besides my plate and family pictures, household furniture of every kind, my own children's and servants' apparel they carried off about £900 sterling in money and emptied the house of everything whatsoever except a part of the kitchen furniture, not leaving a single book or paper in it, and having scattered or destroyed all the manuscripts and other papers I had been collecting for 30 years together, besides a great number of public papers in my custody.[11]

Throughout the night the grisly work continued. Men smashed and trampled the chairs, tables, and picture frames to a mass of splinters. They slashed the mattresses and spread feathers through the rooms. Everything that could be lifted was thrown through the windows into the street, and still many rooms were knee-deep in wine bottles, china, plaster, furniture, stuffing, glass, shredded curtains and rugs. Out of the cellar the rioters brought a dozen barrels of good wine, which helped inflame them until "no demons were more enraged." While the work of destruction went on, a group broke off from the crowd to seize Hutchinson himself. Word came to the Mather home that the houses of the neighborhood were being searched. "I was oblig'd," Hutchinson said, "to retire thro' yards and gardens to a house more remote." Led along the dark paths and alleyways by his young niece, Hannah Mather, he went to the house of Thomas Edes, where he spent the rest of a sleepless night. In later years his young guide remembered her uncle had been "calm through the whole scene."

The weather turned cold toward morning and the coming of dawn drove the looters away. By then only the outer shell and the floors of the house remained, a tribute to the mansion's hardy construction. Surrounding this skeleton of a building were heaps of debris that had been its furnishings, and the streets in all directions were flecked with the tattered remnants of Hutchinson's belongings. Only by burning the house to the ground could the attackers have made the damage more complete, and, given the temper of the crowd, it is a mystery why they did not put it to the torch. When Hutchinson returned with the first light of day, still wearing only a thin frock coat he had worn the night before, he saw a picture that he could not forget for the rest of his life—a shock that he used from then on as a yardstick to measure all the other shocks of his tragic career. The hardest part for him was to see the psychological impact of this savageness in the eyes of his children. He felt the helplessness of a man who at that moment could not provide any assurance of protection to those who depended on him. As he stood amid the wreckage outside the house, staring at his beloved garden, where even the ground was torn, the Reverend John Eliot came up to him with the battered, muddy manuscript of the second volume of his *History of Massachusetts Bay*. He had found it down the street, in a gutter.

This day was to begin the Superior Court session in Boston, and since that was his next duty, Hutchinson went to the Town House. The court rose as he entered, not in the customary scarlet robes, but in his rumpled street clothes of the evening before, his face showing the effects of a stressful, sleepless night. When the court was seated, he spoke to a hushed, emotion-filled room in a quiet voice. Josiah Quincy was present and recorded what Hutchinson said:

Gentlemen:

There not being a quorum of the court without me, I am obliged to appear. Some apology is necessary for my dress—indeed I had no other. Destitute of everything—no other shirt—no other garment, but what I have on—and not one in my whole family in a better situation than myself. The distress of a whole family around me, young and tender infants hanging about me, are infinitely more insupportable than what I feel for myself; though I am obliged to borrow part of *this* cloathing.

Sensible that I am innocent, that all the charges against me are false, I cannot help feeling:—and though I am not obliged to give an answer to all the questions that may be put me by every lawless person—yet I call God to witness—and I would not for a thousand worlds call my *Maker* to witness a falsehood—I say, I call my *Maker* to witness, that I never, in New England or Old, in Great Britain or America, neither directly nor indirectly, was aiding, assisting or supporting, or in the least promoting or incouraging what is commonly called the STAMP ACT; but, on the contrary, did all in my power, and strove as much as in me lay, to prevent it. —This is not declared through timidity, for I have nothing to fear.— They can only take away my life, which is of but little value when deprived of all its comforts, all that is dear to me, and nothing surrounding me, but the most piercing distress.

I hope the eyes of the people will be opened, that they will see how easy it is for some designing wicked man to spread false reports, raise suspicions and jealousies in the minds of the populace, and inrage them against the innocent—but, if guilty, this is not the way to proceed—the laws of our country are open to punish those who have offended. —This destroying all peace and order of the community—*all will feel its effects.* —And I hope all will see how easily the people may be deluded, inflamed, and carried away with madness against an innocent man—

I pray God give us better hearts![12]

Thomas Hutchinson's daughters were so badly shaken by the violent events that he felt he could not leave them in town. On the evening of the 27th, he put the girls in his coach and headed for Milton. Once on the road, however, he ran into small parties of men who pointed at the carriage, saying, "There he is now," as if they had been waiting for him. The girls were terrified and begged him to turn back. He was forced to change his plans and seek the safety of Castle William.

The ultimate responsibility for the riot of the 26th has been laid at many different doors. Hutchinson remained convinced for the rest of his life that the mob was led by men with a purpose in mind. The whole event was too methodical, too well organized, to have occurred without a plan. He could name the men who had participated in the attack—Mackintosh, Will Moore, Atkins

—several were later arrested and jailed for their part in the offense, though they were subsequently released and never stood trial. That Mackintosh led the riot was only too clear. But who controlled Mackintosh, and for what reasons?

It was rumored at the time that the riot was planned to disguise the intended burglary of papers in Hutchinson's possession that proved "the grant to the New Plymouth Company on Kennebeck River was different from what was contended by some claimants," but no evidence has ever been found to support this.[13] The Hallowell accusations were another possibility. Two years earlier, Briggs Hallowell, a Boston merchant returning from London, spread the word about town that he had seen affidavits, sworn before Hutchinson and signed by him, accusing several important fellow Boston merchants of smuggling. At the time this had created a minor stir, but only recently Hallowell had been prevailed on by someone to put his story in writing. Printed copies of his tale were circulating through the town in August, conveying the impression that Hutchinson was the force behind the depositions, although in fact he had signed officially as a justice attesting only to the genuineness of the signatures on the documents, without comment on the information they contained. The revival of the Hallowell accusations could have been intended to inflame the merchants, reasserting the danger of further legal action against them and pointing out Hutchinson as their enemy.

Years later Hutchinson was to refer to the destruction of the house as "being caused by the report of letters having been shown to Briggs Hallowell by one of the clerks of the Board of Trade." This, in the end, he accepted as the immediate cause, although he sometimes thought back to the 1750s, when he had been threatened by men who did not want to see the colony go over to hard currency. Hutchinson, in winning that fight to restore the gold-backed bills, made for himself some powerful enemies who "had retained their rancor ever since."[14] He remembered, too, how in 1750 he had barricaded his house against a mob infuriated by the decision to outlaw paper money, and how, when his house accidently caught fire, the same ruffians cursed him and called, "Let it burn!"[15]

There is still a question as to how much of the assault on

Hutchinson's mansion can be charged simply to the inevitable results of mob violence. The house was in easy reach and, unlike Bernard's town house (owned by the province), Hutchinson's was private property. Mayhew's sermon and others like it and the calls to violence that had appeared in newspapers and pamphlets must have contributed to the temper of the town. But a mob thus formed would not have so carefully sought out Hutchinson's official records. The thoroughness of their destruction attests to the deliberate planning that was part of the riot.

From Josiah Quincy's report it seems that Hutchinson himself was convinced the blame for the riot could be laid to one person, one "designing, wicked man," rather than to a group of men. Indirectly or not, James Otis was to Hutchinson the ultimate cause of the trouble. Peter Oliver did not mince words when he came to tell the story of the riot. "The mob of Otis and his clients," he wrote, "plundered Mr. Hutchinson's house." At another point Oliver concluded that Otis named Hutchinson as the next victim. "Mr. Otis said so, and it was done."[16]

If Otis was responsible, he himself did not believe it. That the riot and the destruction shocked him was evident at the town meeting called the next day. Showing plainly the passion in his speech, Otis begged his fellow townsmen to do everything possible to stop the riots that were destroying property and law in the town, and causing such ruin. They should, he said, immediately send "dutiful and loyal addresses to his Majesty and his Parliament, who alone under God can extricate the colonies from painful scenes of tumult, confusion, and distress." In response, the townsmen voted a declaration of "utter detestation of the extraordinary and violent proceedings of a number of persons unknown." Among those voting their assent were Mackintosh, Moore, and Atkins.

10

Adams in the House

September–December 1765

The power and authority of government is really at an end.

GOV. FRANCIS BERNARD, August 1765

EVEN WITH HIS HOUSE in ruins Thomas Hutchinson gave not an inch to his opponents. Convinced at heart that the Stamp Act was a horrible mistake "unreasonably pushed" onto the colonies, he nonetheless considered himself obliged to support it.[1] His letters show him deeply troubled by the prospect of new violence. He warned that resentment against the Stamp Act was so high that the greater part of the colonies probably would oppose the act with force. If Hutchinson was grimly expectant, the governor was full of fear and foreboding. "The people here are actually mad," Bernard said, "no man in Bedlam more so."[2] He predicted that government would cease on November 1, when the Stamp Act went into effect. He promised to try to establish order when the General Court met on September 25, but he said he could not be optimistic. "If that fails me I have nothing to do but keep out of harm's way, if I can, 'til fresh instructions and powers come from England."

What came across the ocean, however, were newspapers and personal letters too often filled with support for the radicals. He attributed much of the unrest in the colonies to the activities in London. "Most of the political performances reach us," he told Mauduit, "and those which favor liberty and a state the least dependent are most approved." Barré in the House of Commons and Lord Camden in the House of Lords led the opposition to the Stamp Act and a strong following grew up around them. When Townshend painted a picture of the birth of the colonies as a noble gesture in which the British government had planted the settlements with care, Barré, in a fury, refused to accept such a distortion and responded in words he may have taken from Otis' *Rights:*

> They planted by your care? No! your oppressions planted them in America. They fled from your tyranny to a then uncultivated and inhospitable country.

In the elections for the House in 1765, many conservatives who had represented their towns for years found themselves out of a seat. Andrew Oliver, powerful secretary of the province, nearly lost his place on the council. Boston elected Otis, Cushing, Thacher, and Gray as representatives, and Samuel Adams once again drafted the town's annual instructions by which these men were to govern their conduct in the House. He presented his paper to the town meeting of September 18, where it was unanimously approved. In it the representatives were lectured on the dangers of allowing the precedent of taxation without representation and were given strict orders to declare the town's rejection of the Stamp Act and "by no means to join in any public measures for countenancing and assisting in the execution of the same."[3] The instructions, of course, were not intended only for the representatives, who were well aware of the stand their town had made on these issues and were themselves instrumental in that stand; read at town meetings and immediately published in the newspapers, the words of Adams were a solidification of Boston's position and a call for the cooperation of the whole province to repudiate the new legislation.

In a tense atmosphere not helped by Barré and the other British Whigs, Bernard took a deep breath and sallied forth from his defensive position at Castle William to open the General Court on September 25. He had already decided to follow a plan that would keep himself out of trouble and give his people time "to grow cool and considerate."[4] He greeted the House and council with the usual short speech, in which he again hoped there would be no resistance to the Stamp Act. This seemed a futile gesture by the governor, since the delegates already had departed for the Stamp Act Congress in New York and the mood of the House reflected the stubborn insistence throughout the province that the act could not be accepted. Bernard's plan became clear, however, when he said he knew that all the representatives would need to explain to their constituents that the Stamp Act, while inexpedient, had to be obeyed because it was Parliamentary legislation and the colonists were British citizens. He would therefore postpone the session for five weeks in order to give them time to go home, consult with their fellow townsmen, and return without too much hurry and inconvenience. The court would meet again on October 23.[5]

The representatives hardly let Bernard finish his speech before voting that they "were not themselves convinced of the necessity of submitting to the act" and that there was absolutely no need for a recess. Before the House could prepare a formal answer, however, Bernard declared the session closed. This done, he retired to resume his quixotic correspondence with London. He had learned, he wrote to Jackson, that his opponents "grumbled" at the dissolving of the House, but his actions were "well approved by the friends of government."[6]

With the Town House door slammed in their faces, the representatives took to the newspapers for the reply they had been unable to give to the governor. On October 7, the day the Stamp Act Congress opened, the *Boston Gazette* enumerated the evils of taxation without consent and trial without jury, and punctuated these considerations with a call for action:

> AWAKE! Awake, my countrymen, and by a regular legal opposition defeat the designs of those who enslave us and our posterity.

In a cooler vein, the *Gazette* predicted the following week that the expenses of buying stamps would cost the province £40,000 in the first year of operation, "which is more than double what the common charges of government ought to be in time of peace."

In the meantime, James Otis was at the Stamp Act Congress in New York, where along with Timothy Ruggles and Oliver Partridge he met the representatives of eight of the other 13 colonies, most of whom he had known only by their writings or not at all. In response to the request of the circular letter, only New Hampshire had declined to attend, but Virginia, North Carolina, and Georgia could not send representatives because the governors of these states refused to convene their assemblies, knowing that election of delegates would follow. At New York, nevertheless, Otis found 27 of the best political thinkers in the land, among them John Dickinson of Pennsylvania, the New York Livingston brothers Robert and Philip, John Rutledge and Christopher Gadsen of South Carolina, Eliphalet Dyer of Connecticut, and Henry Ward of Rhode Island.

Otis was the man most carefully studied by the rest of the delegates, who had read his tracts and the newspaper accounts of him and expected to meet a dragon breathing fire and calling for independence (John Watts was surprised to discover that in Otis he found an intelligent and impressive man, "not riotous at all"). But when the vote for a leader of the congress was taken, the name of Otis was avoided. The delegates were afraid that he had too often "figured in a popular way"[7] and therefore might prejudice their cause in England. On October 7, Timothy Ruggles was elected chairman.

Ruggles had come to New York only after much urging by Bernard, who hoped to use him as a counterforce to Otis. Bernard's instructions to this old warhorse were to make every effort to get a declaration of the supremacy of Parliament. This Ruggles could not do; even as chairman, he found himself powerless to soften the repudiation of the Stamp Act. After two weeks of work on a series of drafts, the delegates produced 14 "declarations" which followed closely the radical line of colonial political thought: they insisted there could be no taxation without representation (and made it plain that no American representation in London was possible), they emphasized the importance of trial by

jury, and they condemned the tendency of the Stamp Act to subvert the rights of the colonists, adding that free trade would
continue to fill British treasury coffers well enough without taxation. Although called by at least one representative "the boldest
and best speaker"[8] of the congress, Otis' conservatism almost prevailed. He was stunned when a majority of the delegates voted to
strike from the drafts the wording which admitted colonial subordination to Parliament. That, and the lack of adequate expressions of homage and loyalty to the king brought him close to
the position of Ruggles. He delayed his approval until October
25, the final day of the congress, reluctantly putting his name to
the declarations at the last minute after Thomas Lynch of South
Carolina begged him to sign. The stubborn Ruggles refused to
place his signature on the paper; only one other delegate, New
Jersey's Robert Ogden, joined Ruggles in opposition to the final
draft.

When the delegates returned to Massachusetts, the *Gazette*, in
announcing their return, singled out Ruggles as its target: "It is
hoped and expected that a Parliamentary inquiry will be made
into the conduct of one of the members of the late congress
chosen in the lukewarm state of things who it is said has not
signed the resolves and petitions etc."[9] Otis, on the other hand,
received the highest praises of the town for his work at the conference. In contrast to Ruggles, he appeared as the true patriot,
although rumors spread that while in New York he had accepted
an invitation to dine with General Gage, who made his headquarters there. The rumor was true—Gage not only confirmed it,
he elaborated on the story by insisting that Otis told him conditions in Massachusetts would not improve "until the Council
was appointed from home."

Bernard also had grist for the rumor mills. He considered Otis
still the major source of trouble, the man who had contributed
"more than any one man whatsoever to bring us into the state
of outlawry and confusion we are now in."[10] Otis, he said, on his
way to the Stamp Act Congress had predicted, "If the government at home don't very soon send forces to keep the peace of
this province, they will be cutting one another's throat from one
end to the other of it." Bernard, consciously or unconsciously,

was covering his own tracks. He wanted all the Regulars that could possibly be spared for duty in Boston.

On the evening of November 5, Otis was at the rostrum of the Boston town meeting, where he gave a Pope's Day speech. According to Bernard, he "made a most inflammatory harangue," ridiculing the governor's order for mustering the militia with the comment, delighting the crowd, that no one would give the name *rebellion* to the act of pulling down "two or three two-penny houses"[11] when the liberty of the people was at stake. Hutchinson commented in a note to England, "It is not safe to give you a particular account of the deplorable condition we are in."[12] Not safe because the letter might be intercepted and turned against him. Ironically enough, the recipient of this letter was Benjamin Franklin, the man who a few years later would acquire several of Hutchinson's letters and send them to Cushing, contributing in large measure to Hutchinson's downfall. Three weeks later, Hutchinson again wrote to Franklin, telling him it was "not safe . . . to advance anything contrary to popular opinion whatsoever."[13]

The major part of Hutchinson's letterwriting that fall concerned the loss of his property. He wrote to Pownall, Lord Halifax, Jackson, Bollan, Conway, the Lords of Trade, Franklin, Lord Gordon, Earl Loudoun, Lord Edgecombe, and others, all with the same plea for help in obtaining payment for his damages. In the end he was forced to send his son, Thomas, to England to intercede for him.

With the death of Oxenbridge Thacher, Samuel Adams was elected by the town of Boston to fill the empty seat in the House after the Caucus Club gave its support to him rather than to John Rowe or John Hancock, who were also in contention. Adams no sooner arrived than he was voted into the position of clerk, a responsibility he would hold for the next decade, giving him immediate access to every paper and record that passed through the House. Adams was now forty-three, gray-headed and shaking with a palsy that made him seem an old man. His highest official responsibility to date had been the position of town tax collector, and in that job he was still far in arrears. It was a success at last for the unsuccessful man, and the Stamp Act was part of the reason. This legislation forced many loyalists who were quietly fighting the new radicalism to come out into the open and side with England, exposing them to defeat and loss of political influence. It had the opposite effect on men who had fought the administration, who were now elevated in the public eye in proportion to their reputations for opposition to recent Crown policy—and no one in all the colonies had been more vigorously or vociferously opposed than Samuel Adams. The world had caught up with him, and not vice versa; he had not changed since his Harvard days.

In the absence of Otis in the House, Adams had personally taken responsibility for preparing an answer to the governor's address and had written it himself. In this paper the marks of style that characterized Adams in all his later writings are visible in their early form: the eagle's eye for the slightest weakness or the phrase that can be turned around and used with sarcasm against the originator; the polite insolence couched in words of submission; the feigned righteous surprise at assertions made; the surface appearance of objectivity and calm while the fire shows through only too plainly; the lip service to respect for authority, when that authority is actually the target of the attack.

His trademarks would always include the veiled threat, which appeared in this paper as the possibility of a revolt. If Americans are not to be governed in accordance with the British constitution, then "it is greatly to be feared that their minds may in time become disaffected; which we cannot even entertain the most distant thought without the greatest abhorrence."[14] Also present was the subtle undercurrent of ridicule which Adams reserved for men such as Bernard. He concludes with a word of advice to the governor:

> And you will have our best wishes that you may have wisdom to strike out such a path of conduct, as, while it secures to you the smiles of your royal master, will at the same time conciliate the love of a *free* and loyal people.[15]

With James Otis returned from New York, a new, major Otis-Adams collaboration produced the Massachusetts Resolves, a set of 14 declarations[16] which were laid before a full House on October 29. The resolves were a restatement of the two principal grievances associated with the postwar Parliamentary legislation —taxation and the extension of Admiralty jurisdiction to the province. Otis and Adams repudiated any British taxation of the colonies because they were not represented in Parliament, and at the same time declared that representation was "impracticable for the subjects in America." This position was powerfully reinforced by another of the resolves, which stated that "all acts made by any power whatever other than the General Assembly of this province, imposing taxes on the inhabitants, are infringements of our inherent and unalienable rights as men and British subjects and render void the most valuable declarations of our Charter."

That the first joint effort of the two men should produce a rejection of the idea of *de facto* representation of Americans in Parliament was a remarkable achievement on the part of Samuel Adams. Otis, in *Rights* and in his other writings, had insisted that American representation was the best solution. Now he committed himself to oppose any arrangement for representation. The House passed the resolves with a unanimous vote, closing off another possible avenue of reconciliation. Hutchinson later gave Adams most of the credit for the resolves. They were written, he said, in the style of Adams and were "agreeable to his professed principles, which he owned without reserve to be independency."[17] Samuel Adams, in his first few days as a member of the House of Representatives, had become the equal partner with James Otis in the creation of resolutions which were aimed at transmitting to posterity "a just sense of liberty and the firm sentiments of loyalty" as they were understood in Massachusetts.

Boston buildings were draped in mourning black and bells tolled slowly on November 1, the day the Stamp Act went into effect. Bernard felt that the power and authority of government was "really at an end" and that his attempts to moderate the direction taken by the House would soon precipitate a crisis and cost him the governorship. He wanted to go to England, to escape for a while at least, to be relieved of the pressure. While he tried every means to be called back home, he burned both ends of the candle, writing to Lord Colville, "If I stay, I would not have it known that I thought of going."

Bernard prepared for the events that were bound to follow

the closing of the port, and worried because it fell so close to Pope's Day, November 5. With Hutchinson at Superior Court in Salem he ordered the militia of Boston to muster to maintain the peace during the first weeks in November. But at the last minute the militia commanders informed him that the men would not respond. The first drummer to sound the call promptly had his drum broken, and the rest would not go out. Anyway, said the officers, the town would be quiet on Pope's Day.

November 5 dawned, and except for effigies of two of the pro-Stamp Act British politicians, Grenville and John Huske, hanging on the Liberty Tree, there was no indication of trouble. In the afternoon, to the tolling of church bells, an orderly crowd marched with the effigies through the town in a mock hanging. Bernard, however, was not reassured by the relative quietness of Pope's Day. "I am perfectly convinced," he wrote, " that the best step I could take for his Majesty's service would be to set out immediately for London." Three days later he closed the General Court.

The closing of the assembly in November left the province adrift on the question of the stamps. The dissidents as well as the administration avoided responsibility for continuing to do business without them. Since any negotiation or legal proceeding which went ahead without official recognition might later be called void, this was a serious matter that caught the average man in the middle.[18] It was not until 46 days after the stamps went into effect that the Port of Boston was opened and the first ships cleared the harbor.

With the harbor again in operation, the Boston town meeting sent a message to Bernard asking him to open the legal courts of the province, regardless of the lack of stamps. Bernard said he would call the council and discuss that matter, and on Thursday morning, December 19, another town meeting voted unanimously to appoint lawyers Jeremiah Gridley, James Otis, and John Adams as a committee to present the case to Bernard and the council. This gave the three men little time to prepare themselves—especially John Adams, who had no idea he would be asked to take such an assignment. On Friday afternoon the lawyers met in the Town House with the Boston committee to discuss their approach to the governor and council. This meeting was chaired by Samuel Adams, who, though not a lawyer, was now the recognized strategist and coordinator. The planning continued until darkness fell, and then was interrupted by a messenger from Bernard announcing that the governor was ready to hear them.[19]

At the Town House John Adams spoke first, emphasizing the Stamp Act was contrary to the charter and adding that, in any case, it would be impossible to put the act into effect with the mood of the people so much against it. Otis "reasoned with great learning and zeal on the judges' oaths, etc." Gridley spoke of the burden that the act would impose. Bernard, however, remained unmoved. He had seen a loophole already, and when the three were finished, he pronounced the whole case a legal question and therefore one which the executive branch could not handle. On Saturday the town called Bernard's answer "unsatisfactory." John Adams, called on for his opinion, cooled emotions in Faneuil Hall with a warning that legal decisions made without stamps might later be declared void.[20] The troubled citizens left the meeting undecided as to their next move.

For John Adams the call to assist the town of Boston had been one of the great experiences of his life. For a week he had worked in close association with Otis, whom he now saw as a man of fire and fever: "His passions blaze—he is liable to great inequalities of temper—sometimes in despondency, sometimes in a rage." He felt himself drawn closer to his cousin Samuel, a man who he said understood better than anyone else the temper and character of the Massachusetts people. Samuel, he said, was not the best in knowing the law and the constitution, but he had the "most correct, genteel, and artful pen" of them all. John's admiration for Samuel flowed into the famous diary:

> He is a man of refined policy, steadfast integrity, exquisite humanity, genteel erudition, obliging, engaging manners, real as well as professed piety, and a universal good character, unless it should be admitted that he is too attentive to the public and not enough so to himself and his family.[21]

On Christmas Day 1765, John Adams was at home in Braintree, "thinking, reading, searching concerning taxation without consent." Another great man had been drawn into the circle.

11

Hampden

December 1765–May 1766

It is a marvel then, that the colonist, though very artificially and gradually disposed to submission, passive obedience, and nonresistance, should all of a sudden be alarmed, rouse, grow tumultuous, outrageous, and to all appearance as fixed and determinate as fate? What does that bungling, cobbling no *statesman* deserve who by his Quixotism has occasioned such a convulsion and commotion? Did a true politician ever tempt a young lion to try his paws, or a young eagle his wings and talons before the time? The eagles and the lions must have their prey, and 'tis far better that a reasonable portion should be quietly yielded than to have them ranging and prowling at large among the herds of the fields and the flock of the air, if from this consideration only, that when let loose, tho' it is possible that in a combined force of inferior individuals the greatest of them may meet with his match, yet it would occasion much bloodshed.

"HAMPDEN," *Boston Gazette,* December 23, 1765

BEGINNING IN EARLY DECEMBER 1765, James Otis, under the pseudonym "Hampden," accomplished the most sustained writing output of his career, publishing a long article in every issue

118

of the *Gazette* for eight successive weeks. In these columns he argued against the new trade laws and insisted that Parliament showed an appalling ignorance of American colonial economics and a callous disregard for American rights, and he set himself the task of erasing "a thousand old rivetted prejudices"[1] that blocked a better understanding of the colonies in London. On a deeper level, "Hampden" revealed the conflict in his own mind as he attacked not only the intransigence of Parliament but the rationale of the empire itself. He argued that the historical struggle of colonization proved the provinces did not owe a great debt to England, and he insisted that "common law, common sense, and the first principles of a free constitution" showed that the colonies should be governed by their charters, not by Parliament. In London, he said, the picture of American trade was distorted by the West India planters and the influence of hatters and ironmongers who did not realize that by denying trade they were only hastening the development of American manufacturing with their shortsighted ideas.

As Hampden, Otis revealed more clearly his views of the future of the colonies and the empire and the reasoning behind some of his thoughts in *Rights*. For the last time he restated his idea of a "union," meaning an expanding organization of loosely connected self-governing states which would insure stability and long life to the British Empire. Now, however, he was much more pessimistic, admitting that a union would have to be based on such "noble, generous, and disinterested principles, that it is ten thousand to one if any such thing ever takes place."[2] He had come to see the union as overly idealistic, because the first steps would have to be the formation of an entirely new system of commercial laws, the destruction of monopolies, and throwing open all the world's ports to American traders. It was becoming evident to him that all of this could not happen; it would require great statesmen in London, and these were obviously lacking. In the meantime, pettiness ruled Parliament and the middlemen in London took their enormous profits. The colonies, by nature disposed to submission, nonresistance, and obedience, were now like young lions, he said, tempted to try their paws. The American population had reached four million and was doubling every 20 years. In what was for Otis a drastic change, he theorized that America had the potential to be the basis of "a greater empire than the world has yet seen" and even implied that it was up to England to decide whether or not she would be part of that empire. He consistently returned, however, to his loyalty to the monarchy and his hope that the present line of kings would rule forever. But the unmistakable influence of Adams was beginning to show.

Otis' relationship with Adams had now become one of the most significant forces of his life. He began to sense the strength of Adams' convictions and the abilities of Adams in controlling the politics of Boston. On questions of political theory that were extremely important to him, he found himself accepting Adams' view. Adams had convinced him that the idea of American representation in Parliament would work against their aim of maintaining the liberties granted by the colonial charters. Otis now agreed that Americans had to rule themselves under the constitution—as Adams said, London was too far away to be aware of "the internal circumstances" of the people on the west side of the Atlantic. "We think the colonies cannot be fully and equally represented," Adams had said, "and if not equally, then in effect not at all."[3] When Otis reflected this sentiment in the Hampden essay of December 30, commenting on the "pitiful expedient of an American representation in Parliament" as completely impracticable,[4] Hutchinson was quick to perceive the change. "Our great incendiary," he said, "who when it was first talked of became an advocate . . . is now silent because he finds the voice of the people against it."[5]

As he drove himself to write these analyses of the options available to British statesmen, Otis was in fact slashing away his own personal convictions that had tied him to the king, Parliament, and the empire. It was a costly process of psychological and even physical punishment. In late January he experienced a series of nosebleeds[6] over several days, and his father and brothers began to think his robust health had gone.

Rumors coming across with the merchant ships increasingly told of the imminent repeal of the Stamp Act. Bernard fervently prayed that this would happen, complaining that the act itself had now been "swallowed up in the importance of the effects."[7] Hutchinson agreed the colonies were sick, but asked, "Can we bear the cure?"[8] Otis talked to an old friend who had just arrived from England and learned that General Conway saw repeal ahead but cautioned that "the only thing was to do it with dignity." The opposition needed a way to retreat, Conway said. They already were so beaten that "if a million sterling would put them down where they was when they began to tax America, they would be glad to give it."[9] Next day Otis was in high spirits as he talked of his plans for the winter session.

With the court due to open, Bernard worried about the new strength that the Stamp Act had given to Otis, Adams, and the popular party. To carry out such a provocative law in the face of such opposition, he said, "affords a frightful prospect."[10] In early January 1766 the Boston town meeting appointed Otis as head of a committee to visit the governor and insist that the next session of the General Court take place as scheduled, on January 15. The confrontation had its effect. Bernard had planned to delay for two more weeks at least, but he opened the session on time. He was prevented from giving his prepared speech, however—the House waited until a few minutes before he was scheduled to speak and deliberately adjourned, forcing him to wait until it reconvened the following morning. At that time he delivered a curt address of just over a hundred words, indicating that "whenever the time shall come that my service can be acceptable to you, it will not be wanting."[11]

As Otis continued his Hampden articles, he moved ever farther away from his earlier goal of reconciliation with England, omitting the qualifications with which he had previously softened his attacks against Parliament. If there were a *"grand generous plan of union,"* he said, Parliament would have the theoretical right to tax the colonies but would not do so.[12] In such a case, justice and objectivity would hold sway over self-interest, and Parliament could be entrusted with these great powers. But no such marks of judiciousness controlled the legislators in England. Their creation of the current tax system made it obvious that the ideal union was "unpracticable if not impossible."

From the time of the Sugar Act, the American colonies had

made efforts to show their displeasure by nonimportation. They were not often successful in reaching agreement on the campaign to stop trade, nor were they able to coordinate their plans with any real efficiency; nevertheless, the overall result of their sporadic efforts caused a distinct slowdown of British exports to America and a large dent in the pocketbooks of English merchants. The Rockingham ministry began to feel the pressure from British merchants and bankers who were being hurt by the boycott. Parliament was apprised that exports to the colonies already had fallen off 10 to 20 percent, and signed petitions arrived from thirty of the largest English towns demanding repeal of the Stamp Act.

Debate on repeal or continuation of the Stamp Act began as soon as the new assembly opened in December 1765. Grenville, having been forced out of office the previous summer, continued his support of the act in the House until in January he was demolished by a great speech of his brother-in-law, Pitt. Both Whig and Tory had waited anxiously to hear what Pitt would have to say on the issue, and sensing the advantage of a dramatic confrontation, he made the most of it. Pitt declared flatly that Parliament had no right to tax America and told the assembly that "the Americans are the sons, not the bastards, of England!" Conway, following Pitt's line, committed the Rockingham administration to repeal of the act, and the debates continued with testimony by several of England's leading merchants, who provided details of the decline of trade and the fruitlessness of the customs regulations. But there were still powerful forces, including the influence of the king himself, that pressured for continuation of the act. Debates were long and hard, sometimes lasting far into the night, and for weeks the weight swung first to one side, then to the other. In the end the constant, unyielding pressure from the British merchants was successful: after a session in the House of Commons that ran into the early morning hours of February 22, the members voted 275–167 for repeal.[13] By mid-March a new bill had been formulated and signed by the king.

The repeal of the Stamp Act could have been used to show that virtual representation actually worked: astute politicians could have emphasized that American interests had been taken into account and that Parliament had reversed itself when it became clear that the Americans were adversely affected by a law. This is the way that Otis had so hopefully described the actions of an all-powerful Parliament that nonetheless could make mistakes—and could be moved to rectify those mistakes by the objective criticism of reasonable men. Parliament, however, was unable to live up to the idealistic vision of Otis. It followed, instead, a hard line and chose to append to the announcement of repeal a "Declaratory Act," which maintained the right of taxation over the colonies.

While these debates were under way in London, the Massachusetts House in January voted 81–5 to open the law courts of the province and operate without stamps. The resolution then was sent to the council, where Hutchinson tried and failed to muster enough votes to reject it. The best he could do was obtain a delay, postponing consideration until the end of the month, when it was passed into law. His recalcitrance only goaded Otis into reintroducing the bill to exclude Superior Court justices from sitting on the council. Backed by the country party, the bill passed the House, but Hutchinson led the council in rejecting it. Frustrated and angered, Otis on January 27 took to the press as "Freeborn Armstrong" and railed at Hutchinson, "The Chief Justice of the Superior Court, who on this occasion also sits as President of the Council, a place he has usurped after engrossing all the places of honor and profit in the province." Hutchinson, he said, gave the motion "the go-by,"[14] indicating it was beneath the notice of the board.

This was the last straw for Hutchinson.[15] He called a meeting of the council to demand that Otis be reprimanded by the House and that the printers be "sent for." The council vacillated. It would not be feasible to try to force the House into a motion for censure, they said, and to put the printers behind bars would only create martyrs. Instead, it would be better to publish in the newspapers a denial of the charge Otis made. This mild answer to such an affront disgusted Hutchinson, who refused to attend council meetings for the remainder of the session. "They were afraid of a tumult," he said, "and I did not care to remain among them and be so insulted."

In February, Bernard had written another in his series of letters asking to be called home. He first included Hutchinson's
name in the draft, suggesting to Conway that one of the two
ought to return to explain conditions in Boston, but later he
crossed it out. And when Hutchinson asked him for his approval
of a trip to England to try for compensation for his house damages, Bernard would not allow it. At this point Hutchinson, for
the first time, seriously considered yielding to the forces aligned
against him. His house was a pile of wreckage, his children lived
in fear of some new assault, his political organization within the
General Court was faltering, he had lost his influence in the
council, and even the governor seemed to have reservations about
his judgment. It would soon be necessary for him as chief justice
to open the Superior Court again and face the question of proceeding without stamps. He was determined not to act contrary
to the law, and yet he knew there would be no support for him.
He therefore submitted his resignation as chief justice. The governor, however, refused to accept it and promised him that the
problem would somehow be solved. "I will hold out as long as
possible," said Hutchinson, but he did not relish the idea of
fighting alone against the power that Otis now could muster. "To
die by inches," he added, "will please my great adversary, the
present champion for liberty."[16]

Hutchinson saw to it that he was out of town on March 11,
when the Superior Court was due to open. Shrewd Peter Oliver
presided and proved to possess the toughness and decisiveness
that Hutchinson at this time could not summon up. He recognized that, with rumors whispering the impending repeal of the
Stamp Act, few if any of the lawyers would want to risk a case
without stamps, since it might later be appealed on technicalities.
This gave him the opportunity to humiliate the men—in his
opinion irresponsible hypocrites—who had been clamoring for
an opening of the Massachusetts courts. One by one Oliver called
the lawyers forward to the bench and asked each whether he
would now proceed to business "contrary to the Act of Parliament," and one by one the lawyers were forced to admit they did
not want to put cases into court at that time.[17] Otis himself, after
four months of criticizing the courts for remaining closed, turned

down the opportunity to get what he had been asking for. After going through the motions of calling one "continued" case and postponing it, the court adjourned to April. John Adams left the courtroom muttering about Thomas Hutchinson, who had kept out of sight and gained a few weeks more "to trim and shift and luff up and bear away and elude the blame of the ministry and the people."[18] But Adams, too, had declined to open a case in court when Oliver gave him the opportunity.

The courts remained closed, business stayed at a standstill, and the tension continued as ships plowed westward across the winter Atlantic to bring news of the repeal to Boston. Hutchinson was sure a decision had been made in Parliament, and he waited and watched the harbor for signs of a merchantman or man-of-war. He was convinced that, if measures were taken to carry out the Stamp Act, "force will be opposed to force" and the Sons of Liberty would unite in all the colonies.[19] As for Boston, he thought there was little chance now that the town would regain its senses. Otis was "without dispute, a madman."[20]

Though under the influence of Adams he had given ground from his earlier moderation, Otis was more worried than Hutchinson about the explosive situation. He saw himself as a balancing force and told his sister, Mercy, that the Stamp Act had to be repealed soon or America would be "engaged in contests that will require neither the pen nor the tongue of a lawyer." He dare not leave town, he said, until the matter was settled in England because Bostonians were so upset that "every nerve is requisite to keep things from running into some irregularity or imprudence."[21]

The rising spirit of anger and frustration in America continued to be fed by the radicals in London. John Adams, reading excerpts from the British Parliamentary debates, asked, "What has been said in America that Mr. Pitt has not confirmed? Otis, Adams, Hopkins, etc. have said no more." The words of Pitt, condemning the Stamp Act as impolitic, arbitrary, oppressive, and unconstitutional, were widely published in the colonies. Conway and Barré wrote to Otis, who published their complimentary letters in the *Gazette,* causing Hutchinson to feel a twinge of apprehension[22] that Otis was gaining new contacts in

England while he himself stagnated in a lost corner. In the same issue Otis published an "Address to the True-born Sons of Liberty," instructing them to insist on eliminating the province secretary and the judges of the Superior Court from seats on the council and to allow no monopolizing of public offices. A man should hold no more than one public office at a time, he wrote, urging all who called themselves Sons of Liberty to unite and break the power of Hutchinson, Oliver, and the court party. His newspaper instructions were accompanied by a listing, without comment, of 32 representatives;[23] the obvious meaning was that these were the supporters of the Stamp Act, who should not be returned to their seats in the May elections.

The radicals were ready for a renewal of the conflict, using the stamps as their symbol, as time for reopening of the Assembly drew near. On April 5, however, Bernard upset their plans with a proclamation postponing the General Court until further notice. Otis responded in the *Gazette* that Bernard could not dissolve the Assembly unless it was in being, and urged the members to meet on the appointed day, with or without the governor. On the morning of the 9th, although a few representatives appeared at the Town House in answer to Otis' call, he was unable to obtain the necessary quorum of 40. By noon he had nine, and the afternoon added only three more. This small group sent a message to Bernard saying they were waiting for more members and desired an adjournment until the following day, but Bernard remained silent and the loyal dozen melted away in the evening, leaving only Otis and two others. Although Bernard won, he was sobered by the realization that there were many more such confrontations ahead.

Anxious to keep up the pressure on the administration, the radicals insisted that business be conducted without stamps. When the Suffolk Superior Court met again in April, Otis "pressed hard for judgment in his actions,"[24] but Hutchinson ordered all cases carried over for another two weeks. When the court reopened Hutchinson merely again told the assembled lawyers that no legal activity would be carried on without the stamps—"it would not be regular nor prudent at this critical juncture"—and then closed the court once more, reporting to

London that he had been successful in avoiding all civil business "notwithstanding Mr. Otis' efforts to the contrary." John Adams noted, "The times are terrible and made so by Hutchinson."

An unofficial copy of the repeal of the Stamp Act arrived in Boston on Sunday, April 13,[25] and a town meeting was called to discuss a plan for celebrations to take place when the official news arrived. There was some disappointment when the Declaratory Act was read, making Parliamentary legislation binding "in all cases whatsoever," but Otis, as moderator, assured the meeting that the declaratory portion was immaterial and that he was satisfied the struggle had been won. According to Hutchinson, "the Grand Incendiary declared . . . that we could expect nothing less; the resolutions were such as he would have drawn himself."[26] The optimism of Otis carried the day, and an announcement was drawn up in advance, rejoicing that the "incontestable right of internal taxation still remains to us inviolate." The need for a calm and orderly celebration that would enhance the reputation of Boston was emphasized; "all abuses and disorders on the evening for rejoicing, by breaking windows or otherwise,"[27] would be punished by the town.

Bostonians had to wait almost a month before the official document arrived aboard John Hancock's brig *Harrison,* which dropped anchor in Boston on Friday, May 16, 44 days out of London. Captain Shubal brought the new act to the Town House, and in the words of the Massachusetts council, touched off "the greatest and most universal joy that was ever felt on the continent of America."[28] The prearranged celebration, which was scheduled for Monday, May 19, began unexpectedly early when, a few seconds after the clocks struck one in the morning, the church bells all over town began to ring. By two o'clock "music was heard in the streets" and cannon fire reverberated from the shore batteries. Dawn found the Liberty Tree hung with banners and flags flying from many housetops. At noon the cannon fire began again in the batteries and was taken up by ships in the harbor. One group took advantage of the euphoria by collecting from the happy crowds enough money to free all the inhabitants of the debtors' prison. "Joy smiled in every countenance, benevolence, gratitude and content seemed the companions of all."

Rocket trails crisscrossed the evening sky and householders placed candles and lanterns in every window to "illuminate" the town. The Sons of Liberty built a wooden pylon on the Common, lit by 280 lanterns and displaying sketches of the king, the queen, and 14 "worthy patriots" who had argued for repeal of the bill. John Hancock and James Otis, among others, held open house; at Hancock's a barrel of wine at the front door announced free drinks for all. The only casualty of the evening was the carefully constructed pylon, the fruit of such enthusiastic labor: left lit and unattended after midnight, the obelisk with its kings and lords and promises of loyalty set itself afire and was totally destroyed.[29]

12

The Partnership

May 1766–September 1767

It will be of some amusement to you to have a more circumstantial account of the model of government among us. I will begin with the lowest branch, partly legislative, partly executive. This consists of the rabble of the town of Boston, headed by one Mackintosh, who I imagine you never heard of. . . . they are somewhat controlled by a superior set consisting of the master-masons, and carpenters, etc. of the town of Boston. . . . When anything of more importance is to be determined, as opening the custom house on any matters of trade, these are under the direction of a committee of merchants, Mr. Rowe at their head, then Molyneux, Solomon Davis, etc.: but all affairs of a general nature, opening all the courts of law etc., this is proper for a general meeting of the inhabitants of Boston, where Otis, with his mob-high eloquence, prevails in every motion, and the town first determine what is necessary to be done, and then apply either to the Governor or Council, or resolve that it is necessary the General Court correct it; and it would be a very extraordinary resolve indeed that is not carried into execution.

THOMAS HUTCHINSON, in a letter marked "not sent," March 8, 1766

THE SPRING BROUGHT ELECTION time again to Massachusetts. Remembering the reversal they had suffered with Jemmibullero, the opponents of Otis tried a new approach: Instead of attacking Otis as a Whig, which only won him more sympathy in Boston, they tried to prove him a Tory and thus alienate him from his supporters. Two columns of quotations from *Brief Remarks* appeared on the front page of the *Evening Post* supplement of April 28, along with a commentary that asked readers to decide for themselves whether Otis could really be called "a true patriot and an enemy of the Stamp Act." The quotations were edited and arranged to show Otis supporting the right of Parliament to impose taxes on America.[1]

The following week the *Post* writer asserted the quotations were "diametrically opposite" to the position of Otis in *Rights*, and accused Otis of being a chameleon and a "double-faced Jacobite-Whig" who lived in a chaos of inconsistencies. The most ingenious assault on Otis, the inspired invention of the character Bluster, was continued with new variations that included a short biography of the comic bad boy:

> When any disputes arose, as disputes will arise when a number of lads get together, Bluster would leap into the middle of the school, strip to his buff, and clenching his fist, threaten to knock the first man down that contradicted him. In short, he grew so mischievous and troublesome, that the Scholars once or twice got him to the door to thrust him out.[2]

But Otis was too strongly entrenched to be "thrust out" by his enemies. The many hours he had spent with John Rowe, Isaac Royal, and the other politically active members of the Merchants' Society helped to convince them that he kept their interests at heart, and that the road to liberalized trade laws lay in the direction he and the Whigs were taking. His years of productive work in the service of the town served him well with the hardheaded townspeople who knew the difference between words and deeds. As elections neared, Otis intimated that the severe pressures of the day-to-day political infighting were affecting his health, and this confession met with much sympathy, especially when the

Tory writers referred to his problem as "the unhappy influence of weak nerves, or, as it is vulgarly called, cowardice."[3] Otis' response was to announce himself the champion of the people and to challenge Grenville to a duel on the floor of Faneuil Hall. His flamboyance struck the right tone and the elections were once again a victory for him and for the popular party. The town returned Otis, Adams, and Cushing along with John Hancock, who took Gray's place. Of the 32 men on Otis' blacklist, many of them strong local political figures, only 13 were returned to their seats in the House.

The bitter election fight carried over into the General Court when that body convened on May 28. Otis, who had served earlier as speaker pro tem, was now elected speaker, subject of course to Bernard's approval. Some of the governor's friends advised him to acquiesce and approve Otis as a gesture of conciliation, but Bernard had had enough of such gestures; he could not stand the thought of Otis in the chair. He was backed by Hutchinson, who reminded Bernard that the governor would be held answerable to the Ministry at home "if he should approve of so obnoxious a person in any post of consequence." When the House sent up the name of the newly elected speaker on the morning of the 28th, Bernard promptly returned the note signifying his "disapprobation of said election," and Otis was out. Cushing was then elected and accepted by Bernard as speaker. Adams continued as clerk since that position, under the charter, was not open to the governor's challenge. But Bernard could not hope to win that kind of game. Otis and the radicals were given another opportunity to emphasize the existence of a plot to consolidate control in the hands of a few power-hungry men. The Stamp Act had been repealed, and this was a time for reconciliation. Instead, the governor had chosen to emphasize the old controversy. And Hutchinson soon found cause to regret his advice to Bernard; the governor's refusal to allow Otis to be speaker "raised the resentment and increased the strength of the opposition, when the choice of Councilors came on." On the same afternoon, the angry representatives sent up a list of councilors which eliminated Bernard's four conservative mainstays, Hutchinson, the two Olivers, and Edmund Trowbridge.

Bernard, in turn, revenged himself by cutting five of the six new radical council members from the list, including Colonel Otis, whereupon the House refused to elect any replacements for them, leaving him with a decimated council whose radical members, including James Bowdoin, now exercised a far greater influence. It was little consolation to Hutchinson that he and the other conservatives had been eased out of the council by a very narrow majority of one or two votes apiece; he had to agree that Otis had carried the field. "I was the principal butt," he said, "of Otis and his myrmidons."[4]

With the help of Adams, Otis had now reached the goal he had sought for five years—a united and strong popular party in the General Court—and he was determined to take advantage of his success. This, however, would be no easy matter. His margin of strength was narrow, and the Massachusetts representatives were proud of their independence of any faction. Each issue created its own problems of coordinating a position, since Otis' followers were a political entity in name only. Otis kept constantly in the center of turmoil, under great pressure from his opponents and not always enjoying the support of his friends. His aims were simple and direct: he wanted to reestablish the dominance of the charter and purge those who plotted against it. Bernard, the outsider, was to Otis only a figurehead; it was Hutchinson who controlled the Tories of Massachusetts and saw to it that the important positions were filled by members of the cabal. Hutchinson therefore remained the mark.

Bernard on June 3 addressed the House on the subject of the Stamp Act's repeal, digressing to chide the representatives on their choice of council members. He made the mistake of saying what he thought—that the men excluded from the council had been precisely the men who were best fitted for it, and he compounded his error by threatening the House with loss of the right to select the council. Adams was quick to respond that "no unprovoked asperity of expression on the part of your Excellency can deter us from asserting our undoubted Charter rights and privileges."[5] The province, he added, had flourished to the entire approval of Parliament and the king when there were no Crown officers seated at the council board, and he trusted that it would do so again.

Bernard was making other mistakes. In his eagerness to show London that he could implement decisions from home, he converted a recommendation by Secretary Conway into an outright requisition for immediate compensation for the sufferers of the August 1765 riots, and peremptorily ordered the House to provide a motion for payment. Adams, of course, attacked the arbitrary aspect of Bernard's ultimatum, snapping that if the letter precluded any disputation, then the House "should be glad to know what freedom we have in the case."[6] He was also quick to use Bernard's words later as an excuse for the slowness of the House to act on this issue, telling a London correspondent in November that Bernard's cavalier treatment was the cause of resentment that led to the delay. The House finally refused to reimburse the victims of the riots, postponing action by appointing a committee of inquiry.

The loyalists fought back, attacking Otis as a mad dictator and an unnatural monster with some "dark and poisonous end to serve."[7] An article in the *Post* again accused him of saying, "This province never could be happy till the government was changed and the Council appointed by the King," and ended with four lines of prophetic verse:

> Is there not some chosen curse,
> Some hidden thunder in the stores of heaven
> Red with uncommon wrath, to blast the man
> Who owes his greatness to his country's ruin?

Otis was angry, and hard words passed on the floor of the House the following day. Samuel Otis, writing to brother Joseph, said Timothy Ruggles asserted Otis was lying, but "James proved Ruggles a liar and so it ended."[8] Such fights did not end, however, and Otis became progressively more deeply involved in personal feuds with the men he opposed politically.

On the following Thursday, June 12, the House radicals overrode violent court-party objections to approve the construction of galleries for spectators to observe the debates and voting of their representatives. This had the full support of Otis, a sign of the change taking place in him as he came to rely more and more on the counsel of Adams. Simple railings were set up within a week, and the first onlookers to use the galleries found themselves intimately involved—they could reach out and touch the legislators. The galleries worried Thomas Hutchinson, who recognized that the arrangement gave the popular party "great additional weight and influence over the people." Hutchinson set out on the 15th for Falmouth and Casco Bay, the first stops on his three-week journey for the Superior Court circuit, leaving Bernard to struggle against a hostile House. On June 25 the representatives killed the motion for compensation by referring it over to the next session in order that they could have an opportunity, they said, to discuss it with their constituents.

The newspaper war, which normally died down after elections, this year continued into the summer. The loyalist writers recognized that Otis could be upset by repetition of the accusation that he had vowed to "see the country in a flame" over the chief-justice affair, and they used it repeatedly. They were correct; it was a soft spot in the armor precisely because Otis was so strongly loyal to his own idea of the British constitution. "Reflect," they told him, "(in your intervals from your rage) how basely you have betrayed your country's interest."[9] These were harsh and provocative words for Otis, who above all considered himself a patriot.

In London, Pitt came back to take charge of the king's ministry that summer after Rockingham, who had engineered the repeal of the Stamp Act, was dismissed. Pitt, now Lord Chatham, kept the Rockingham cabinet but wanted to be rid of Townshend, who was still chancellor of the Exchequer. With Pitt pressuring to replace him, Townshend grasped at a straw—a bill that would bring new revenues for England and therefore increase his popularity. The act he proposed would levy taxes on paper, lead, glass, and tea entering the American colonies, and would establish a board of customs to oversee the collection of money. These revenues would then be used to pay the salaries of American governors, judges, and minor Crown authorities in the colonies. With the Stamp Act barely dead, Townshend thus led Parliament into a new and far more dangerous confrontation with the colonies. He was at once meddling in colonial trade, adding to the hierarchy of "pensioners" in America, and taking away the old charter rights that allowed most of the colonies to pay—and thus control—their key officials.

With the opening of the courts, Bernard added to his long string of errors in judgment. He had received a very complimentary letter from Secretary Shelburne ("It is with great pleasure, sir, that I have observed the manner in which you have conducted yourself . . ."), and he could not resist reading the letter in full to the House, once again completely oblivious of the mood of his audience and the effect the letter, which not only puffed Bernard but contained disparaging comments on the province. Where Bernard hoped it would show support for his policy, the letter actually gave away the fact that he had been complaining to London about the state of affairs in Massachusetts. Shelburne wrote that he had shown two of Bernard's recent letters to the king, and that "His Majesty is extremely sorry to observe any degree of ill temper remaining in his colony of Massachusetts-Bay, or that points should be so improperly agitated as to tend to the revival of disputes."[10] The House overlooked Shelburne's flattering comments and, instead, accused Bernard of misrepresentation of the province to the king. Adams wrote a long report to the London agent, on the surface designed to offset Bernard's correspondence but actually part of the effort to undermine the governor's position and force his recall.

The committee to consider compensation for the riot victims had reported to the House in October that it was unable to learn any new facts or place the blame for the violence on any individual or group. Otis, looking after the interests of his constituents, stubbornly blocked the grant of compensation until a motion was made for the province as a whole, rather than the town of Boston, to pay it. The final recommendation was tied to an amnesty for all those accused of participating in the riots, and in this form the compensation bill was signed by Bernard. Hutchinson received £3,194 sterling, Oliver, £172, Benjamin Hallowell, £385, and William Story, £67. When much later the amnesty portion was disapproved by the Crown, it was too late—the matter had passed into history.

James Otis, who had kept up his extensive legal practice, made a special effort to champion those who ran afoul of writs of assistance. In September, customs men prepared to break into the house of a Captain Malcom to search for smuggled wine. Malcom sought out Otis, who stalled the customs men and the sheriff until sundown, after which the writs were no good. When on the following day Bernard began to take depositions as evidence in the case, a Boston town meeting was called. Otis became chairman of a committee to procure copies of the governor's depositions in order to give those who were accused a chance to defend themselves. When the General Court met in November, Otis had not forgotten this episode. He moved for a censure of Bernard for attempting to use the writs. The House may have supported writs in the past, he said, but now "the times were altered; they now knew what their rights were; then they did not."

Otis' strength intimidated the conservatives. "The language he uses in the House of Representatives is extravagant to an immoderate degree and he meets with no check,"[11] said Hutchinson, who still held Otis indirectly responsible for the destruction of his mansion and considered him a far greater danger than Adams. He saw that the erratic behavior of Otis was in this period a kind of strength, making him unpredictable, bold, feared, and making even his blatant errors seem somehow noble. "If some way could be found," Hutchinson said, "to destroy the influence of one man, the people of this province would recover themselves."

For all his violent, erratic ways, Otis was a far better behind-the-scenes organizer than is now recognized. For six years he had spent his evenings and often full days on the business of the town of Boston, on committees for school inspection, bridge repair, traffic control, market practices, smallpox inoculations, chimney inspections, and other mundane assignments which, even during the period after he became the regular moderator of the meetings, he was willing to undertake. He was in constant attendance at coffeehouse meetings of the Boston merchants before and after the formalization of their society in 1763, and he figured in all the gatherings of the Sons of Liberty and the Caucus Club. Not even Adams could match him. He now had not only the backing of the provincial towns but also entree into the mechanics' groups as well as the Merchants' Society.

As 1766 came to a close, the repairs to Hutchinson's house were completed and he moved back to Garden Court Street. He had spent much of his time throughout the year working on the second volume of his history of Massachusetts, bringing events up to 1750. Whether he knew it or not then, the 130 years covered in these two volumes would be a prelude to the third, which was to deal in detail with the era in which he himself had lived. The pressure of his combined duties as Superior Court chief justice and lieutenant governor was too much for Hutchinson, however, and now, at fifty-five, he began to show the strain. He was experiencing short spells of dizziness,[12] and he sometimes found himself wishing that there were some way he could quit the political world and return to his mercantile business. "It adds to my misfortune," he wrote, "that from my present station I cannot return to my former condition with honor."[13] At the same time he watched Samuel Adams growing stronger, calling for "a union and a correspondence"[14] among the merchants of North America and pronouncing the Stamp Act a blessing in disguise which had at last shown the colonists how London intended to make slaves of them.

Hutchinson, after losing the election to the council, had used his position as lieutenant governor to justify continuing to sit *ex officio* at the meetings. Precedent for this had been established early in the life of the colony, when several of the lieutenant governors also had been members of the council. But Adams and Otis felt differently about it, and the House, accusing Hutchinson of a "lust for power," demanded that he cease his appearances at council meetings. When the council approved the House resolution, Hutchinson was obliged to withdraw, as he put it, "to avoid further controversy."[15] Though his many duties were wearing him down, he could not reconcile himself to the loss of any office; to do so would mean relinquishing a dream of eventually succeeding to the governorship.

In May, Hutchinson suffered a slight stroke. Bernard reported that the lieutenant governor "has lately been ill to a degree alarming but is much better"[16] and said he thought the political pressures of the times had caused Hutchinson's illness. Judge Lynde noted in his diary that Hutchinson was absent from the opening of the Superior Court in May, having suffered "a paralytic stroke." Hutchinson himself explained it away as "a nervous disorder which I have been under for 6 or 7 weeks past and which I attribute myself to crossing the water in a cold evening after 12 or 13 hours attending a very crowded capital trial,"[17] but he admitted that the diagnosis of his close friends might be correct, that the true source might be "the mortification I feel from the slights and injuries offered me by my own countrymen." This, he concluded, has had "some influence." On advice of his physician, he stopped all his official activities for several weeks, rode out into the country often, and began to feel his health returning.

May elections came, and Boston voted for Otis and Adams as usual, along with Cushing and John Hancock, who was now popular enough to receive 100 percent of the town's votes. Bernard, impressed with the continuing strength of the popular party, tried again to strike a politician's bargain: he would support Colonel Otis for the council, along with one other member of the popular party, if he were allowed to have Thomas Hutchinson and Andrew Oliver back.[18] This was summarily rejected by Otis, however, and no deal could be made. The House submitted the names of all the six men rejected for the council the previous year, and Bernard again refused all but one.

The hard spadework by Otis and Adams had created a popular party which for the first time matched the court party in strength. Although Bernard tried to say that Otis had come to the end of his rope and that "it is generally believed that even now his reign is quite over,"[19] this was only posturing. The radicals, in one session, had blocked Hutchinson and Oliver from the council, criticized Bernard for his speech on the Stamp Act and the Shelburne letter, forced the dismissal of Hutchinson's friend, Jackson, as colony agent, delayed the compensation motion, moved galleries into the House, and had driven Hutchinson to the verge of complete collapse.

PART III

The British Respond With Force

13

The Townshend Acts

September 1767–May 1768

If from the bottom of my heart to disapprove of
all tumultuous and riotous proceedings, and upon all
proper occasions to bear my most humble testimony
against them is to be a Tory, I am, and ever have been,
so far a Tory. On the other hand, if to stand like men,
for the rights of men, be a distinguishing characteristic
of the Whigs, I hope I am, and ever shall be so far a
Whig. I profess however to be not altogether devoted to
any party but that of truth and right reason, which I
think I am ready to embrace wherever I find it.

JAMES OTIS, 1768

To PUT IT MILDLY, James Otis was not an easy man to understand. Never was an American political figure so torn by diametrically opposed—but coincident—emotions and convictions. His
strong, original, searching intellect was challenged at every
crossroads by his equally strong inhibitions, making his life a
running battle. He was at once a radical political innovator and
a conservative guardian of the status quo; a fearless attacker of
his enemies and an obsequious, apologetic eater of humble pie;
a gregarious party boss and a lonely theorizer. No one individual
of his time was described by contemporaries with such disparity
of impressions. To Hutchinson he was a mad incendiary; to

James Putnam he was "the most able, manly, and commanding of his age at the bar"; to Peter Oliver he was "rash, unguarded, foul-mouthed, and openly spiteful." Catherine Macaulay called him "the greatest guardian of American liberty," and the American Tories said he was the destroyer of his country. Otis himself added to the contradictions: he could upbraid his contemporaries for their "shameful silence" in the face of the Sugar Act in 1764, and ten months later write, " 'Tis the duty of all humbly and silently to acquiesce in all the decisions of the supreme legislative." Every part of him seemed opposed by another: for his rebelliousness, a profound respect for authority; for the unrelenting logic of his reasoning, a long series of emotional outbursts and temperamental gestures; for a legal expertise buttressed by years of painstaking research, a propensity to misconceive the simplest statement.

Many despaired of ever really knowing the unpredictable Otis, but one man knew him well. Samuel Adams had sharpened his keen understanding of men in years of work in the political clubs and on the town committees, watching, listening, helping with decisions that placed men in the jobs for which they were most suited. More important, he was a man who could see into himself without the slightest distortion and he was utterly committed to the radical cause with no thought of personal advantage. This helped him to comprehend the psyche of Otis. The relationship, however, was a complicated and difficult one which only Adams could have handled. Nor were the difficulties all on one side. Adams himself, for all his objectivity and manipulative ability, was a stubborn, self-righteous, and unchangeable man. He knew, however, that there was much to be gained in the combination of himself and Otis—too much to risk a confrontation with his unpredictable partner—and only Adams was self-effacing enough to carry out his role in such a relationship. He often found that what was gained in the morning might be lost in the afternoon, but he was always ready to start over again.

By the summer of 1767 the details of the Townshend Acts were clear; everyone in Boston realized that the port had become the customs capital of the North American coast and the object of a growing list of regulations that could only be called punitive legislation. What began in London as a collective ignorance of the trading system grew to a stubborn and simpleminded vindictiveness as the swiftly changing ministries followed one another, helping Parliament along a stony and blind path of self-defeat. The series of repressive moves undercut the power of Hutchinson and the court party and also turned away the normally conservative Boston merchants, who had long been the stabilizing force in the politics of the town. The harsh enforcements and new, tough laws goaded Boston's radical mobs to violence and gave fresh support to Otis and Adams.

The newspaper attacks against Adams as early as the spring of 1763, in which he was seen as Otis' "pimp" and "journeyman scribbler," showed that he was already a thorn in the side of the loyalists. Although he much preferred to work behind the scenes, Adams found that the personality of Otis and the changing times, and growing radicalism, were forcing him out into center stage. Now Boston was ready for him; he became more and more the symbol of a new feeling. As clerk of the House, he was in the highest position unaffected by Crown control, where every paper that passed in or out of the House went through his hands. The gradual effect of his unyielding pragmatism on the idealistic and highly theoretical mind of Otis would now begin to be evident.

By the late summer of 1767 Adams had convinced Otis that the immediacy of articles in the press at this stage was far more important than the scholarly essays that had served in the past to articulate the basis for radical political action. Thus the theoretical reasoning and legal expertise of Otis, the journalistic energy and style of Adams, and the presses of Edes and Gill were brought together. Here began a period of anonymous productivity for the two writers, who met each Saturday at the printers, carrying manuscripts and notes to prepare the *Gazette* columns to be printed and distributed on the following Monday. Together, the two men would work the weekend through, writing and correcting columns of print on Parliamentary oppression, nonimportation, the decay of the charter rights, searches and seizures by the customs men, and the latest moves of the Hutchinson "cabal." They attacked the idea of Crown salaries for colonial judges and insisted that Massachusetts was being misrepresented in London by some of "her own children"; they ridiculed the customs commissioners and other "pensioners" who lived "in luxury" at the expense of colonial taxpayers; and they smothered the Tory writers who attempted to reply.

In September, amid the talk of nonimportation as a response to the Townshend Acts, while Adams and Otis were publishing the Bill of Rights and parts of the Magna Charta in the *Gazette*, Jeremiah Gridley died in his sixty-sixth year. For a moment all controversy stopped, and Otis joined Hutchinson and Trowbridge at Gridley's coffin, where all three were bearers.[1] The passing of this immensely influential man, foremost lawyer in the province, Grand Master of all Masons in North America, colonel of militia, left a gap that was difficult to fill, but Hancock wrote in his ledger that, with Gridley gone, Otis was now the best lawyer in Boston,[2] and he advised his London agents to retain Otis for their business affairs in Massachusetts. Men such as Hancock and John Adams recognized that, for all his instabilities, Otis was a legal mind without peer in the colony. In the same week Townshend died in England and was succeeded by Lord North as chancellor of the Exchequer. With Chatham ill at home, isolated from the business of government, North did nothing to change the Townshend program.

A series of town meetings in Boston called to urge a reaction to the new taxes resulted in a vote to refrain from purchasing a number of British products, beginning in the new year, two months away. Adams saw to it that copies of the Boston motion were sent to all the Massachusetts towns urging that they do likewise. While sanctioning this move, Otis, who had played a very conservative role in his leadership of the town since the riots of 1765, insisted that the worst was over in the confrontation with England and that the colonies were well along the road toward resolving past differences with Parliament. Drastic acts, he said, could only delay and possibly damage the good relationship now returning. Adams, on the other hand, did no theorizing on this question. His interest now lay in getting the merchants committed to action on the side of the town. It was the merchants, after all, who would do the importing or nonimporting.

The arrival of the new customs commissioners provided Adams with a good opportunity to exploit the tensions brought on by the Townshend Acts with a symbolic gesture that would echo through the colonies: Bostonians en masse would go down to the docks and resist their landing. Otis, however, wanted to use the arrival for a different purpose—to show London that his beloved Boston was not ruled by a mob. When some diehards insisted on posting a brash letter on the Liberty Tree, Otis called a town meeting for repudiation of violence as an approach to the problems of the times, reminding his fellow townsmen of the riots two years earlier, when Thomas Hutchinson's house had been destroyed. He could not countenance the kind of action that was threatened by the letter, he said. This was "to act like madmen," against all the rules of conduct, and would destroy the reputation of the city. Boston, he said, had had enough of violence. It was absurd to blame the customs men for the new taxes. If the laws were burdensome, "we ought to behave like men, and use the proper and legal measures to obtain redress."[3] The king, he insisted, was accessible and there was no doubt that "our humble and dutiful petitions and remonstrances would, sooner or later, be heard, and meet with success, if supported by justice and reason." Nothing could justify mob action, no possible circumstances, "though ever so oppressive."

Otis' instructions were enough for the Bostonians. The customs officials, debarking on the evening of the celebration, were understandably wary of coming into town, but their fears were quickly dispelled. Bernard reported that they came ashore "and even passed by one of the bonfires without receiving any affront whatsoever."

In effect, Otis had counseled compliance with the Townshend Acts. Bernard, taken aback, thought Otis' words showed him to be "entirely on the side of government,"[4] and the watchful court-party writers seized on the contradictions in his successive statements. Otis, in turn, angrily defended himself from what he deemed were personal affronts. He was becoming ever more emotionally involved, ever more vulnerable. He adhered to his earlier statements that the province must seek redress in a legal, constitutional way. His friendly correspondence with John Dickinson of Pennsylvania, whose philosophy was close to his, helped him fend off his detractors. Dickinson sent Otis a manuscript draft of *Letters from a Pennsylvania Farmer* (later printed in the Boston newspapers). Like Otis, Dickinson was ready to argue with Parliament but believed in the constitution and the empire.

The Townshend Acts had gone into effect on November 20. Bernard delayed the opening of the General Court until December 30 in order to put as many days as he could between the acts and any response by the House, hoping that time would soften the anger and frustration, but that was not the case. Once the routine of affairs in the House began again, Adams and Otis were quickly back at their collaboration. The former, who always favored establishment of connections to England and to the other colonies by correspondence, now saw a new opportunity. From the exchange between Otis, Barré, and Conway during the previous year, he had recognized the psychological value of letters that would link them with members of Parliament. Using the excuse that the House wished to set right the false picture that Bernard had painted in his correspondence with Shelburne, Adams succeeded in getting approval to write to every major political figure in London who seemed favorably disposed to the colony, providing them with facts that could be used in Parliamentary debate. The committee of correspondence included Adams, Otis, Cushing, and Hawley. Letters were prepared to Shelburne, de Berdt, Rockingham, Camden, Chatham, and Conway. The letters, showing stylistic marks of Adams, differed enough one from another to be considered as personal correspondence, but they were for the most part rearrangements of the same basic statements. The old themes were repeated: taxes made slaves of the colonists; lawmakers in London and even the king failed to understand the American issues, which were continually misrepresented by deceitful underlings.

Adams and Otis immediately followed this series with an attempt to expand their correspondence to all the colonies. They had tried on January 21 to push through a motion for a circular letter presenting the Massachusetts view on the Townshend Acts, but were defeated by about 2 to 1 in the full House.[5] They therefore waited and worked to build support until near the end of the winter term, when many representatives had left for home, and with a cadre of popular-party men they tried again. The letter which they presented was a good combination of the subtle psychology of Adams and the moderation of Otis. Without appearing to dictate to the other colonies, and shunning all references which might credit Massachusetts as the leader, the paper asked for agreement that what was repulsive to Massachusetts about the new duties was also repulsive to the rest of America. On February 11 the bill carried. Bernard attributed the success to "cabals." Not content with merely passing the bill, Adams called for a vote to erase from the House *Journal* all records of the earlier defeat, and in this, too, he was successful.[6]

In late January, Bernard—who never learned—allowed Secretary Oliver to read to the House a letter he had received from London supporting his negativing of the councilors elected in May of the previous year. Otis immediately delivered a blistering attack on Bernard, and the House followed this with a message which Hutchinson called "the most rude I have known sent to a Governor."[7] Bernard, shaken, would only comment that this latest act "outdoes even Otis' outdoings."[8] He continued to press for a job elsewhere—anywhere that could get him out of Boston—but once again his greed got in his way. He qualified his plea—he wanted only to be relieved of the responsibilities in this broiling town—he did not want to retire—he needed a new governorship. Predicting that peaceful government would be restored to Massachusetts by summer, he asked Barrington for a leave of absence for a year. Hutchinson agreed that prospects were good for a quiet period ahead. "We have, however, now and then flashes from our firebrand," he added. "I wish I could think them presages of his extinction."[9]

Hutchinson had insisted that it mattered little to him whether or not he sat with the council during their deliberations, but in fact he was much disturbed. Deprived of participation, he had no opportunity to exercise any political power, since Bernard did not include him in other governmental activities. Except for the opportunities to represent the province in such matters as border disputes or Indian conferences, Hutchinson was left out of the picture; he considered himself a "mere cypher" and saw his chances for the governorship fading away.

On February 29, 1768, Joseph Warren, writing under the

pseudonym "A True Patriot,"[10] violently attacked Bernard in the *Gazette*. Accusing him of "insolence," Warren said Bernard had misrepresented the state of the province to Lord Shelburne, with the result that Shelburne had turned against Massachusetts. Charging Bernard with manifold abuses and a "diabolical thirst for mischief," Warren threatened the governor and announced he would say no more on the subject of the letters "lest a full representation . . . lead . . . to an unwarrantable revenge."

Bernard, deeply shocked, asked the council to take action against the writer. The council voted agreement with Bernard that the anonymous letter was offensive and censured its author. Otis, according to Bernard, then attacked the council with "oaths and imprecations,"[11] promising that there would be a purge of the council in the next elections. In the House, debate over the letter began one afternoon and was continued into the next day as Otis and Adams fought to keep the *Gazette* from censure. Finally a motion was prepared stating that "the liberty of the press is the great bulwark of the liberty of the people." The House refused to agree that the article warranted any legal action or even censure, and Bernard, in response, characterized Otis as "the canker-worm of the constitution of this government."

Hutchinson was determined to stop the newspaper campaign against the governor, the council, and the courts. If the legislature was afraid to act, the courts would not be. As chief justice, he arranged for the *Gazette* to be charged with libel in the Superior Court when it met a few days later, but even in his own bailiwick he was unable to stop Otis. The jury, which had reached the point of requesting the attorney general to prepare a bill for libel, changed its mind overnight, apparently under the influence of Otis and the Sons of Liberty. When the court met next day, the jury opposed the bill in phrases that Bernard said were "almost word for word the same Otis had before used in public." Hutchinson's report of the event shows his frustration:

> I never gave any offence to the grand jury with more zeal than I did this and I told them almost in plain words that they might depend on being damned if they did not find a bill but they were unwilling to run the risk of it. This has convinced me

as much as anything that has happened among us that the laws have lost all their force.[12]

On March 4, Bernard, stung by the results of the "True Patriot" affair, sent an angry note to the House and abruptly prorogued the General Court. Otis and Adams, in a House almost evenly split, had been the better manipulators, and the popular party came out ahead. The last act of the representatives had been to approve Boston's nonimportation agreement with only one dissenting vote, that of stubborn Timothy Ruggles.

Bernard now increased his emphasis on the need for military control in Boston. He knew that the council would never agree to the arrival of British Regulars, no matter how desperate the situation, and he was well aware that a request on his part would ruin him as a political figure in the province and possibly in all America. Writing to Hillsborough in March he said,

> Ever since I have perceived that the wickedness of some and the folly of others will in the end bring troops here, I have conducted myself so as to be able to say, and swear to, if the Sons of Liberty shall require it, that I have never applied for troops. And therefore, my Lord, I beg that nothing I now write may be considered as such an application.[13]

Gage wrote from New York, pointedly asking Bernard whether or not he needed troops and again the governor was evasive, stating that his failure to apply for troops "is no argument that they are not wanted."

With increasing pressure for nonimportation, the Sons of Liberty once more became active with physical harassment of recalcitrant merchants and customs men. The familiar drums and horns of riot sounded in the Boston streets, commissioners Paxton and Williams were hanged in effigy, and a cargo of undutied wine was escorted openly from ship to warehouse by a group of toughs. Saint Patrick's day celebrations were postponed one day (to March 18) in order to coincide with the anniversary of the repeal of the Stamp Act, and a near-riot occurred in the evening. The results of this combination of political pressure and physical intimidation were evident in an agreement signed by a hundred Boston merchants not to import manufactured goods and to encourage American industry. The success of the Boston radicals, however, was not mirrored in other colonies. In April, Philadelphia refused to join in, and although New York merchants signed up, they did little to enforce the agreement and eventually repudiated it. Since the Boston merchants had agreed to nonimportation on the qualification that the plan would be acceptable to the other major port towns, the resolution lost its force and went unheeded.

At the town meeting of May 4, Adams and Otis were once again chosen as Boston's representatives to the General Court, along with Cushing and Hancock. The vote was a foregone conclusion, and Otis invited Adams to dinner that night to mark the beginning of another political year. There was cause for celebration, since they also had engineered a refusal to provide the use of the Town House to the governor for his annual councilor's dinner to celebrate the opening of the court. They would not give him the hall, they said, unless he first promised to exclude the commissioners from the dinner.[14] This, of course, he could not do.

Before the spring elections Bernard had made his perennial offer, sending word to the Otises that, if Hutchinson were chosen for the council, "the Governor would probably admit Otis Sr." This, said Bernard, would provide an opportunity for reconciliation. Colonel Otis, however, was not to be bought off. His answer, reported by Hutchinson, was that "he had rather not only renounce any share in the government himself but also lose his whole estate which is not a small one than the Lieutenant Governor should be chose."[15]

On the first round of voting in the House, Hutchinson received 68 votes for the council, three short of the required majority. His supporters called for another count, which probably would have given him the council seat, but as the roll call began, Adams interrupted to ask the House "whether any gentleman was certain that the Lieutenant Governor was a pensioner," linking Hutchinson to the hated Townshend Acts and also to repressive British policy in Ireland. A few weeks earlier the *Gazette* had complained that "in a short time there will be as many pensions upon the American establishment as on the *Irish*." Otis immediately answered Adams, saying he knew for a fact that Hutchinson was one of the pensioners, paid by the Crown out of the American revenues, and that no man who valued his country should vote for him. Otis then circulated through the room repeating "pensioner or no pensioner"[16] and calling on individual representatives to vote for Hutchinson's opponent, Artemus Ward. The "pensioner" label, which, as Hutchinson admitted, "among Americans conveys a very odious idea," cost him his council seat.

Hutchinson often appears to possess a calm and objective evaluation of events in which he is personally involved, but his correspondence shows that his view of this episode underwent a change as he continued to smolder over the defeat. On May 26, the day after the elections, he wrote that Otis "in a very irregular manner" had interrupted the ballot and "declared" he knew Hutchinson to be a pensioner. Five days later he wrote (more correctly) that Adams had interrupted the vote, whereupon Otis "ran about the House . . . crying out pensioner or no pensioner and so carried his point." Ten days after the event, Hutchinson said, "Our great Incendiary was enraged and ran about the House in a fury . . . crying pensioner or no pensioner." Finally, when two weeks had passed since the election, he wrote to Pownall that Otis, "like an enraged Demon ran about the House . . . crying pensioner or no pensioner."[17]

Hutchinson now considered letting it be known that he would take the position as London agent for the province, but he could not muster within himself any real desire for the job. He might have to support political principles that he found absurd, such as the claim of exemption from certain acts of Parliament, and this he could not do. What he still wanted, in fact, was the governorship of the province, and the opportunity "to introduce a better spirit." He had by this time decided that he would never serve in second place under another governor. He felt that he deserved the chance to run the province. "No Lieutenant Governor since the Charter," he said, "has suffered so much as I have done."

14

The Liberty Incident

May–June 1768

The vessel seized was the property of a private
gentleman, a merchant, but the manner in which it
was seized was judged a public affront, an unwarrantable action; yet the people suppressed their just resentment.

SAMUEL ADAMS, August 1768

HIS MAJESTY'S SHIP of the line *Romney* arrived in Boston harbor
on May 17, with orders to assist in the regulation of trade by inspecting American merchant shipping for contraband. A high
square-rigger mounting 50 guns, the *Romney* was a first-class fighting vessel in every way, but her captain, John Corner, had sailed
with many empty berths among the crew. He needed men to fill out
his working shifts, and he meant to get them by whatever meth-
ods necessary, including impressment—seizing sailors off commercial ships for forced service. This practice, a sure method of re-
cruitment, was common at the time and legal under Admiralty
regulations—except in North American waters. In order to assist
the shipping trades along the American coast, British Parliament
60 years before had declared colonial sailors immune to such
seizure. But Corner needed men.

Corner's experience in American coastal waters had given him little reason to respect colonials. The crews of merchantmen he stopped at sea were insolent and uncooperative and the inhabitants of port towns in the provinces were unfriendly. This was especially true of Boston, which in Corner's mind was "a blackguard town ruled by mobs." He was anxious to show the ill-mannered citizens of that place what he thought of them. Besides, as far as Corner was concerned, his need to fill out the *Romney's* crew was justification enough to ignore an old law, especially when most American sailors were nothing but smugglers anyway. Corner's attitude fed the rumors then in circulation and increased the enmity between the dockhands of the port and his sailors, making *Romney* an ominous and hated word in Boston.

In the first week in June, Corner sailed his man-of-war close up into the Boston commercial dock area, dropping anchor only a few hundred yards from the merchantmen tied up at the wharves. He wanted the dominating presence of the ship to serve as a grim sign that the hand of the Admiralty rested heavy on the harbor: more men would be impressed; more ships would be searched; more merchants would be discovered and named as smugglers.

The commissioners of customs, who held jurisdiction over the entire North Atlantic coast, were now well settled in Boston. Since their arrival in November, they had published continual notices to shippers in the molasses trade, warning them that the easygoing days were over and that inspections from now on would be in earnest. No one believed such talk at first, even when a few ships were boarded and searched. Then seizures had come and ships were confiscated, though no incident had yet taken place within Boston harbor. The governor, of course, profited to the tune of one-third the cargo of each vessel seized.

Heartened by the presence of Captain Corner and his man-of-war, the commissioners resolved to put their authority to the test while they were sure of naval support. They turned their attention to the merchant whom they felt had most openly flaunted the trade regulations—John Hancock. At that moment his ship *Liberty* lay at dockside, having arrived a few weeks earlier from Madeira with a cargo that included wine, one of the taxable items. Hancock's captain, Nathaniel Barnard, declared his wine cargo at the customs house, paying the tax on 25 barrels. The ship was unloaded in the presence of customs inspectors and later reloaded with 200 barrels of oil.

Customs Collector Harrison then announced that Thomas Kirk, who had inspected the unloading of the *Liberty*, had come forward with new evidence that Hancock was a smuggler. Kirk changed his routine inspection report, which originally disclosed no irregularities, to say he had been roughly treated by one of Hancock's captains, who first tried to make him look the other way while additional wine above the declared 25 barrels was unloaded. When this didn't work, Kirk said, the captain had imprisoned him deep in the *Liberty*'s hold for three hours while the unloading continued. Captain Barnard could not be called to contradict this account; he had died of a heart attack the day after the unloading. Kirk produced no witnesses—not even his partner, who had failed to show up for duty that day. Nevertheless, the commissioners decided Kirk's word was reason enough to seize the ship. Hancock had been high-handed and rude with several of the customs men, and his all too obvious disdain made it that much easier for them to act. The job of actually taking over the ship was given to Benjamin Hallowell, comptroller of the port, the man who had suffered along with Hutchinson in the riots of 1765.

Hallowell was quite aware that he was dealing with danger. Few men were as popular along the waterfront as John Hancock, a town selectman, a merchant known for his consideration for the dockhands, and an employer who often provided make-work jobs just to keep salaries coming when business was slow. But with the *Romney* in port, he knew the opportunity for firmness should not be lost. Admiral Montague had agreed to provide a ship's party from the man-of-war to help the customs men take over Hancock's ship. Near sunset on Friday afternoon, as Hallowell along with collector Joseph Harrison and their deputies walked down the dock, the *Romney* lowered two longboats filled with sailors and marines. Rowing hard, the boarding party crossed quickly to the *Liberty*. While Hallowell was discussing the matter with Hancock's new captain, Corner's sailors clambered on deck and took over the merchantman. In the meantime, Hancock's wharf was filling up with a crowd of angry townspeople.

Hallowell spoke to the leaders of a gathering crowd, including Otis' friend Captain Malcom, insisting that there was no cause for trouble, that this was simply an administrative action. But when the British sailors cast loose the ship from the dock and began to tow her off, the watching crowd expressed its disagreement, first with words, but soon with the ubiquitous Boston cobblestone. These traditional missiles filled the air and clattered in the long-boats while sailors ducked, shouted back obscenities to match those of the rock throwers, and rowed as hard as they could to get the heavy ship moving. Within minutes, drawn by an outgoing tide and by the two longboats, the *Liberty* was drifting back down on the *Romney*.

Admiral Montague, who had found himself a convenient observation point at a second-floor window in a dockside house, had the advantage of a safe and spectacular view of the proceedings, but Hallowell was less fortunate. With the ship now gone, he was left standing on Hancock's wharf, too close to the action long to enjoy the sight. He perceived the danger and bolted into the crowd, trying for a quick escape, but managed only a few steps before he was knocked to the ground. He got to his feet and wormed his way through angry men who pummeled and kicked him, bringing him to earth several more times before he finally staggered off. His assistants on the dock met a like fate. Harrison escaped through a back alley, but not before he was "much bruised," while his son, who had accompanied him, was soundly beaten and dragged up the street by the hair. Cheers, cries, and the sound of shattering glass and splintering panes rang along the docks as the spectators vented their anger on the houses and shops of other customs officials. Singling out the home of Inspector Williams, the mob broke a hundred panes of glass, and then repeated the performance at the homes of Harrison and Hallowell. This accomplished, some of the rioters discovered a small pleasure boat that belonged to Harrison and carried it ceremoniously through the streets to the Common, where they set it afire. This achievement capped the night's events, and the next day (Saturday, June 11) was quiet again. The *Liberty* swung sedately next to the *Romney* on the tide a few hundred yards off Hancock's wharf.[1]

There were indications, however, that the battle had only begun. A paper attached to the Liberty Tree invited the Sons of Liberty to meet at six that evening "to clear the land of the vermin which have come to devour us." This was more than enough for the battered commissioners, who, fearful of more reprisals, seized the opportunity to get themselves and their families out of harm's way; 67 people took refuge aboard the *Romney* that afternoon.

On Saturday night Joseph Warren, chosen as a go-between, went to see Comptroller Hallowell, who was confined to his house recovering from his beating. Hancock, Warren said, wanted his ship back and would give bond for her if she were returned to the dock. Harrison said he would think it over, and asked Warren to return the next day. On Sunday, the 12th, when Warren returned, Harrison gave him a note for Hancock, agreeing to return the *Liberty* to the wharf on condition that Hancock would post bond to guarantee the ship's presence pending court proceedings. Warren returned to say that he had delivered the note and that the matter was now settled.

On Monday the town of Boston was quiet and calm on the surface but boiling with speculation. Bernard received word that there was to be an uprising, a fact which he readily believed. A Tory friend told him the plan was to get rid of all Crown officials. More handbills issued by the Sons of Liberty appeared around town, calling for a meeting at the Liberty Tree on Tuesday morning. The frightened tax men, crowded with their families aboard the *Romney*, asked for asylum behind the protection of the guns at the castle. Bernard decided he would remain out of sight at his Jamaica farm, where he continued to receive secondhand reports of the Boston activities. With Hutchinson away on the eastern circuit of the Superior Court, the governor was left to face the crisis alone, and the prospect of a new confrontation frightened him. He refused to come to town and debated with himself over whether or not to send for his lieutenant governor.

Samuel Adams, of course, saw the political possibilities of this new situation and conferred with Otis, Warren, and Hancock, with the result that a strategy meeting was arranged for Monday at Hancock's house. Otis began by arguing that the customs men had exceeded the law; no process papers had been served, and the time of seizure was after sundown, which was legally prohibited. Since there were very good odds that Hancock could win a court fight over his ship, Otis urged him not to weaken his case by any out-of-court agreement for its return. Adams added another reason, characteristic of his sensitivity to the psychological aspects of the confrontation: the presence of the *Liberty* lying idle under the control of the Admiralty would serve as an excellent and highly visible symbol of British coercion. The name of the ship, of course, was a stroke of luck for the radicals.

This was not an easy decision for Hancock, who had to consider, in addition to the politics involved, the very real financial problems of an idle ship. Even if he won the case in the end, Hancock said, the delay would be costly. Otis and Adams prevailed, however, and at midnight Warren was again at Hallowell's. He was extremely sorry, Warren said, but the matter was not settled after all. Mr. Hancock, at the advice of counsel and friends, now would "have nothing to do with the business, but would let it take its course" and would provide no bond. The challenge was given, and Hallowell had to inform the commissioners that Hancock and his lawyers were planning to fight the seizure in court.

While the radicals laid out their strategy in complete disregard of Bernard, he imagined them plotting his overthrow. He spent a restless Monday night, and by dawn on Tuesday he had made his decision, sending his son riding to Exeter, New Hampshire, through a cold rain to find Hutchinson, tell him the situation was desperate, and order him to hurry to Boston. While he waited for his deputy's return, Bernard tried to decide whether or not to make his escape by running the gauntlet to Castle William.

The rain on Tuesday did not stop a very large gathering under the Liberty Tree to protest the seizure of Hancock's ship. There were 1,500 people milling around the big elm before the Sons of Liberty guided the crowd to Faneuil Hall for a spontaneous town meeting, calling for Otis as moderator. Otis came forward to take the rostrum amid a clamor of cheers and applause, and assured his audience that there would be no giving in to the customs men. Hancock joined Otis at the rostrum and drew shouts of acclaim when he defiantly announced that he would take the case into the courts, no matter what the cost. Otis then adjourned the session, calling for an official town meeting that afternoon at the Old South Church. This motion passed with great fanfare and the crowd dispersed. By the time of the later meeting Otis had prepared a petition to the king, which he read from the pulpit.

The petition, created in haste, drew great roars of approval from the crowd, but it was a disappointment to Samuel Adams. It lacked focus. In order to arrive at the specific subject, the seizure of the merchantman, Otis journeyed through the familiar theory of the British constitution as a basis for the right of a citizen to be taxed only when he is represented; he asserted the well-known fact that previous petitions had been prevented from reaching the king; he numbered the usual complaints—the invasion of soldiers, the seizures, and the impressments; he reported intimidation by Crown policy and the threatened destruction of American trade; he declared Boston was "in a situation nearly as if war was formally declared against it." Any thought of war with Britain, said Otis, was "the most shocking and dreadful extremity,"[2] but the only alternative was so humiliating and base as to be unthinkable. As he drew near the end, he finally came to particulars. Even then there was no mention of Hancock's *Liberty,* but only a request to move the *Romney* out of the harbor and to prohibit the customs commissioners from resuming their activities.

This rambling and inconclusive harangue was approved and a committee of 21 was appointed to present it to the governor at Jamaica Plain. Another vote called for drawing up a letter on "some late occurrences in this town" to be sent to the agent in London. But still no one made any specific complaint about the *Liberty* affair. At the last minute, near the end of the meeting, an exasperated Adams managed the appointment of a committee of three—himself, Benjamin Church, and Joseph Warren—to draft a motion expressing the town's "great dislike" of the procedures used in carrying off the *Liberty,* but this action came too late to have any influence on events that day. Otis adjourned the meeting with fiery words demanding removal of the people's grievances against the administration; if not, he said, and if Boston were called on to defend its liberties and privileges, "I hope and believe we shall, one and all, resist unto blood; but, at the same time, pray Almighty God it may never so happen."

That afternoon Bernard received word at Jamaica Plain that a large part of the Boston faction was on the way out to his farm. From his door he watched and waited until the long column of 11 carriages came into view. As it approached he recognized Otis, whom he had so often called the grand incendiary, in the lead, but the group seemed peaceful; what he feared as an ugly mob turned out to be a polite if unusually large deputation from the town meeting. Breathing easier, the embattled farmer became the governor again and ordered wine handed around to his many uninvited guests. In a relaxed and gentlemanly atmosphere, Otis announced he had a paper to read to the representative of the king's administration. As Otis read his vague document, Bernard realized he was indeed out of trouble, if only for the time being. His courage returned, along with his condescension and his view of the Bostonians as bumpkins. "They left me highly pleased with their reception," he said, "especially that part of them which had not been used to an interview with me."[3]

He had indicated that he needed time to study the committee's petition, and when they left, he composed a reply, which was read at another town meeting on the following day. Since he was responding to a weak complaint, he could afford to be conciliatory. He had no authority, he said, to change the customs procedures, but he promised to stop impressments and to do whatever he could to improve relations between the town and the administration. This, said Bernard, pleased Otis so much that he read the governor's words to his fellow townsmen with the comment that Bernard was "a well-wisher to the province." Samuel Adams, however, was unimpressed. "Thus saith Governor Bernard," he wrote, "but no one remembers or believes it."[4]

While this exchange was being consummated, Hutchinson was galloping back on muddy New Hampshire roads.[5] He knew there would be unrest in town, though, unlike Bernard, he refused to believe stories of an impending revolt. Nevertheless, he remembered the riots three years earlier that had cost him so much. There was little hope, he later said, of controlling a Boston mob once it started—especially since all those who normally might help the sheriff were Sons of Liberty. After a hard ride, he arrived at Jamaica Plain, where he found an ebullient Bernard, who announced that he had personally restored the town to a state of order and that all was well; the road-weary Hutchinson could go back to his duty on the circuit.

At the town meeting Otis, delighted with Bernard's reply, nearly overlooked Adams and his committee report on the *Liberty* seizure, and as the meeting drew to a close on a self-satisfied note, Adams could generate very little interest. After an indecisive debate it was recommended to enlarge the three-man committee of Warren, Church, and Adams to seven members and to absorb the draft motion into a set of instructions for the Boston representatives to the General Court. With John Adams, Richard Dana, Joseph Warren, and Edward Payne on board, the new committee was given until Friday afternoon to draw up the paper.

Adams felt keenly the failure of this series of meetings, where bombastic prose took the place of hard reasoning and the threat of action. Later the Tory Richard Sylvester would swear to the truth of a deposition that he heard Samuel Adams call for revolution on that day. "If you are men, behave like men," Adams was supposed to have said, adding the exhortation, "Let us take up arms immediately and be free." Sylvester said Adams assured the Boston firebrands that 30,000 men would join them from the countryside if a fight began. Whatever he might have said, it is certain Adams was not pleased with the turn of events surrounding the *Liberty* affair. For all the activity, little had been accomplished. He resolved to correct that by making the instructions a compendium of grievances against the Crown, with the *Liberty* incident as centerpiece. The committee worked from noon Tuesday into the evening,[6] and again Wednesday until late afternoon, when the town meeting reopened.

The resulting instructions, unanimously approved, were very different from the petition which Otis had read to Bernard. After a pro forma profession of loyalty to the king, Adams insisted that the Stamp Act, though repealed, had been continued in spirit by other unconstitutional taxes and by the maintenance of "swarms of officers and pensioners in idleness and luxury." He recounted in detail the illegal seizure of Hancock's ship. He said that a catalogue of new rumors and reports had alarmed the province—there were more Crown officials to "suck the life blood of the body politic while it is streaming from the veins,"[7] more warships to inhibit trade, more troops "to dragoon us into passive obedience," and more impressments of New England sailors. Harking back to the old British law for Encouragement of the Trade to America, which prohibited seizures of American mariners, Adams ordered Boston's representatives to insure that the law was upheld.

As had been the case in the past, the petitions and instructions were successful in building a spirit of resistance in Massachusetts, but they were read with indifference when they finally arrived in London. Even before the *Liberty* riot, the king had made known his decision to station enough Regulars in Boston to insure better control of the port and the province. On June 8 Hillsborough had written secretly to Gage, ordering him to send at least one regiment to Boston to assist in "preservation of the public peace" and to protect the revenue officers. The secretary of state followed this with a letter to Bernard telling him that troops were on the way and that the ministry remained convinced a firm stand would encourage the administration in the other colonies. Regardless of the continued objection of a minority in Parliament (Barré insisted that the riots proved only that the province was "mimicking the mother-country"), the ministry from this time on took measures that consistently were designed to punish and isolate Boston, characterizing the town as the only place on the continent where there was real opposition to the Crown.

15

Troops to Boston

June 1768–January 1769

> Are we a garrison'd town or are we not? If we are,
> let us know by whose authority and by whose influence
> we are made so: If not, and I take it for granted we are
> not, let us then assert and maintain the honor—the
> dignity of free citizens and place the military, where
> all other men are and where they always ought and
> always will be plac'd in every free country, at the foot
> of the common law of the land.

SAMUEL ADAMS, December 1768

ANY RESPITE BERNARD MIGHT HAVE GAINED from his conciliatory reply to the town of Boston was quickly dispelled when on Saturday, June 18, word arrived that British Regulars were on the way to Boston.[1] To add to the governor's discomfort, the mail packet from London that day carried a Hillsborough letter instructing him to demand that the Massachusetts House immediately repudiate and rescind its circular letter on the Townshend Acts. Bernard did as he was told. He addressed the House on June 21, informing the representatives that they had no choice but to call back the circular letter—and his announcement caused an explosion of anger. Otis took the floor that afternoon, speaking for two hours in a harangue that was, according to Bernard, "the most violent, insolent, abusive, treasonable declamation that perhaps was ever delivered." Otis did not insult the king personally, wrote Bernard, but he did everything else—he "traduced his government with all the bitterness of words."[2] His majesty's ministers, Otis said, were mere boys who played with titles and badges, leaving the real business of government to clerks. The ministry was full of venal, corrupt, and debauched wretches who were useless because they had been brought up all wrong. "They are sent to . . . Oxford and Cambridge—and pray, what do they learn there?—Why, the outside of a monkey. What are they when they return home again? Complete monkeys themselves."[3] As for the House of Commons, it was "a parcel of button-makers, pinmakers, horse jockey gamesters, pensioners, pimps, and whoremasters." The Massachusetts House need not be intimidated by such people—it should not rescind the circular letter; let Hillsborough tell Parliament to rescind *their* acts, and let the minister take back his own letter. If he did not, then England, not America, was lost forever.[4]

Spurred by the violent rhetoric of Otis and the backstage maneuvering of Adams, the debate continued for nine days. Adams, elated with Otis' response, drafted a paper incorporating the Otis position that the circular letter, conceived and approved by an earlier House, could not be withdrawn by a new and different legislative body, nor could the present representatives be held responsible for it. The letter, he said, was an accomplished fact. It had been received in the other colonies, and several of them had replied enthusiastically in favor of the Massachusetts position. No letter from England could change all that. Adams professed respect for the king but condemned the ministers who surrounded him for isolating the sovereign and misrepresenting the conditions in the colonies. He refused to consider rescinding the circular letter, which he said was justified and within the rights of the representatives "even if they had invited the union of all America in one joint supplication."[5]

Once again he had read very accurately the minds of the other representatives, who knew they would destroy themselves by backing down at this point. He asserted that Massachusetts had the support of the rest of America and pointed out that the sympathies of a great many Britons lay with the colonies. He and

Otis also threatened reprisals against those members of the House who intended to vote for recission, promising to publish the proceedings and the vote in the newspapers. On June 30, the House voted 92–17 to refuse to rescind the letter. Bernard then had no other recourse but to dissolve the General Court, which he did on the same day. True to their word, Adams and Otis published two lists in the next *Gazette*—the "famous ninety-two" and the "blacklist"—the 17 whose names would be "handed down with infamy to the latest of posterity."[6]

Hillsborough's letter was a turning point, the first outright challenge to the Massachusetts radicals. The Crown's heavy-handedness made it almost impossible for the representatives, even the most moderate, to back down, and gave Otis and Adams the opportunity to force a dramatic confrontation and gain a prestigious victory. It was now necessary to publicize that victory in order to gain additional support for the radicals. When Bernard's prorogation had eliminated the House as a forum, Adams as usual sought a wider battleground. He told Otis that he wanted to publish the letter from the House to Hillsborough in order to inform the whole province of this latest turn of events. Otis was not in favor of this move, and argued the point with Adams in a conversation reported, probably with embellishments, by Bernard:

> OTIS: What are you going to do with the letter to Lord H?
>
> ADAMS: To give it to the printer to publish next Monday.
>
> OTIS: Do you think it proper to publish it so soon that he may receive a printed copy before the orginal comes to his hands?
>
> ADAMS: What signifies that? You know it was designed for the people and not for the minister.
>
> OTIS: You are so fond of your own draughts that you can't wait for the publication of them to a proper time.
>
> ADAMS: I am clerk of this house and I will make that use of the papers which I please.[7]

Whatever the actual words might have been, the conversation probably did run along the lines reported, with Otis, as outspoken as he might be in the House, unwilling to appear immoderate in London. Adams must have won the argument with

Otis; the *Gazette* published the Hillsborough letter to Bernard
on July 4, followed two weeks later by the reply of the House.
Reaction in the province strongly supported the House, and the
17 representatives who voted against the refusal were ruined politically. The episode did much to sound the death knell of the
court party. Bernard recognized it as a disaster. "Immediately
after the vote in the House for not rescinding," he said, "the
Council suffered so great a change that they don't appear to be
the same persons."[8] His council was intimidated, he concluded,
and could no longer be depended on for advice and consent.
Hutchinson agreed with the governor, and reported that Adams
and Reverend Samuel Cooper "say it is the most glorious day
they ever saw."[9]

In the weeks that followed, both Hutchinson and Bernard
asked for troops to control Boston. Hutchinson said that the provincial administration had to be "aided from without" or it
would fall.[10] "I fear you have in England a difficult task," he
wrote, "to retain the colonies in a due subordination and at the
same time to continue the benefit you receive from their commerce."[11] Bernard also wrote that a change in measures had to
originate at Westminster and that "the first orders for quartering
troops in Boston would come from thence,"[12] since it would
mean the end of the governor if he attempted to bring soldiers
into town. The urging was unnecessary. While these words were
being written, Hillsborough was preparing a letter ordering Bernard to obtain enough information for prosecution of those persons overtly resisting British law to provide a basis for their arrest
and transport to England for trial.[13]

The merchant ship *Liberty* during all this time languished in
Boston harbor, creating the kind of symbol that Adams had foreseen. He, of course, assisted in bearing out his own prediction;
writing for the *Gazette,* he used Hancock's predicament to stir as
much sentiment as possible against all the Crown representatives
in the town. Hancock's case came before the Admiralty Court in
early August and continued for two weeks, with a verdict against
him. The ship was taken over and sold—and the buyers were the
same customs commissioners who converted the *Liberty* into a
revenue cutter. Hancock was then personally charged as a smug-

gler, but after a long and indecisive trial the case was dropped.

Bernard's clumsy threats were often boomerangs—the force he put into them was turned back on himself. On June 21, when he ordered the House to rescind the circular letter, he added that, if it became necessary to dissolve the House, he would not be able to call the General Court together again until the king's pleasure had been made known—a statement contrary to the Massachusetts Charter, which gave the governor full power to call the Assembly into session whenever he saw fit. This kind of mistake played into the hands of Otis, who knew the law better than any man in the province, and Adams, who if anything was ready to publicize the governor's failings.

On June 27 Adams republished the circular letter in the *Gazette,* along with the replies of Virginia, New Jersey, and Connecticut. Peyton Randolph, Virginia's speaker, wrote that the House of Burgesses applauded Massachusetts for its "attention to American liberty" and insisted that "no power on earth has a right to impose taxes on the people, or take the smallest portion of their property, without their consent." Speakers Cortland Skinner of New Jersey and Zebulon West of Connecticut sent messages of concern and support. A letter from Georgia's speaker, Alexander Wylly, dated May 11, was published on July 4, stating Georgia's admiration for the wise and spirited conduct of Massachusetts. The governor had prorogued the Georgia assembly until November to avoid any participation in a united appeal to England, but Georgia had sent instructions to its London agent, Benjamin Franklin, telling him to "join earnestly with the other colonies' agents" in working against the new acts.

Early in August, a *Gazette* column by Adams chided those who saw Boston as a mobbish town, while the "orderly and very polite cities of London and Westminster" lived in fear of "the weavers' mob, the seamans' mob, the tailors' mob, the coal miners' mob, and some say the clergy's mob."[14] Characterizing the *Liberty* incident as only "a stirring" in which a few panes of glass were broken, Adams said that Boston remained in perfect peace, even though the plundering British navy still held Hancock's ship as its prize, "secured under the mouths of hundreds of cannon."

In meetings that ranged from the coffeehouses to Faneuil Hall,

Adams and Otis were again busy organizing a new revival of sentiment against importation of British goods.[15] In August, working through the Merchants' Society, they convinced nearly 100 merchants (two-thirds of the total) to pledge not to import any goods for six months, beginning on the first day of 1769.

In the first week of September, in response to Hillsborough's orders, Gage sent his aide-de-camp, Captain Sheriff, up from New York with a message for Bernard: the 14th Regiment would soon be on the move from Halifax for Boston. If Bernard wanted more troops, he need only say the word and the 29th Regiment would follow. Bernard now would have the troops he wanted so desperately and had begged for so often, and the thought frightened him. He knew the coming of the troops would be a great shock to the city and he feared the violence that might result, but he was committed.

There was already an uncanny, instinctive conviction running through the town, a knowledge that the troops were coming. The *Gazette* ran an article under the heading "READER AT-TEND!,"[16] threatening that, if troops come, "we will put our lives in our hands," and urging the towns to disregard the postponement of the General Court and send members to a meeting whether the governor wanted it or not. To Bernard this was "exceeding all former exceedings," and he was convinced that "the cabinet of the faction" would attempt to excite armed resistance. In view of this, perhaps it might be best, he thought, to avoid any formal announcement and to let the coming of the troops be "gradually communicated." How he imagined that such news could seep by degrees into the consciousness of the townspeople he did not explain.

On Thursday, September 8, Bernard dropped a hint to one of the members of the council who, he guessed, could not keep a secret for long.[17] He was correct. The news stormed through Boston; before nightfall the whole town talked of nothing but the coming of the Regulars. Bernard was reported to have said that three regiments were destined for Boston—two to garrison the town and one to take over Castle William. The immediate call was for a town meeting to decide what action to take, and on Friday it was said that shopkeepers were sold out of all available firearms. Posters announced a meeting at Faneuil Hall on Monday, September 12, and the Sons of Liberty placed a barrel of turpentine on a pole atop Beacon Hill, ready for use as a fiery call for reinforcements from the inland towns. Bernard watched the reaction in the town and saw his worst fears confirmed: there would be a bloodbath when the troops tried to force their way into Boston. By Saturday he had retreated again to Jamaica Plain, where members of his council sought him out to plead for a meeting to discuss measures to be taken. He agreed on the need for a conference but would not come to Boston. The council thereupon gathered in a house halfway between Boston and Jamaica Plain, the closest that Bernard would come, but even there the governor was too preoccupied to accomplish anything. He had convinced himself by this time that Adams and Otis were plotting to seize the castle, which was his own last resort, and the thought of its loss unnerved him.

On Monday night Otis took charge of the town meeting in a Faneuil Hall filled to the walls with angry Bostonians. The 400 Brown Bess muskets belonging to Boston's militia had been taken out of storage and placed in chests on the floor of the hall much earlier, when fire damage had made their storage room unusable, but now Otis called attention to them as a symbol of a determination to resist further intimidation. "There are the arms," Otis with appropriate drama pointed out from the platform; "when an attempt is made against your liberties, they will be delivered."[18] In the excitement a motion was taken to distribute the weapons, but Otis saw to it that this did not pass.

Finally, amid the noise and confusion a committee was appointed—Cushing, Adams, Dana, Rowe, Hancock, Kent, and Warren—to confront the governor and question him directly on the information he possessed concerning the arrival of Regulars. Armed with a call for an immediate General Assembly, the group marched to Bernard's office the following morning, where the governor received them, read their petition, and gave them his answer in writing. His knowledge of the impending arrival of the Regulars came from "information of a private nature,"[19] he said. He swore he had received "no public letters notifying to me the coming of such troops," and as for an immediate assembly, he could not convene the General Court again until the king approved it.

Bernard's fear of the Boston mob led him in this case to an outright lie that soon would come to light. Even for the moment, the lie helped him very little. That night, at the reopened town meeting, the assembled citizens resolved that the keeping of a standing army among them was a violation of their rights, and that they would defend themselves "at the utmost peril of their lives and fortunes." Samuel Adams then called for nomination of representatives from Boston to a "committee in convention" to meet with "such as may be sent to join them from the several towns of this Province" at Faneuil Hall on September 22. Adams and the three other regular representatives to the General Court (Otis, Cushing, and Hancock) were named, and with that motion the Bostonians defied Bernard, created an outlaw convention, and called on the rest of the province for support. It was the boldest move yet, engineered by Adams while an unwilling Otis held his tongue.

As a result of the meeting a circular letter, signed by the selectmen, went out to all the towns. It is a strange composition which showed the mark of different hands in the writing—a portrait in miniature of the Otis-Adams struggle taking place at this time: bellicose words are closely followed by humble self-examination, and outright rejection of Crown policy is linked to lame excuses for the conduct of the town. Starting with a complaint against unconstitutional taxes, the letter rambles into other subjects—standing armies, the Hillsborough correspondence, and the news of troops on the way. Then it moves to an assertion that the people are worried about "an approaching war with France," an excuse that had been used to keep the muskets on display in Faneuil Hall. This is followed by a plea for the convention as a way to "prevent any sudden and unconnected measures" which in their present anxiety the people of Boston may be in danger of falling into. Only then does the letter announce the convention scheduled for the 22nd.[20]

For all its incoherence, the letter did what it was written to do; the towns by now were so far along the trail blazed by Adams that perhaps any letter would have served as well. It was sent out to the towns on the 14th and printed in the *Gazette* on the 19th. Bernard considered putting out a proclamation forbidding the assembly, but his courage failed him once again. He would do it, he said, "but I dare not take so spirited a step without first securing my retreat."[21]

On the appointed day, September 22, delegates arrived from 66 towns; this group swelled to 96 towns and six districts before the convention was over.[22] Cushing was elected speaker, Samuel Adams became clerk. Otis, who had been so much in favor of a convention a year earlier, pointedly remained away for the first two days, his absence disconcerting the delegates and muting their spirit. A motion for adjournment after the first day was fought off by Adams, who led and encouraged the work of the convention committees, but he could not carry the convention toward a stand against the troops. The atmosphere was definitely cool; the delegates were not prepared for rashness. That they had come did not necessarily mean that they supported the actions of Boston. The hinterland conservatism was evident from the start, and Adams found that radicalism was not the style of this group, which perhaps had read the Boston letter with care and did, indeed, desire to prevent any "sudden and unconnected measures."

With the convention tottering and ready to fall, Otis finally yielded to the pressure of Adams and the Sons of Liberty, and attended the session on the third day. He was not convinced so much by Adams as by the realization that a failure of the convention would seriously damage the popular party. When he finally arrived, the atmosphere changed. The convention closed its doors and busied itself in secrecy to produce a petition to the king. The words of this statement were by no means earthshaking. It asserted the charter rights, promised to adhere to the British constitution, and emphasized the need for peace and good order. But the major step had been taken, the precedent set, and the job of establishing the committees of correspondence and the provincial conventions would be that much easier.

The convention and the town meetings that preceded it showed the power Otis held over the Massachusetts provincial mind. The return of his unshakable conviction that the problems of the colonies could be solved within the existing political structure led him to eviscerate the town's attack against Bernard and to destroy the idea of physical opposition to the landing of troops in Boston. Adams had pushed too hard, and Otis stopped him, but now that the province was back on a program of moderate and constructive opposition, Otis threw himself into the battle at Adams' side and produced the plan by which Boston would make life exceedingly difficult for Gage's Redcoats.

The town of Boston, Otis said, included Castle William. Boston was obliged by act of Parliament to quarter the troops and would do so by allowing them to stay at the castle. If the troops tried to stay in the town proper, no barracks would be provided. No person in his right mind would rent any buildings to General Gage, and therefore the troops would be forced to stay out of town or to take the building by force. The law in such cases stated that any officer of the military forces who took it upon himself to quarter his men by commandeering private buildings would be "*ipso facto* cashiered." If the Regulars decided to take such action, Otis said, "we may resist them with the law on our side."[23]

On the first day of October, just as the convention broke up, two regiments of British infantry, supported by a company of artillery with five brass field pieces, arrived in Boston harbor. With muskets loaded and ready, the 29th Foot marched from the docks to the Common while the 14th assembled near Faneuil Hall. The commander of the force, Lieutenant Colonel William Dalrymple, reported to Governor Bernard that his men would require quarters.

When the selectmen declared that they had no authority to provide barracks, Bernard tried to get the council to authorize other quarters in houses and buildings of the town. The council pointed out that barracks were provided at Castle William and that under law troops could be quartered in private buildings only when there were no other dwellings available for them. For the moment, Bernard's only choice was to use the province buildings, and for the first few weeks troops lived in Faneuil Hall and even in the Town House, where they used all the rooms except the council chamber. The fight over quartering the troops continued for more than a month, forcing Gage himself to leave his headquarters at New York and come to Boston. By this time Bernard had designated the "manufactory house"—a brick building that belonged to the province—for use of the troops, but this building held a number of the town's poor, who clung tenaciously to their squatter's rights. Gage's attempt to take over the building resulted in a comic siege. The Sons of Liberty shifted destitute families from the workhouse to fill every chink of space in the manufactory, which they opened to all comers. In a circus atmosphere the sheriff, attempting to oust the tenants, entered through a window and was quickly locked in, where he remained imprisoned until Gage used British soldiers to rescue him.

To Hutchinson the landing of the troops staved off a disaster for the Crown. "We were upon the brink of ruin," he said, "and their arrival prevented some most extravagant measures; the party now say they were not in earnest and that it was all a puff."[24] Otis continued to believe that his own activities were correct and within the bounds of propriety in attacking a Parliamentary policy that eventually would be recognized as illegal. He therefore saw no reason for enmity on either side. He had dined with Gage in New York, and now he returned the invitation (Gage declined). He also attended a dinner at John Rowe's along with officers of the 14th and 29th Regiments. Bernard wrote to London accusing him as the prime enemy of Crown government in Massachusetts and asked whether "so open and notorious an attempt to raise a rebellion" would go unpunished.[25]

The pressures on the colonies were growing and Otis once again argued the possibility that the blunders of Parliament were irreversible. In a letter at this time, he made a surprising prediction which showed one of the swings of his fluctuating viewpoint on the relationship of America and the empire. "You may ruin yourselves," he wrote to England, "but you cannot in the end ruin the colonies. . . . We have been a free people, and if you will not let us remain so any longer, we shall be a great people."[26] The measures taken against the colonies, he predicted, could only lead to events which every man might wish delayed for ages or prevented forever. He was beginning to see where the path led.

Adams had been unable to stop the troops from coming into the town; now he would make the most of their presence. He created the "Journal of Occurrences,"[27] a series of anonymous newspaper articles that appeared not in Boston but in the *New-York Journal*, from which they were widely reprinted in the colonies and even in England. The articles were written by Adams and by every Boston Whig writer he could cajole into helping, including Church, Joseph Warren, Cooper, Edes, Josiah Quincy, and probably Henry Knox, William Greenleaf, and even Isaiah Thomas, later editor and publisher of the *Massachusetts Spy*. The "news" purported to describe the horrors of a town under military rule, where without provocation officers wantonly attacked the Boston citizens on the street, where an unbridled soldiery insulted, molested, and raped their daughters, where the military were free to commit every sort of crime, turning the streets of town into a hideous chaos. Hutchinson, who knew the stories were being written in Boston, called the series "a scurvy trick at best," by men who would "stick at nothing."[28] The tales of misconduct and atrocities in a captive town stirred emotions all along the Atlantic coast. Although some were outright fabrications, most were elaborations of actual events, carefully arranged to show the Bostonians as long-suffering innocents under the harsh realities of a military occupation. Loyalist attempts to disprove the allegations of the "Journal" led only to more accusations.

While the energies of Adams drove him into this new endeavor, Otis was tiring; with a fast-paced law practice and with his political responsibilities as leader of the popular party and moderator of Boston town meetings, he began to feel himself too far extended. He may have sensed a deterioration of his own physical and mental condition; whatever the reason, he wrote to England announcing that he was "winding up" his law cases and would take no more of the suits for debt which had long been a heavy portion of his work. At forty-three, Otis seemed to be aging beyond his years, while Adams, who looked decrepit and shook with palsy, grew ever more active. In addition to the "Journal," Adams wrote an article every week for both the *Gazette* and the *Evening Post*. In the *Post* series, as "Candidus," Adams ridiculed the customs officials, while as "Vindex" in the *Gazette* he attacked the Crown for placing a standing army in Boston. How easy would it be, Vindex wrote, for the soldiers, with weapons at hand, to act outside the law of the province. "How long can we imagine it would be . . . before the tragical scene would begin?"[29]

Reading these essays, Hutchinson became less confident that the presence of troops had averted disaster. He reported that the leaders of the rebellious faction were unafraid of the soldiers, believing that "no troops dare fire without the order of a civil magistrate and no civil magistrate dare give such orders." They might be right about the first part, he said, but no one would know for sure whether the second part were true until some actual event forced a test. Fourteen months before the Boston Massacre, Hutchinson wrote that, unfortunately, he could see that Boston had some people "bad enough to take every measure in their power to bring on the trial."[30]

16

The Decline of Otis

January–September 1769

I have been young, and now am old, and I solemnly say, I have never known a man whose love of his country was more ardent or sincere; never one, who suffered so much; never one, whose services for any ten years of his life were so important and essential to the cause of his country, as those of Mr. Otis from 1760 to 1770.

JOHN ADAMS, 1818

ON A COLD WINTER'S DAY just after the turn of the year 1769, a weary Hutchinson sat down to write a letter to Thomas Whately in London. As he took up his pen, the events of the immediate past came to mind in a procession that almost overwhelmed him. The riots, the illegal convention, the almost daily incidents involving the Regulars, the horrid "Journal of Occurrences" repeating its lies and gross exaggerations, the chaos in the House of Representatives that blocked all efforts of the Crown to regain control of the colony, the increase in smuggling, the intimidated and unreliable juries—it was an appalling scene, a travesty of the meaning of the Massachusetts Charter, and it had all come about because misguided demagogues had convinced an ignorant populace that there was no limit to their freedoms. As long as these firebrands were allowed to do and say anything they wished, the province would continue to smolder, ready at any moment to burst into a conflagration. Only the presence of the Regulars, he thought, had saved the town from the kind of mob violence that had destroyed his own home and had caused so much damage to others, and even the troops themselves posed a danger in this volatile town.

In response to Hillsborough's orders, Bernard had given Hutchinson the job of gathering evidence that could be used against Otis and Adams if they were brought to trial in England for treason. Hutchinson had recorded the statement of Richard Sylvester, accusing Adams of calling for an armed insurrection, but he knew that a few depositions would not be enough. Only drastic steps could be of help now, he wrote to Whately. And then he added the comment that would soon come back to torment him:

> I never think of the measures necessary for the peace and good order of the colonies without pain. There must be an abridgment of what is called English liberty. . . .[1]

Thus an anguished Hutchinson penned the words that his opponents would display years later to show that he was an enemy of the province.

While Hutchinson gathered evidence, Adams continued his newspaper theme of the risks inherent in placing a "standing army" in Boston. Some people, he wrote in late January, are trying to say that an insurrection had been planned and that only the arrival of troops prevented it. It would be just as easy to say that certain others, "in calling for a military force under pretence of supporting civil authority, secretly intended to introduce a general massacre."[2]

This was a period of intense activity for Adams, who in addition to editing the "Journal of Occurrences" was fighting for nonimportation and keeping up his work as clerk of the House. He and Otis continued their weekends of typesetting at the *Gazette,* quoting such material as Lord North's boast that there would be no repeal of the Townshend Act until America was prostrate at England's feet, or a letter which appeared to be written by a naval officer in Boston, who concluded that in the town "the men are all hypocrites and the women w——s; there is not an officer on the sea or land service nor a common man down to a drummer that cannot have his bedfellow for the winter, so that the Yanky war, contrary to all others, will produce more births than burials."

Deeply involved in the war of words, Adams nearly forgot an old problem: he was still far in arrears as a tax collector and his enemies had brought new pressures to make him pay. Since the tax collector was a very influential political figure in a town that never could balance its books, Adams had probably accepted the collector's job originally not only because he needed the commission money, but also because he recognized the leverage that the position would provide him. Collecting the taxes, however, was almost an afterthought, and each year he had fallen short because he did not press hard enough against the debtors who, "thro' poverty and misfortune, were unable to make payment." For this reason, as he himself said, he had to "make use of the first moneys . . . in a new year, to make good the deficiencies of the former,"[3] thus always drifting further into the red.

By 1763 Adams was £2,179 behind in his collections (two other collectors were short about £1,000). After four more years of collecting he had fallen farther behind, owing £4,029 (five other collectors then averaged a debt of £780 each). He was allowed to resign after 1766, and over the next two years he made up a part of his debt, so that by 1768, after having collected a total of over £51,000 for the town, he was still £2,009 short of his commitment.[4] The debts were then so old he had little chance to collect them, and he therefore petitioned the town for abatement of the final £2,000, as other collectors had done in the past (though none for so large a debt).

Those who wished to hold Adams to his debt motioned for a committee to study the facts and reply to the town. When this motion failed, they demanded a detailed list of outstanding taxes, but this too was shouted down. In the end it was moved that Adams be pardoned of his debt, and the question being so put "passed in the affirmative by a very great majority."[5] Robert Pierpoint was empowered to collect whatever of Adams' outstanding taxes could be dredged up.

A few minutes later Adams was elected to a committee "to consider what may be still necessary to be done for vindication of the town." James Otis and Joseph Warren were also members, along with Cushing, Dana, John Adams, and Samuel Quincy. This group set about preparing a petition to the king, which was approved by the town on April 4 and sent to the London agent by Adams a few days later. The petition strongly objected to the censure Parliament had passed on Boston for being in a state of disorder. Adams also dispatched the latest piece of news: letters written by Bernard had been sent back to Boston and were in the hands of the radicals. "There are some things in them," wrote Adams, "which it can be made clearly to appear are very gross and material mistakes."[6] In these letters Bernard had said that Boston and the province were "influenced by mad people" and that he was happy to see the troops arrive.

The letters, obtained by Bollan, the Massachusetts agent, were addressed to Hillsborough by Bernard, Admiral Hood, and General Gage. It was plain from these fragments of a much larger body of correspondence that Bernard had, in fact, pressed hard for British troops to control the province. Other comments made it obvious that the governor had little reverence for the rights which the radicals insisted were a part of the Massachusetts charter. To Otis and Adams the letters represented yet another confirmation of the plot to destroy the colonial freedoms and impose a dictatorial rule; the *Gazette* carried the word that the House of Lords had heard a proposal to seize Otis, Cushing, and as many of the other radicals as Bernard thought proper, and carry them to England "to be tried for high treason."

With the May elections coming up, the outcry and commotion over Bernard's letters was enough to smother the court party for the second successive year, leaving only a handful of old reliables who were able to squeak through and retain their seats. The newspaper campaign of Adams and Otis against the 17 representatives who had voted to rescind the circular letter had been successful—while 82 of the "famous 92" were returned to the House by their towns, only five of the "black 17" were reelected, and of these only two thought it appropriate to attend the session. The election of the Boston representatives to the House was close to unanimous. Hancock, as the hero of the *Liberty* incident, received the highest number of votes, 505 out of 508, but Adams, Cushing, and Otis were only one or two votes behind.

The Assembly convened on May 31 and proceeded to elect a council that disgusted Bernard, who vetoed every new member except two. Since four council members (Thomas Flucker, Nathaniel Roper, Timothy Paine, and John Worthington) who invariably sided with the governor had been dropped, Bernard was once again faced with a small council whose support for him was uncertain. In the House he faced an overwhelming opposition. From a strength of 120 the court party had dwindled to ten men who could be expected to back the governor or the Crown. In the first few days the House demanded that the troops be removed from the town and refused to do any other business "under the guns of the Regulars." Bernard seized this opportunity to achieve a modicum of quiet in Boston by moving the General Court to Cambridge, where they at least could not complain of intimidation by the troops (and where he would not be troubled by the Sons of Liberty in the galleries).

At Cambridge, Otis was as effective as he had been in Boston; it was said that the young Harvard undergraduates were moved to tears by his eloquence, but they may have been more interested at that time in the eccentricity that had become his hallmark. With Timothy Ruggles in the middle of an oration in support of the Crown, a bored and angry Otis suddenly cried out, "Oh Mr. Speaker, the liberty of this country is gone forever! And I'll go after it."[7] With that he abruptly left the chamber, amid no small amount of humor and confusion.

By June, Bernard had received permission to go to England, leaving the lieutenant governor in charge. He had been waiting for this news since 1768, when he first stopped hinting for an invitation to return and simply asked outright. His dream was to be given the opportunity to explain to Parliament and the ministry his theories of the political control of the colonies. This, of course, would be far easier to do than to put any of the changes into effect, or indeed to maintain the present status quo. What he admitted between the lines of his letters was that he was tired of the rough and tumble of the American political scene, tired of

Boston and the Massachusetts factions, and ready for a quiet assignment at home. By this time he had given up his old dream of a transfer to a comfortable province such as Bermuda; now he simply wanted to be rid of it all.

On July 2, Bernard told the House in a message that he had been called to England for consultation, and since there existed the possibility that he might be absent for an extended period, he desired his salary be paid a year in advance. He added that the appropriation of this advance should "precede the other business of the session,"[8] an unsubtle hint that he might be forced to hold up all legislation if he did not get his pay. The House, however, recognized that Bernard would be pilloried in England for such a move. Otis, selected as chairman of the committee to prepare a reply to Bernard, succeeded in a motion to refuse the grant on the grounds that it was not logical to expect Bernard to remain in office after the king heard the truth about the situation in Massachusetts; the House, he said, therefore cannot provide any money "for services which we have no reason to suspect will ever be performed."[9] Bernard, in response, prorogued the General Court until January 1770. The session over, he could now go home.

As he prepared to leave, Bernard was called to make yet another decision. General Gage, mindful of the many incidents and accusations stemming from the presence of troops in Boston, wrote to ask whether or not it was still necessary to keep a force in the town. If the troops were still required, he asked, would a single regiment suffice? Bernard acquiesced in the removal of two regiments, the 64th and 65th, but said he could not answer for the consequences if the last two, the 14th and 29th, left town.[10] Gage then ordered half the force back to Halifax.

While the troops prepared to depart, the Massachusetts House drew up a petition to the king, listing Bernard's sins—his letters misrepresenting the town, his many proroguings of the General Court, and his general lack of love for the province.[11] The petition concluded with the wish that Bernard might be "*forever* removed from the government of this province." This the House approved by unanimous vote. Adams meanwhile had been preparing a set of resolves to parallel those of Virginia. These he pushed through the House and published in the *Gazette* on July 3, just as the two regiments were about to embark from Boston. Among his assertions, he stated that no man is bound in conscience to obey any law to which he has not given his consent in person or by his representative. In response to the bold move of Adams, Colonel Dalrymple, under pressure from Bernard, stopped the regiments, sent them back to quarters in town, and wrote to Gage in New York to explain the situation and ask for orders. At this point the radicals realized it would be better to get the troops out of town; the House reconsidered its vote and issued a new set of resolves in which they muted the words of Adams, merely emphasizing that the power of levying taxes was constitutionally vested in the legislative body.[12] With Bernard thus satisfied, the troops were sent on their way.

In July, Boston received the two-month-old news that the supporters of the Townshend Act had been defeated in Parliament. All the duties associated with the act were repealed except the tea tax, which was to be kept as a symbol of Parliamentary supremacy. Word of the repeal provided an excuse for the Boston merchants to renege on the nonimportation agreements. Adams fought to keep up the pressure on London, but the other large towns along the American seacoast were importing and the merchants saw no reason to continue the battle alone.

It was time for Bernard's departure, and Hutchinson, forgetting his first moments of hesitation at taking over at such a difficult time, became as anxious to assume the governorship as Bernard was to give it up. After his years as lieutenant governor, always patching up difficulties but never making decisions, he found that he wanted the leadership of the province, come what may. "No Lieutenant Governor since the Charter had done and suffered as much as I have done," he said. "Each of them was a great part of his time commander-in-chief. In eleven years I have had a run of only two months."

Thunderstorms rolled over Boston on Monday, the last day of July, and lightning split the masts of two ships in the harbor. After the storms, when the afternoon grew to a quiet close, Bernard slipped out of Boston and stayed the night at Castle William. Next day he was rowed out to the warship *Rippon,* which made sail and started down the harbor, heading for England. But Bernard was not spared one last humiliation. The wind died to a flat calm and the *Rippon* was forced to anchor again, still within the harbor, where it remained becalmed for three days, while from the town Bernard could hear church bells signaling joy at his departure and cannon firing all the first day.[13] That evening the harbor was lighted by two large bonfires, one on Fort Hill in the south end of town and the other across the river to the north in Charlestown, while crowds turned out in the streets to celebrate the governor's departure. Finally, at noon on Friday, August 4, the wind came up and Bernard was free of the town at last. The following Monday's *Gazette* noted that the governor had sailed on the *Rippon,* captain and ship "both worthy of a better cargo."

With Bernard gone, Hutchinson at last held the reins of government in Massachusetts. Although he was only an acting governor, he nevertheless had his opportunity to reverse the trend of past days and bring the town to its senses. Certainly he could do no worse than Bernard, and if the province, on the point of disintegration, could be brought back to its former state of subservience to the Crown, Hutchinson would be on the brink of a new career. At the same time he had few illusions. He knew that Otis and Adams now would turn the full power of their attack against him, and he expected little help from the shambles of his own party.

The first moves against Hutchinson were indirect. Within a week of his takeover, the merchants began a series of meetings, first in the British Coffee House and later, as the size of the meetings grew, in Faneuil Hall, where Otis was observed to come out of the building "smiling at his success."[14] The nonimportation agreements, which had been in force since August 1768 (and which Boston started in October 1767 to fight the Townshend Duties) were strengthened. Importers were named in the newspapers and became marked men, subject to insults and physical attacks on the Boston streets. Handbills called them "enemies of the constitution" who could expect their "base designs" to be blocked at every step. This directly affected Hutchinson, because two of his sons were involved in merchandising tea and had on hand 130 cases which they had imported in defiance of the merchants and their agreements. Business was poor, however, and his sons were forced to deal under the counter to get rid of the tea.[15]

August 14 was the anniversary of the Stamp Act riot of 1765, and the Sons of Liberty saw to it that the celebration did justice to the day. A procession of 118 carriages with Hancock in the lead and Otis bringing up the rear filed south across Boston Neck to Dorchester. Under the sign of the Liberty Tree there were speeches, toasts, and songs until evening, with Otis and Adams moving among the 350 celebrants, mostly Boston workmen, welcoming new members and talking of nonimportation and recalcitrant merchants, of charter rights and bad governors, of Boston's sea trade and corrupt customs men. As darkness fell, the long column, now festive and noisy and punctuated with raucous cheers, wended its way back to glorious Boston, resolving to right the wrongs of the universe.

London Whigs had turned over more letters to Bollan, including a batch from the customs commissioners in Boston. These he packaged and sent to Cushing, who promptly showed them to Adams and Otis. Adams was delighted to have more fuel for the fire, but Otis was dismayed; among the letters were several in which Otis saw himself portrayed as an enemy to the Crown and a traitor to his country. He publicly accused six commissioners—Henry Hulton, Charles Paxton, William Birch, Joseph Harrison, Benjamin Hallowell, and John Robinson—of representing him as "inimical to the rights of the Crown and disaffected to his Majesty."[16]

Otis had been accused of many things and had taken many drubbings in the Boston press, and often he had responded with emotional rhetoric. But these insinuations came at a time when he took great pride in his moderate course and cherished his friendly correspondence with several of the ranking British politicians of the day. Worse still, they came from London, where the accusations could have been seen by the king himself. Otis immediately placed a statement in the newspapers declaring his faithful allegiance to the Crown and desiring the "principal Secretaries of State, particularly My Lord of Hillsborough," to pay no regard to these lies of the customs men. Faced with these charges, he fell back to his earlier loyalties, repudiating his more recent warnings that a growing America was becoming irreconciliable with the political attitudes in England. He declared himself a staunch and loyal supporter of the king, a man whose allegiance to the British constitution and belief in the final triumph of the empire could not be questioned. How then could he be singled out for such pernicious abuse, except by power-hungry members of Hutchinson's "junto" who plotted to destroy good government and replace it with their own controls? It was part of the plot, "which cabal may be well known from the papers in the House of Commons and at every great office in England." When Joseph Harrison apologized in print for any offense he might have caused Otis, declaring he had no intent to censure, Otis was too far gone in his anger to accept any apology. Anyone who could write such accusations and then deny them, he said, must be either a liar or senile.[17]

Adams saw the mounting distress in Otis, and acted to stave off trouble.[18] Through his efforts, Otis met twice with the commissioners to discuss the letters, and several apologies of sorts were made. But Otis would not be satisfied. He refused an invitation to talk the matter over at the home of one of the commissioners, but did accept a meeting at the British Coffee House, where he asked Birch several "improper" questions on the letters, which Birch refused to answer. Otis then sent Birch a note to his home: "Mr. Birch, I have reason to think and take occasion to tell you that you are a poltroon and a scoundrel, J. Otis."[19] Birch went to see Hutchinson, who advised him not to take up the challenge. He took the governor's advice, but Hutchinson was worried. "I expect some bad consequences of this affair," he wrote to Bernard. As for Otis, he announced publicly that "satisfaction has been personally demanded, due warning given, but no sufficient answer obtained."[20]

Ominously, Otis began to focus his anger on a single member of the group, the most truculent, John Robinson. John Adams, who met with Otis and Samuel Adams at the *Gazette* offices on Sunday, September 3, to help prepare the Monday edition, noted in his diary that Otis was unusually garrulous. "Otis talks all," he wrote. "He grows the most talkative man alive. No other gentleman in company can find a space to put in a word—as Dr. Swift expressed it, he leaves no elbow room. There is much sense, knowledge, spirit and humor in his conversation. But he grows narrative, like an old man. Abounds with stories."

In the newspaper issue they were preparing, Otis that Sunday unconsciously parodied his own political stand, writing of Robinson, "If he misrepresents me—I have a natural right if I can get no other satisfaction to break his head." He threw down the gauntlet to Robinson, calling him a "superlative blockhead" and threatening bodily harm. Robinson, unlike Birch, was not one to back down. He had been roughed up before at the hands of Whig radicals; he had been thrown in jail in Taunton in 1765[21] and his house in Newport had been threatened by Whig mobs; there were old scores to settle. He bought himself a heavy cane and let it be known that he would use it if necessary. Otis, when he heard this news, went to the same shop and ordered "the fellow of it."

On Monday evening Otis attended a meeting of the Merchants' Society, where he again could not be still. He pestered his friend, Henderson Inches, and others for not calling a town meeting to discuss letters that had been so insulting to him, charging them with "timidity, haughtiness, arbitrary dispositions, and insolence of office." All evening, said John Adams, was "nothing but one continued scene of bullying, bantering, reproaching, and ridiculing the selectmen" by Otis, with a complete lack of politeness, delicacy, taste, and sense.[22]

The next day, Tuesday, September 5, at about seven in the evening, Otis left his house. Many people were out in the Boston streets that night, watching a large comet move across the sky.[23] He went to the British Coffee House, carrying his heavy cane. Robinson was there with several friends, including some British officers, and words were exchanged immediately. Otis asked Robinson to step outside, where each could seek "a gentleman's satisfaction." As Otis started for the door, Robinson tried to twist Otis' nose, a gesture of supreme insult, and Otis pushed him away. Each then attacked with his cane, and the exchange of blows lasted for about a minute. The canes were lost as both men resorted to fistfighting, and Otis began to gain the advantage. At that point some of the British officers joined in, either to help Robinson or to keep him from being beaten. A young man, John Gridley, nephew of Otis' old friend, Jeremiah Gridley, stepped into the coffeehouse, attracted by the noise of the scuffle. Seeing Otis in trouble, he tried to go to his aid, shouting that it was "dirty usage" to gang up on Otis. He was knocked down and dragged outside. Attempting to return to help Otis, Gridley was struck again, suffering a head laceration and a broken wrist. In the confusion Otis was struck a hard blow. He fell, the fight broke off abruptly, and Robinson left by the back door, guided by his friends. Otis, minus his hat and wig and bleeding heavily from a gash in the head, was assisted to his home. Dr. Thomas Young attended him, judged that he had been wounded by a sharp instrument but that the wound was "not dangerous," and left him in good spirits.

Hutchinson reported to London that Robinson had given Otis "a very decent drubbing,"[24] but lamented that "most people believe it to be a confederacy to destroy Otis and that he had very unfair play." This was unfortunate because it raised Otis even higher in the view of Boston townspeople and thus gave him greater influence. "There is no knowing where his frenzy will stop." Hutchinson was convinced the town had such great sympathy for Otis that, if the radical leader should hang himself, the commissioners would be charged with his death.

Indeed, the call for revenge already was strong as word of the fight spread. For Adams it was another opportunity to place the Crown politicians in bad light. In the week following the fight, the *Gazette* provided an account indicating that Otis had been attacked by several of the persons with Robinson, and that young Gridley had been overpowered by numbers in the same way. Gridley's own "testimony" was published on the following week, corroborating this, and on the third week a long account by Otis appeared, commenting on the story that Robinson had given of the encounter. A month after the event, the fight was still the major news in the *Gazette,* with several columns devoted to a condemnation of Robinson. Adams appeared under the pseudonym

"An Impartialist" with a strong attack that argued there was a "preconcerted plan" to kill Otis, pointing to preparations that had been made earlier in the day to procure swords and to make boats available for an escape. Adams emphasized that cries of "God damn him, kill him!"[25] were heard while the gang in the coffeehouse "were actually endeavoring to perpetrate the murder by the utmost of their power." He insisted that the evidence that more than one person struck Otis indicated there had been a plot to ambush and kill him. Though Robinson said no sword was drawn, Adams announced that a scabbard found on the floor after the fight was in the possession of the sheriff, "where the owner *if he thinks proper* may apply for it."[26]

Adams could not keep the town excited over the Otis-Robinson affair forever, and near the end of the month Hutchinson saw some slacking of the tension in Boston. He breathed a sigh of relief. "If the troops had not been here," he said, "there would have been more than a cudgelling match between a demagogue and a commissioner of the customs, and I am not sure that we are yet out of danger. I know many people are enraged to a degree of frenzy."[27] Hutchinson was appalled by the emotionalism and prejudice surrounding the reaction to the fight and by the distortions he saw in the newspapers. He was afraid that the inland towns, so long solid in their conservatism and loyalty to the government, were more and more drawn to the side of Otis and the radicals. "If we could keep off the influence of Boston for one twelve-month," he said, "I think we could bring the rest of the province to their senses."[28] But he knew such an event was impossible. His own power to control the colony was almost entirely gone, and it seemed as if even London had deserted the Boston loyalists. Hutchinson appealed to Bernard in London to use his influence to convince the ministry that the acting governor in Boston needed a sign of official support. If not, he said, he would be "left to be triumphed over by such wicked men as now have the lead."

Otis was recovered enough from his wound to attend town meetings on September 28 and October 4, where he read portions of the letters that had caused the fight. The words of Gage, Bernard, and the commissioners aroused the assembly, which then roundly condemned the merchants who had imported British goods. Otis was named to a committee, along with John and Samuel Adams, to write a defense of the character of the town and answer the charges in the letters. It was Samuel Adams, however, who wrote in the end most of the report, an essay which he entitled "An Appeal to the World," approved by the town on October 18.

Adams barely mentioned General Gage and ignored the other writers of letters critical of the town in order to concentrate on Bernard. Five of Bernard's letters had been published earlier in the *Gazette*. All were to Hillsborough, dealing with the problem of obtaining quarters for the troops and with his troubles in attempting to control the Council. Adams called the letters a "monument of disgrace" for which Bernard would always be remembered.[29] He then drew quotations from the letters in 37 pages of ruthless analysis and with his now perfected tone of suppressed outrage and righteous anger, he carefully and deliberately demolished Bernard once and for all in the eyes of Bostonians. It must have been chilling for Hutchinson to read.

Much ugliness and violence now flourished in the chasm between the two parties in Boston, and John Mein became its next victim. A confirmed Tory and a brave, stubborn man, he owned a bookstore and published the *Boston Chronicle,* a thorn in the side of the radical movement. Just as Adams finally began to exhibit some success with the nonimportation movement, Mein (who had a friend in the custom house) published week after week the lists of merchants who were quietly continuing to import British goods. Worse still, he was specific in naming the cargoes in detail, the dates of arrival, and the merchants involved. The effect was demoralizing. It pointed out a strong vein of cynicism in these Boston merchant-smugglers who talked in one direction but acted in another. His campaign to destroy the movement and humiliate the Whigs was only too successful, and the Sons of Liberty resolved to drive him from the town. He was insulted whenever he went out, and threats on his life convinced him to carry a pistol. Finally, on October 28, he was surrounded by a crowd and abused and threatened to the point where he drew his pistol and fired it. Even though no one was injured, it became impossible for him to appear on the street without danger to his life. Hutchinson was helpless to answer his appeals, and Mein finally boarded ship for London, defiant but beaten, recognizing that further resistance was suicidal.

For a time, Otis seemed to have recovered completely from his wound. John Adams talked with him on October 9 and found him "conversable enough, but not extravagant, nor rough, nor sour." Hutchinson placed him in a group with Molineux, Adams, and Cushing, four radicals whose influence, he complained, "is as great as ever it was," making it increasingly difficult to think of attempting any vigorous measures to return the province to its old loyalty. Otis resumed his law work, won some important cases, and appeared at all his old haunts. But he told his doctor that his hopes now hinged on a "grand revolution in England" that would vindicate the Bostonians. "May his hopes perish and he with them," said Hutchinson, "rather than he should be saved in that way."[30]

With the coming of another Boston winter, however, Otis again lost ground, and for the first time it became evident that he was drinking heavily and that alcohol was enough to tip him over the brink into frenzy. Hutchinson noticed this and told Bernard that Otis behaved extravagantly in court, lamented that he was dying, and in rational moments was contrite enough to confess his wrongs:

> D. Gardner met him a few days ago and desired him to appear in an action he was concerned in. He replied he was in a bad state of health and believed he had but a little while to live and must quit business. His constitution was gone and concluded thus: *I have done more mischief to my country than can be repaired. I meant well but am now convinced I was mistaken. Cursed be the day I was born.*[31]

John Adams said Otis definitely was "not in his perfect mind," and began referring to the "assassination"[32] of Otis by Robinson. "He loses himself . . . he rambles . . . attempted to tell a story which took up almost all the evening. . . . He talks so much and takes up so much of our time and fills it with trash, obsceneness, profaneness, nonsense and distraction. . . . In short, I never saw such an object of admiration, reverence, contempt, and compassion all at once as this. . . . I mourn for the man and for his country. Many others mourn over him with tears in their eyes."

17

The Massacre

October 1769–March 1770

Our Heroes for Liberty have still a dernier resort.
They say, be the tumults what they may no troops dare
fire without the order of a civil Magistrate and no
civil Magistrate dare give such orders. In the first part
of their opinion this may be right in the second they
cannot be sure until they have made the trial and we
certainly have some bad enough to take every measure
in their power to bring on the trial.

THOMAS HUTCHINSON, 1768

WITH THE DECLINE OF OTIS and his consequent inability to continue as a counterbalance to Adams, it became more evident that
the Boston radicals had been led by two men whose aims were
divergent. Adams was now in undisputed control of the popular
party and the Boston political machine, and the course of the
radicals veered sharply toward violent resistance to repressive
Crown policy, toward emphasis on regrasping lost charter rights
—and toward independence. Adams, however, still did not have
a free rein; he, more than anyone else, was forced to come to
terms with the failing mind of Otis. The intensity and persua-
siveness of Otis' personality continued long after his sanity was
shattered, thereby magnifying his contrariness, his inability to
hold to a single course, his violent emotionalism, and the confu-

sion of his lucid intervals with the times when the curtain fell again.

Throughout the winter the Sons of Liberty held their coffee-house meetings and built their strategy for the opening of the new General Court session, but in the end Hutchinson beat them at their own game. He waited until January 9, one day before the House was due to convene, and announced a postponement until March 24 on the basis of "his Majesty's expressed command." Adams responded immediately in the *Gazette,* reminding the acting governor that, when his predecessor, Bernard, kept the House out of session, it produced the Massachusetts Convention, "which tho' legal in all its proceedings awaked an attention in the very soul of the British empire."[1] Hutchinson read the anonymous column, commented that it was undoubtedly from the pen of Adams,[2] and remained unimpressed by the complaint that the acting governor intended to keep the House out of session, possibly through the summer. "We have some mad, desperate people among us," he said, "who would be for resistance to the last drop of blood" rather than submit.[3] The only answer was a Parliament determined not to be intimidated.

Although Adams was still busy with his contributions to the "Journal of Occurrences," his principal concern was to strengthen the ability of the Boston merchants to enforce the nonimportation agreements. For several months he had been the key figure in a series of meetings to consolidate public sentiment in support of nonimportation and to coerce the merchants who continued to defy the agreement. The only pressure that would work on the toughest of these holdouts was the threat of mob violence—which Adams was quite willing to use.

In mid-January Faneuil Hall was the scene of several meetings of the Boston merchants as Adams tried to force the Hutchinson brothers and a half dozen other merchants "voluntarily" to impound the goods they had imported contrary to the pact. Otis backed Adams: the general idea of nonimportation appealed to him as a legitimate, nonviolent way to bring pressure on London, and the specifics in this case included a harassment of the Hutchinsons. A march on the houses of these merchants was approved and Otis volunteered to lead it.

The march at first seemed abortive. Hutchinson was at home when the merchants, their numbers strengthened by Adams' legion of mechanics and laborers, reached his Court Street mansion. He spoke for his sons, facing down a vociferous crowd with his usual poise, refusing to agree to turn over the large stocks of tea his sons were storing. Seeing Otis at the forefront, Hutchinson asked him how he could be a part of such an action when as a lawyer he had to realize the unlawfulness of it. Otis, strangely quiet, made no answer. That evening, however, Hutchinson changed his mind when several other merchants who had been equally stubborn in speaking to the crowd met with him to say it was time to give in. Adams, they warned, would not allow his followers to be defeated on this issue. There would be violence. On the following day, in a move he would later regret, Hutchinson sent a letter to the moderator of the town meeting promising that his sons would give up the tea. Adams could count another success: his use of the mob not only achieved the immediate aim of bolstering nonimportation; it kept the "cause" of the Sons of Liberty in the forefront, allowed the Bostonians an opportunity to let off steam, and helped provide the sense of unity that would be the mainstay of Adams' political strength.

Adams had returned to the use of the mob, and the importance of collective violence, or the threat of it, increased the stature of the mob's petty leaders. Boston, like any densely populated town of the time on either side of the ocean, was vulnerable to mob violence. There was virtually no law enforcement on the streets. The sheriffs and justices of the peace were ineffective, the council wavered, and the legislature refused to act. The lawlessness that flamed so often in Boston in those years now grew up again around the cause of nonimportation. Houses of importers were splattered with outhouse excrement and with tar and feathers. Soldiers, customs men, and recalcitrant merchants were the targets of violent abuse. Finally on Thursday, February 22, a mob of boys and young men harassed one of the customs "informers," Ebenezer Richardson, driving him into his house and pelting the building with stones. Richardson, in fear and anger, fired from an upstairs window into the crowd, and an eleven-year-old boy dropped with a fatal wound. The crowd then surged into the house, overpowered Richardson, and would have lynched him on a signpost if one of their leaders, William Molineux, had not stepped in to save his life.

It was another ugly and brutal affair that Hutchinson was helpless to rectify. The merchants, unable to stop a few of their number from importing, were willing to countenance mob action to intimidate the violators. The more radical Whigs accepted the mob's existence because it led to a weakening of the administration; some citizens supported it as a counter to the soldiers; others simply liked the excitement.

Hutchinson, powerless, searched desperately for some way to return the province to peace and quiet. Like Otis, he was troubled by visions of the colonies set adrift in the world, easy prey for the hungry European powers. Instead of uniting, the Americans might tear themselves to pieces in fraternal strife. He remembered the colonial congress of 1754 and the talk then, 20 years earlier, of a colonial legislature. Was an American parliament possible?[4] He reasoned that formation of a colonial central government might allow the opportunity to "reform" the constitutions of the individual provinces and reassert the authority of Parliament. He agonized over these problems in letters to Bernard but did nothing further about them, no doubt realizing that the day was too far gone for such remedies.

In essence the situation was ironic. Hutchinson, more than any other loyalist in Massachusetts, had the capacity to understand the province and lead it through the period of adjustment after the Seven Years' War. For 20 years he had observed the foibles and failures of half a dozen Massachusetts governors as they contributed to the decline of Crown authority in the province. But he had kept silent. He had expressed his reservations many times in letters, but just as often he had undercut these with his optimism and his willingness to accede to the superior wisdom of Parliament, never establishing a coherent position on the questions of vital interest. His essays on trade and taxes were outspoken and accurate—but anonymous and almost furtive. His sense of propriety inhibited his newspaper contributions, putting him at a disadvantage in the rough and tumble of the newsprint battles. Now, when at last he had control of the colony, he was acutely aware that the time of great possibilities had passed; he still had no other interest in life than to be governor, and he believed he could hold the province loyal and intact until the political storms blew over.

Perhaps it was just as well that Hutchinson did not know what was ahead of him; even his ardor might have cooled. The encounters between soldiers and Boston workmen grew more frequent and more violent at the end of February and into the first days of March. The town was full of premonitions of terrible things to come. The barracks were seething cauldrons of rage, the British soldiers barely under control of the officers, while the townsfolk brushed aside helpless sheriffs and watchmen (who along with the posted soldier sentinels constituted Boston's law-enforcement agency) and prowled the wintry streets in gangs that the soldiers likened to wolf packs. Many people, from the governor to the dockyard hands and the soldiers, knew that the point of no return had been passed and that only some miracle could prevent a deadly outburst of violence.

On March 5, nightfall came early to the cold, blustery, snow-covered streets of Boston. A Redcoat guard at his post before the custom house struck a boy who was teasing him. The boy ran off in search of help and brought back a small group of companions, who continued to molest the guard. This group served as a magnet, attracting more and more of the citizens who were roaming the snowy streets that night, looking for trouble. Then someone rang a church bell, a signal that meant "fire in the town." The sound of the bell brought out hundreds more townsmen into the streets, leather buckets in hand, ready to help put out the fire. Many of these men, after discovering the false alarm, were drawn by the hue and cry at the custom house, where the guard had been reinforced by a squad of seven soldiers under the command of Captain Thomas Preston.

From that point the story proceeds on its mythic track: the moonlit crowd increases in size and violence; the soldiers dodge flying pieces of ice; Captain Preston is distracted by several people trying to advise him while others threaten him; the growing crowd presses ever closer; a soldier is struck and falls; the cry is "Fire!" and a single shot cracks in the dark, followed by a ragged volley; the crowd parts in panic. Four men lie dead in the snow while the wounded crawl and stagger away.

Hutchinson was at home in his North End mansion when six excited citizens burst in a few minutes later, imploring him "for God's sake" to go to King Street, where the soldiers were firing on the people. He started out at once. As he hurried through the streets, angry dockworkers armed with clubs challenged him, forcing him to scurry through back yards and alleyways.

The firing was over when Hutchinson arrived near the Town House, although to all appearances it had just begun. The milling crowd, now a thousand strong, filled the wide expanse of King Street while the guard company, reinforced by the whole 29th Fusilier Regiment, stood its ground in the narrow part of the street between the Town House and the guard barracks. The prospects of an all-out massacre grew stronger with every passing minute.

Hutchinson spoke first to Preston, who tried to explain what had happened; then to Molineux, who demanded withdrawal of the troops; then to Belknap, who called for a conference. Finally, rejecting all advice, he listened to the crowd's shouts of "Town House, Town House!" and climbed to the balcony facing down King Street to speak in the darkness to a churning mass, torches illuminating isolated islands of upturned faces.

Although he had to shout over the voices that continued to hurl defiance and abuse at him, he quieted the crowd enough to make an appeal for calm judgment, to promise a court inquiry into the shootings, and to insist that the law would take its due course if the people would only allow it. Most of the townsfolk, however, would not be satisfied with words; they wanted to see the troops withdrawn before they themselves would disperse. Hutchinson had tried to avoid this. He did not want to have the Regulars moved away, because that would be considered an admission that they were in the wrong. At the same time, if he favored the troops, he would lose his last vestiges of support from the ordinary people of Boston.

He had learned to read the spirit of these crowds, and the angry faces in the darkness below his balcony told him that no solution was acceptable so long as the red and white ranks stood at one side of the square. At last he was forced to go to Lieutenant Colonel Carr and recommend the troops be sent back to the barracks. Carr promptly agreed to do so, and passed the order. As the soldiers moved off, the crowd thinned out and soon King Street was virtually empty.

No evidence has ever been found to place Otis or Adams at any of the scenes in Boston that night, just as there is no indication that either man was at the wrecking of Hutchinson's home nor at any of the other mob actions. Adams was a fire ward whose duties would have made him respond that night to the bells and calls of "fire" even if he were innocent of any knowledge of the events in King Street, and his house was only a few blocks away. Loyalist writers tried for several months to link Adams with a tall man in a red cape and white wig[5] who was supposed to have harangued the crowd and urged violence in Dock Square earlier that evening. Nothing would have better painted Adams as a man dedicated to violence—which would have helped the cause of the court party and the administration—but the effort to put that red cape on Adams was unsuccessful. A man so well known as Adams could not have made a speech to a crowd that night without being recognized, and the absence of anything more than weak insinuations would indicate that the tall, red-caped man was only one of the many who jumped up to urge the mobs in one direction or another.

At eleven o'clock on the following morning, however, Adams was the most active man in town, speaking before a large crowd at Faneuil Hall. A delegation must be sent to the governor in council, he said, requiring the immediate departure of the troops from Boston. He, of course, would be glad to lead the group. Otis was present and called for a moderate approach to prove to the world that the town was not at fault, but Adams exemplified the spirit of the town in his desire for action. The voters agreed that a vindication could come later. Adams was chosen, along with John Adams, John Hancock, Molineux, and Deacon Philips, to go to see Hutchinson. While the townspeople were occupied in giving depositions and discussing the events of the night before, this committee marched forthwith to the Town House, where the council was in special session. Adams made his way through the crowd already gathered outside. He was confident, nodding to his many acquaintances and repeating the terms that in an instant became a motto and password of the townspeople—"Both regiments or none!"[6]

In the hall, wearing the white wig and crimson robe of office, Hutchinson awaited the town's petition. Once again, as with Otis and the writs, the administration was under challenge, and there was by no means a solid front in support of the governor. Several members of the council already had advised removal of the troops. Lieutenant Colonel Dalrymple, commander of the 29th Regiment, and Lieutenant Colonel Carr, of the 14th, were present; neither objected to this advice.

Adams had with him a piece of paper on which was written, "It is the unanimous opinion of this meeting that the inhabitants and soldiery can no longer live together in safety; that nothing can rationally be expected to restore the peace of the town and prevent further blood and carnage but the immediate removal of the troops."[7]

Adams could produce a draft resolution and guide it through a committee and obtain a vote of approval on it in the House; he could compose a letter to the London agent or a reply to the governor's speech or an article for the press; but he was uncomfortable in front of the council. He was not at home on his feet, feeling perhaps too strongly the lack of long experience in the Boston courtrooms, where many of the lawyers who were his political contemporaries had formed their style. But when he was committed to a cause, his natural reticence disappeared and his fiery words, cousin Adams said, "made a strong impression on spectators and auditors."[8]

This was one of those occasions in which Adams was carried along by the thrust of his own convictions and by the attitude of his fellow townsmen. His determination was clear to Hutchinson, who said Adams pressed the case "with great vehemence,"[9] insisting that the cause of the massacre of innocent citizens was the presence of a standing army in the town,[10] and that the removal of these troops could be the only solution. He implied that responsibility for the deaths could be linked to the colonial administration and to the Crown. If the governor refused, the rage of the people would vent itself upon him. Adams then left the room with his deputation, and the governor turned to his council.

Hutchinson knew that in the eyes of the province an order sending the troops out of Boston would be equal to an admission of their guilt. To do so at the request of Samuel Adams would compound the difficulties, making it appear that the governor had sided with the troops but was forced to yield under pressure from the popular party.

Hutchinson had come to the council meeting determined not to allow this incident to work to the detriment of the troops or the administration, but he was quick to see that he had little support from the military officers and from his own party. Secretary Andrew Oliver was no help. Unlike Hutchinson, he had been quickly intimidated by the Boston mob four years earlier, when he signed away his stamp commission under the Liberty Tree, and he now saw the same kind of trouble brewing again. The rest of the council were openly for getting the troops out of town, and even the military officers wavered. Hutchinson refused to order the troops out, on the grounds that he had no authority over them. The raising of this technicality turned all eyes to Colonel Dalrymple, who in that case, as ranking army officer in Boston, became the only man capable of giving the order to march the troops out. Dalrymple could have evaded an answer by claiming that he could not act until he received orders from Gage. As the commander of the troops, however, he was living with the visions of the night before, when his soldiers, drawn up in street fighting formations, faced a wild crowd, and a few moments on the brink of chaos had convinced him that a bleak future lay ahead if the 29th remained in town. Hutchinson found it hard to conceal his surprise[11] when he heard Dalrymple recommend withdrawal of the regiment to the castle, where, the colonel reminded the council, they were to have been quartered in the first place when they came down from Halifax five months earlier.

Hutchinson once again had to face Samuel Adams and his deputation. He conceded that it might be possible to remove the 29th Regiment, which had been in the thick of the trouble, and quarter it in the castle. Adams immediately recognized the advantage he had gained from Dalrymple's move, and pressed hard: if *one* could be removed without further reference to higher Crown officials, then *two* could go—and it was at the peril of the troops if they did not.[12] Adams warned that, in view of this incident, the people of Boston and the surrounding towns would not let the occupation continue, even if this meant that more blood would run in the streets.

With all his support fallen away, Hutchinson adjourned the meeting simply to avoid making the only further decision possible, which would be to order all the troops out; but he was forced to agree to call another meeting later in the day, after allowing "further study" of the matter by all sides.

Adams knew that his strength lay in the credibility of his assertion that the mood of the city was violent and ready for more trouble, and his symbol of that mood was the "meeting" crowd, which he needed to keep active until he forced Hutchinson to a decision. He returned to Faneuil Hall to report that the governor seemed ready to move one of the regiments, perhaps, but not two. He then read the message hastily written for him by Hutchinson: "From the particular concern which the 29th Regiment has had in your differences, Colonel Dalrymple . . . has signified that that regiment shall without delay be placed in the barracks at the castle."[13] Adams then asked the meeting whether this report was satisfactory, and when "it passed in the negative," he announced that the meeting had grown too large for Faneuil Hall and would have to move to the Old South Church, a walk that would take the 4,000 townsmen directly under the windows of the council room at the Town House.

Later that afternoon Adams and his committee returned to see Hutchinson and to reiterate the message of the town: the only way to avoid far more serious bloodshed was to order all British troops from Boston. Hutchinson still held his ground, warning Adams that those who led the Boston people to violence would be charged with high treason. Adams countered that Hutchinson would be answerable for consequences, and all the blood would be charged to the governor alone for "refusing to follow their unanimous advice." Adams was correct; the town deputation, the governor's council, the province secretary, and the army commander all said he must give in. Councilor Royall Tyler warned that, in his estimation, 10,000 men of the province were ready to try to oust the soldiers and probably could do it, "should it be called rebellion—should it mean the loss of our charter, or be the consequence what it would."[14] Councilors Russell of Charlestown and Dexter of Dedham confirmed Tyler's analysis—the countryside was in arms and probably would come in to Boston if the troops remained. Councilor Gray emphasized that the governor had received unanimous advice from his council and that, if he chose to take a different course, the responsibility for the results would be laid at his door.

Now, with the council against him and even Secretary Andrew Oliver, his friend and closest advisor, calling for removal of the troops (when Oliver saw "how artfully it was steered he whispered to me that I must either comply or determine to leave the province"), Hutchinson knew he had run out of time. He had begged the councilors to reconsider carefully what the removal of the troops would mean to the prospect of future control of the town, but the answer he received was still the same: let us get the troops out at any cost, since nothing could be worse than the rising of the countryside that was sure to come. Hutchinson could delay his answer no longer. Night was falling and the meeting crowd could easily be converted into another ice-throwing mob—and 10,000 armed men in nearby towns watched for the tar-barrel signal from Beacon Hill. As he told Adams that both the regiments would be taken from the town, Hutchinson was unable to conceal the strain of the past 18 hours: "I observed his knees to tremble," said Adams, "and his face to grow pale—and I enjoyed the sight."[15]

Adams, self-righteous and exultant, took the governor's message back to the assemblage at the Old South Church. His triumphant announcement must have been an anticlimax to his confrontation with Hutchinson a few minutes earlier. After cheers and celebrations, the meeting broke up peacefully. The horrors of another night of rioting had been avoided—at the cost to Hutchinson of the remnants of his popular support in the town. As it was, Adams won in two ways: he forced the troops

out, but at the same time made it plain that the governor complied with the wishes of the people only reluctantly and after
much pressure.

Hutchinson had his own thoughts on the matter. "That the
country would have been in arms and come in nobody doubts,"
he wrote in a letter of which only a fragment is preserved.
"Whether 10,000 of them could have drove out 600 Regulars is
another question, but an attempt to do it would have been like
passing the Rubicon."[16]

In the absence of any support from the Crown, from Gage,
from the General Court, or from the people, Hutchinson used
the only tactic that remained for him. Hoping for any kind of
help, unable to change his point of view as he saw others doing,
unyielding in his convictions regardless of committee-room maneuvers, he continued to delay the actual move of the troops.
Adams, however, knew better than to underestimate Hutchinson,
and he had been watching carefully for any signs that the governor's promise was a trick to gain time. On March 10, after four
more days in which the troops made no move to leave, Adams
called another town meeting, and once again Hutchinson faced
Adams and his committee. The previous time Adams had emphasized the danger of new fighting between the people and the
soldiers; this time he said the threat of "the rage of the people"
was aimed directly against Hutchinson himself. Adams in effect
was telling the governor in public, and over the council table,
that the summer of 1765 might happen again. But images of riot
did not frighten Hutchinson as they did Andrew Oliver. He dismissed the committee without giving them any reply.

The deadly game of delay could not continue, however, and
preparations must have been under way to move the troops;
Adams and his group spoke to Dalrymple that day and within
hours the 29th Regiment began its move to the castle, with the
14th following next day. This second town meeting cemented
the conviction of Bostonians that Samuel Adams, practically by
himself, had moved the Regulars out of town, and the British
units ever after would be known to Bostonians as "the Sam
Adams Regiments."

The accomplishment of the move was, to Adams, only the beginning of this episode. Since the night of the 5th he had been

preparing the verbal assault that would make use of the events to discredit Hutchinson and the Crown. Words in the press were not enough; the emotion could better be conveyed by pictures. Paul Revere engraved a scene of carnage, and his print was distributed throughout the colonies and in England. The massacre was a concrete, undeniable base from which the power of the word could be put to use, and the next such event would be the trials of Preston and the soldiers. Adams now exerted every energy to get these trials under way.

His plan was frustrated when the Suffolk County Superior Court opened as scheduled on March 12 and decided to postpone the trials until June. Believing this was proof that the "cabal" intended to obstruct justice, Adams called the Sons of Liberty to action. He and Joseph Warren, followed by a "vast concourse" of townspeople, proceeded to the courthouse and "harangued the justices,"[17] in Hutchinson's words, demanding an immediate trial. The chief justice maintained that for a court proceeding as significant as this, all the judges should be present. Since one judge was sick at home, and another had been injured in a fall from his horse, postponement was in order.

At the town meeting the following evening, March 13, Adams moved to create Boston's own committee to investigate the "horrid massacre." James Bowdoin, Joseph Warren, and Samuel Pemberton were appointed and within a week drew up the infamous "Short Narrative," a document which amassed a considerable number of depositions to "prove" two points: the customs men were involved, and the soldiers had plotted and entered into "a combination"—in other words, the shooting was premeditated as an act of revenge.

The narrative produced six witnesses who saw guns being discharged from the windows of the custom house during the street firing and one expert who examined the strike of the musket balls on two houses across the street and judged they came from "the westernmost lower chamber window of the Custom House." Another 12 witnesses gave evidence that in one way or another depicted the British soldiers executing a planned attack on the people of the town. Some Redcoats warned their American friends that trouble was coming, said the witnesses, who spiced their depositions with salty quotations overheard that night: *"The town was too haughty and proud. . . . Many of their arses would be laid low before the morning."*[18]

The General Court opened in Cambridge on March 15, and Hutchinson was again besieged by the House, demanding an immediate return to Boston. Hutchinson blamed London, saying he was only following orders and had no authority to bring the assembly back to Boston. He was never discovered in this lie; actually, Hillsborough had only *suggested* the move of the court to Cambridge and had left the decision to Hutchinson.[19] When the House refused to do any business, the governor dissolved it and wrote to Hillsborough asking him to be careful that no copy of the secretary's letter be made public. On the 16th, John Robinson slipped out of town aboard one of Admiral Montague's ships, carrying with him accounts of the recent events written from the loyalist point of view, but the town's version, sent by a specially chartered fast schooner, would arrive first.

On the same day that his old antagonist, Robinson, left town, Otis took another step down the road to insanity. John Rowe reported that, on the afternoon of March 16, Otis returned to the Town House, scene of many of his great victories, and in an uncontrollable frenzy smashed several windows before he could be stopped. Brother Samuel Otis wrote home to the Colonel that James was much worse, "for which I am deeply troubled (may God support you under this severe affliction). . . . My heart sinks at the thought of his being lost to the world and his family."

As Hutchinson had foreseen, the removal of the troops to the castle did not mean the end of trouble for him. The legislature was beyond his control and the town was becoming a law unto itself. Samuel Adams had rightly judged that two regiments were enough to constitute a provocation but not enough to bring Crown control to Boston. For that it would take much more. Hutchinson once again began to express doubt in his own capabilities[20] and a desire to be free of the responsibilities of the governorship. He repeatedly told Hillsborough, Bernard, and others in London that Massachusetts now needed someone of much greater influence than "any common leader" could carry, adding that the job was too much for him and "the fatigues of it make their impressions on my constitution." But the leadership of a man of power within the British nobility was not enough. "I need not suggest to you what is necessary to be done," he wrote, in words that echoed those of Bernard. "The longer we are neglected the harder our cure will be."

As Hutchinson later admitted, he came dangerously close to a physical breakdown in these weeks. He was attempting to carry the full weight of government alone, with no support from council, House, party, or people, and the pressures were enormous. "I had the utmost reason to expect a further succession of trying scenes," he said later, "and that on my death or incapacity for business the government would be in a greater confusion than it ever had been." He summed up his feelings in a plea for relief which he sent Hillsborough at the end of March. "I find, my Lord, that I have not the strength of constitution to withstand the whole force of the other branches of government as well as the body of the people united against the Governor in every measure he can propose." At one point in the draft of this letter, he found himself forced to admit the physical and mental strain of the continuing battle with Adams and the radicals. He wrote and then scratched out the words asking that "I may be excused I may be allowed to resign my office," substituting in the final draft a less specific request that "a person of superior powers of body and mind may be appointed to the administration of the government of the province." On April 26 he dissolved the recalcitrant General Court assembly and closed his Boston town house, taking the family to Milton, where he sought the peace and rest that he so badly needed.

It was at this time, with the shooting incident much in the minds of the people of Boston, that the neighbors of James Otis were startled by the sound of musket shots coming from his house. A gathering crowd watched apprehensively as Otis stood at an upstairs window firing his musket into the air. It was then discovered that he had burned his remaining papers. His daughter said he could not be stopped; "he had spent much time and taken great pains to collect together all his letters and other papers, and in one of his unhappy moments committed them all to the flames." This time he was methodical, taking two days to complete the destruction by which, as John Adams commented, the true history of the American Revolution was lost forever.

18

Candidus

April 1770–May 1771

> Facts are stubborn things, and whatever may be our
> wishes, our inclinations, or the dictates of our passions,
> they cannot alter the state of facts and evidence: nor
> is the law less stable than the fact.
>
> JOHN ADAMS, at the "massacre" trials, 1770

IN EARLY MAY 1770, the *Gazette* ran a notice in oversize print
announcing that "our friend James Otis, Esq, has already received very great benefit by his tour in the country" and that the
prospect of his full recovery was very good. The loss of his health,
the notice concluded, was "principally if not altogether" owing
to his unremitting efforts in the cause of American liberty. The
optimistic tone, however, could not hide the hard reality: for the
first time in ten years, Otis was not present in the House of Representatives. For Hutchinson the absence of Otis was a welcome
relief, but his problems were by no means solved. From this time
forward, he said, "Mr. Samuel Adams may be considered as the
most active member in the House."[1]

Adams took over the full leadership of Boston and the popular
party, and soon proved how much he needed the counsel of Otis.
Without him, Adams returned to old battlegrounds; at this inop-
portune time he attempted to reopen the campaign for nonimportation, oblivious to the mood of the merchants and the prov-

ince in general. With the help of the Boston Sons of Liberty, he began anew the physical threats and harassment against individual importers. Offending merchants were castigated by name in the newspapers and the scorn of the people was called down upon them, under the motto "By uniting we stand, by dividing we fall."[2]

The town elected James Bowdoin to replace Otis, and returned Adams, Hancock, and Cushing to the House. Even though it was obviously impossible for Otis to serve, he received 70 votes from townsmen,[3] who were confident he would soon recover. Josiah Quincy wrote the town's instructions to its representatives, urging them to "cultivate a union with the other colonies." Hutchinson commented that these words were written by "a young lawyer, a coxcomb,"[4] who appeared to be trying to take the place of Otis and added, "It is much if he does not run mad also." Quincy was writing articles for the *Gazette* at this time, and on his drafts he often noted, "Let Samuel Adams, Esq., correct the press." Adams could not have written all the anonymous columns that appeared in the *Gazette* and all the provocative short pieces that Edes and Gill fitted into the empty corners of the newspaper, but it is evident that he served as the *Gazette's* unofficial editor for all political commentary. He kept up his correspondence with friends in England, watched events there, and was quick to emphasize the political violence that had become commonplace in London. (In May the British experienced a "massacre" of their own when the Regulars fired on an unruly crowd that was demonstrating in support of the imprisoned Wilkes.) He carefully reprinted in the *Gazette* the reports of angry debate in Parliament over the policy for controlling America. Hutchinson repeated Bernard's conviction that the unrest in Britain and the "illiberal, even savage harangues" of the House of Commons only aided and abetted Boston's radicals. "You do not consider the extensive consequences of such irregularities," he wrote to England. "We ape you in everything, especially in everything which is a reproach to you, and for fear of falling short we go beyond you."[5]

Boston was outwardly calm, however, and Hutchinson could find no argument to override Gage's withdrawal of the 29th Regiment from its bottled-up discomfort in overcrowded Castle William. Ferried from the island across the harbor to Dorchester, south of Boston Neck, the soldiers of the 29th began a march that took them to Providence, where they boarded transport ships for New Jersey and garrisons southward along the coast. Hutchinson now began to feel more confident that, with Otis gone, perhaps the worst was over. When Bowdoin was elected to the council, the Boston delegation and the town as a whole expected that he would be vetoed by the lieutenant governor before he could take his place, but Hutchinson chose to allow him to sit. This opened an additional seat for Boston in the House and to fill it John Adams was elected by a very large majority—418 of the 536 total votes—even though he had placed himself in a tenuous political position by agreeing to defend Preston and the soldiers in their upcoming trials.

On the night of the election a large dinner was held in Faneuil Hall, with "the principal gentlemen" of Boston and the neighboring towns present. After the meal, while a score of toasts were being offered to the king, the queen, the glorious minority of both Houses of Parliament, and to Chatham, Camden, Barré, Burke, and the other Whig heroes, James Otis unexpectedly entered the hall. He was welcomed with fanfare and obvious affection—toasts were interrupted as all drank to the "confirmed health of the patriot Otis."[6] Deeply moved, Otis acknowledged the compliment and lifted his glass in return to "prosperity to the present company, to the town of Boston, to North America." The jubilant crowd, encouraged by the resurrection of their old leader, celebrated far into the night and long after Otis had departed; the final toast of the evening was to the House of Representatives, "our suffering brethren at Cambridge, whose hearts are with us, while their bodies are unconstitutionally torn from us."

On Wednesday morning the province troop of horse guards assembled at Hutchinson's hilltop home in Milton to convey him to Cambridge for the opening of the new session of the General Court. An hour's escorted ride brought him to the Charles River, where Brigadier Brattle waited with the Cambridge militia company to see him into town. After the parade and the usual installation ceremonies, however, the House muted Hutchinson's welcome with another remonstrance against holding the assembly at Cambridge. But he was determined to countenance no more of what he called "the old story over again,"[7] the endless maneuvering on this point; he refused to meet a deputation headed by Hancock and, instead, abruptly walked out of the council chamber. The response of the House was to vote 96–6 against doing any business until Hutchinson moved them back to Boston.

Throughout the month of June, Hutchinson tried to be reasonable and to cajole the representatives into acting on the required legislation. There were taxes to be collected, he pleaded, troops to be levied for frontier service, and much routine business to be done. In vain he countered their arguments with his own interpretations of the charter. In vain he promised them that a decision on the move would be forthcoming in "important advices"[8] from London that he expected from day to day. Finally, on Friday the 23rd, he ran out of patience and gave the House until the following Monday to proceed to business, adding that, if the representatives refused to comply, he would give them "a short recess." On Monday the council was ready to accede, but the House again refused, this time by unanimous vote, and he prorogued the General Court to July 25—once more at Cambridge. But he knew he could not keep up this confrontation. "In the winter," he wrote Bernard, "I must meet them at Boston or not meet them at all."[9]

While he refused to concede any ground to the complaints of the radicals, Hutchinson nevertheless sought new ways to ease tensions in the colonies. On June 8 he asked Pownall, as he had urged Bernard a year earlier, to use his influence with the ministry to suggest a commission that would come to America to inspect the colonies[10] and, hopefully, to recommend Parliamentary reforms that would undermine the radical movements. Such a commission would allow the Crown to fight the opposition in Parliament while making the needed changes. Something had to be done to reestablish Crown control, and as he faced the problem Hutchinson was acutely aware that he was only an acting governor. At a critical time, when he might have thrown himself into the responsibilities of the governorship with a new energy,

he was held back by the knowledge that any of the men-of-war or
merchantmen entering the harbor might announce the presence
of a new governor. Once again lack of a decisive policy in London
had weakened the Crown administration in the colony at a time
when strong and clear leadership was necessary. The consumma-
tion of Hutchinson's ambition was withheld from him. He was
in the governor's chair, but with no firm assurance that he would
ever be there permanently, and under these circumstances he
knew London would expect him simply to move along with routine business, avoiding major decisions that might be reversed
or altered by a new governor. It was the opposite of all that he
had aspired to do.

Hutchinson's next hurdle would be the upcoming trials of
Preston and the soldiers, which could not be delayed any longer.
Preston, he felt, had made a grave error in allowing to be printed
in London a narrative of the events of March 5 authored by him.
Hastily republished by the Boston Whigs, the captain's self-pro-
tective version enraged the town. From his cell Preston at the last
minute tried to stave off bad feelings by a submissive note to the
Gazette in which he thanked the townspeople for their objectivity and kindness. The *Gazette* appended the note to its reprint of
his account of the shooting, making it appear obvious that his
contrite statement was an attempt to cover his tracks.

Hutchinson believed in the innocence of Preston, but he
thought the captain's judgment was poor. He was critical of
Preston's order to load muskets, convinced that a good officer
would have realized that, once loaded, the muskets probably
would be fired. "They are in general such bad fellows in that
regiment," Hutchinson mused, "that it seems impossible to re-
strain them from firing upon an insult or provocation given
them."[11] He intended to wait out the trials and to reprieve Preston
if he were found guilty. The problem of the moment was to get
the captain to the trial alive. There was no way to control the
Boston mob, and considering the "flame in the minds of the people," Preston's life was in their hands. Hutchinson knew there
were people in Boston who wanted to see Preston hang. He
vowed to himself that this would never happen. On the evening
of June 25, when there were signs that Preston's unfortunate nar-

rative had stirred up the beginnings of a mob, Hutchinson with his usual calm courage came in from Milton and sat up until midnight with Preston while Dalrymple's troops patrolled the town, ready for trouble. The night passed quietly, marking one of the few times that Hutchinson's determination was not put to the test.

The General Court met again on July 25. The first order of business was the now-perennial petition to the governor to move the session back to Boston. Hutchinson repeated his earlier assertion that the king had not given permission to return and therefore the session must stay at Cambridge. In a long and carefully reasoned reply which he had composed in his Milton study, Hutchinson reconsidered and dismissed each argument that Adams had presented a month earlier. He now ordered the House to proceed to business, adding a flat statement that "if you shall persist in your refusal, I must prorogue you to some future time." On the following day, as he more than half-expected, the House unanimously resolved to do no business.

Hutchinson spoke once again to the General Court, giving his reasons for holding the assembly out of Boston, and Adams replied for the House. Hutchinson, in turn, attempted to answer Adams with another speech to the assembly. Adams in his role as clerk asked him for a copy of the new speech to insert in the records. When Hutchinson told him the speech had not yet been polished as a final draft, Adams pleaded lack of time and said he would have the speech copied into the record and return it to Hutchinson, who could make corrections at his leisure in the journals of the House. Instead, Adams gave the rough draft to the *Gazette*, which immediately printed it, errors and all. He followed this with articles signed "a chatterer" in three successive issues of the *Gazette*, in which he mentioned the "little inaccuracy" that he found in the lieutenant governor's writing, adding that, since Hutchinson had taken only one day to reply, it was a wonder there were not more imperfections in the work. Hutchinson was enraged at this underhandedness.

On Saturday, August 11, with the General Court now out of session, Hutchinson was at home in Milton when a drunken and maudlin James Otis surprised him with a social call.

Mr. Otis stopped at my house at Milton, in his way to Plymouth, and after some salutations, desired to see me in private; though in the morning, about 8 or 9, he smelt strong of rum, and carried the disorder of mind which had increased in his countenance. He said he was an unhappy man, and had been cruelly persecuted, and he knew I had been so; "But," says he, "God knows," clapping his hand to his head, "that I had no hand in it." He went on that he hoped he had a right to travel the road for his health, that he was in the place of God and the King, that he considered me as the representative of the King, and has come to apply to me for protection. I made him a very soft reply, assured him of all the protection in my power, and he, with great ceremony, took leave.[12]

The General Court reopened on September 25 with Samuel Adams fully in command. Hutchinson complained that Adams and his "Bostoneers" intimidated old Tory stalwarts such as Worthington, Ruggles, and Murray, who had long supported the Crown, and in this manner kept the House from doing any business. "You certainly think right when you think Boston people are run mad," he told William Parker. "The frenzy was not higher when they banished my poor pious grandmother, when they hanged the Quakers, when they afterwards hanged the poor innocent witches, when they were carried away with a land bank."[13] Adams was an organizer, with great influence over the other representatives; other radicals were willing to go to any length under orders of the "pale lean Cassius."[14]

In mid-August, Gage had written Hutchinson from New York, asking for advice on the best way to replace the provincial garrison of Castle William with a contingent of royal troops. Hutchinson gave the matter some thought, but supposed it to be only a distant possibility in case further trouble should arise. He had wanted to transfer Preston from his cell in the town jail to the castle for his own safety, a suggestion originally made by Bernard in a letter. Certainly Preston would be in better hands with a royal garrison holding the fortress. On September 8 Gage sent Hutchinson a note enclosing a Hillsborough letter of July 6 ordering the takeover of the castle by Regular troops. Though surprised, he acted quickly and decisively. On the following day,

Sunday, he called the council to a meeting in Boston, swore them to secrecy, and read Hillsborough's order to them. He then went directly to the castle, turned the ring of massive keys over to Lieutenant Colonel Dalrymple, and returned to Milton, where he waited for the inevitable reaction.

By Tuesday the town was filled with excited anger and rumors of riot, to the point where even in Milton Hutchinson did not feel safe. When his brother, Foster, begged him to take his family to the castle, Hutchinson decided to go. "Adams in particular was inflaming the minds of the people," he told Bernard.[15] Adams, in fact, was one of a committee of five that presented a remonstrance to Hutchinson on the takeover of the castle, asking why this was done. Hutchinson replied that Boston's instructions to its General Court representatives, published in April 1769, "were the immediate occasion of his Majesty's orders to me to replace the provincial garrison with Regulars" (these instructions had ordered the Boston representatives "by no means to comply" with requests for quarters and supplies for the Regulars).

Adams, without the ballast that Otis had long provided him, moved quickly and dangerously. He was by this time convinced that the united American colonies had the military strength to stand up to England in a war.[16] London boasted of a superiority, he said, that might be found wanting if brought to the test. He began to take an active interest in the betterment of the Massachusetts militia, which had been allowed to deteriorate as the intransigence of the province became more evident. In late November he successfully pushed through a motion to urge the lieutenant governor to fill the many empty spaces in the officer ranks of the province. Hutchinson rejected the idea, and in a letter to Bernard added a grim new piece of information which had convinced him his decision to retreat to the castle was correct. "A serious proposal was made by S.A. of which I have one very good witness, to secure me and then to raise twenty thousand men to retake [Castle William]."[17]

The days passed, however, and nothing happened. This was the beginning of another turning point in the struggle for control of Massachusetts, and for a short time everything went Hutchinson's way. On October 9, the House voted to proceed to

business in Cambridge. Unable to stop this swing toward cooperation with Hutchinson, Adams tried to make the first business
of the House a recognition of the nonimportation agreements,
but the news that New York and Philadelphia had given up and
were beginning to import British goods again was enough to stave
off his effort. The Boston businessmen saw themselves too close
to ruin and wanted no more of this political game, especially if
they had to play it alone. Adams had pushed too hard. Nonimportation in Boston was in effect discarded, eliciting a cynical
comment from General Gage, a constant watcher of the Boston
scene: "After a fair struggle between patriotism and interest, the
latter seems to have gained a complete victory."[18] Although
Adams complimented the merchants for holding on to the nonimportation agreements "much longer than I ever thought they
would or could,"[19] he resolved to push them away from the center of Massachusetts politics and seek his support with the people.

The long-postponed trial of Captain Preston began in September, to be followed by the trial of his soldiers. John Adams
and Josiah Quincy had consented to defend Preston and his men
—an arrangement that called forth no objections from Samuel
Adams. The chief prosecutor was Robert Treat Paine, who was
assisted by Samuel Quincy and Robert Auchmuty. The trial was
the first significant test of the merits of John Adams, and he rose
to the occasion. With masterly control of evidence and law, he
guided a basically sympathetic jury to the acquittal of Preston
and all but two of the soldiers, who received the light punishment of branding on the hand for manslaughter. Coming as it
did after the failure of the nonimportation agreements and the
collapse of opposition in the House, the result of the trials made
Hutchinson feel that the prospects for Massachusetts were favorable. "I have more hopes of healing our divisions," he said, "than
I have had at any time since they began."[20] As for the assembly in
Cambridge, "I have fairly beat them, and they must be content
to sit wherever I am instructed to carry them."[21]

With this new confidence, Hutchinson aggressively pursued
Adams and the faction. He appealed to London to change the
province charter, which, he said, gave too much legislative and
executive power to the people and was thus inconsistent with the

interest of the parent state or the welfare of the colony itself.[22] Attempts by Adams to regain his old power must be stopped, and this now should not be too difficult. With the faction weakening, he said, "I think I could find bones to throw among them to continue contention and prevent a renewal of their union. This in some cases would be very criminal but when designed to prevent much greater mischief . . . is allowable and laudable."[23] The end justified the means.

The outcome of the trials stung Samuel Adams into a fury of writing. In the 18 months from December 1770 to June 1771 he turned out 36 political essays for the *Gazette,* an output not matched by any other writer of the time. The first 11 of these articles—the series written under the pseudonym "Vindex"—appeared in a space of two months following the massacre trials and confirms that Adams in fact had lost his way and was thrashing about in a vain attempt to reestablish the collapsed radical position. Otis was gone, Hancock was estranged, John Adams was exhausted after his work on the trials, Hawley was back home, the Sons of Liberty were quiescent, but Samuel Adams struggled on, his impulses leading him into pointless and profitless attacks that wasted his abilities and his precious time.

It was incomprehensible to him that Preston and the squad of soldiers might be found innocent of murder by a Boston jury. He did not attend the trial—just as he did not appear in the rioting that caused the shootings—because he knew he might be charged with having affected the outcome. Dumbfounded with the results of Preston's case, he resolved to be present at the trial of the soldiers, where he belatedly attempted to assist the prosecution, writing heavy-handed and presumptuous advice to Paine on ways to improve the cross examination of defense witnesses.[24] He was angered to find that the jury had been selected from out-of-towners, complaining that they would not know the character of each Boston witness and would be unable to judge truth from lies. He recognized that in these trials the reputation of the town of Boston was at stake, since if the soldiers were not guilty, then the townsfolk were.

The major part of his writing in these weeks following the trials concentrated on the defense of Boston as the home of a quiet and loyal people who were driven to violence by a brutal soldiery—a point stressed by Otis but generally ignored by Adams in earlier days. He had already sketched an indelible picture of the character of the Regulars in his articles for the "Journal of Occurrences"; now he heightened that picture by contrast with the good, gentle, long-suffering people of the town. He was anxious to offset the allegations of a plot on the part of the citizens, who had been accused of preparing "bludgeons" and patrolling the streets, eager to attack the soldiers. On the contrary, he wrote, the plotting was accomplished by the soldiers and even by the officers, and the townsfolk were the innocent victims. In a relentless recital Adams raked hot coals out of the smoldering fire of Boston resentment, trying to show his readers that the trials left many questions unanswered and that justice was not done.

Saving the good name of Boston was only one of his aims. He knew that the continual rehashing of the massacre story kept one fact always in the forefront: the imposition of a "standing army" on Boston had been the cause of all the problems. But Adams could not change with his pen alone the becalmed drifting of the popular party and the trend toward revival of Crown power and influence. Regardless of the inconsistencies of the trials, they were over now and the public was satisfied. John Rowe, visiting James Otis, found him "in a gloomy way."[25] Hutchinson, on the other hand, was elated over the obvious change in the temper of the people, which he felt had come about quicker and to a greater degree than anyone could have predicted. In view of this, he again called for an aggressive follow-up with tighter political control of the province, which he now saw as ready to receive a change in the constitution. He suggested "lopping off the territory east of the Penobscot,"[26] that is, separating what is now Maine from Massachusetts and placing it under a new jurisdiction. He wrote to Hillsborough that "a firm persuasion that Parliament is determined, at all events, to maintain its supreme authority is all we want."[27] Although earlier he had asked to be excused from further service, Hutchinson was pleased when his commission as governor arrived in mid-March. On Sunday the 17th he was proclaimed governor, with Andrew Oliver lieutenant governor and Thomas Flucker secretary. He resolved to keep the General Court in Cambridge for the May opening; this, he judged, would not cause him the trouble he had experienced earlier. Referring to "our demagogues," he remarked with an unaccustomed jauntiness, "They are such bad managers of so bad a cause that they give me no sort of concern."[28]

When March 5, anniversary of the massacre, came around, Thomas Hutchinson's dry wit did not fail him. From his desk he could hear the ringing of church bells all over the town. Boston was showing, he wrote, "that the persons who have the direction of the town differ from the law in their construction of the action this day twelvemonth." The Sons of Liberty saw no such humor in the first anniversary of the shootings, and that night the windows of Paul Revere's house were illuminated to reveal large sketches, political cartoons aimed at keeping alive Boston's hatred of the Regulars and the tax commissioners. The latter were represented in a graphic and gory drawing of young Seider reeling from a shot by Richardson, a hand on his wound to stop the gush of blood, while weeping friends stood by in helpless grief. Another Revere window displayed the soldiers firing on the people, over which were inscribed the words "FOUL PLAY."[29] A third lighted a woman, the symbol of America, with her foot on the head of a British grenadier who lay prostrate before her. The *Gazette* announced that the exhibition was viewed in solemn silence by an awestruck crowd of "many thousands."

Like Bernard and many others before him, Hutchinson never seemed able to give London a clear picture of conditions in Massachusetts. The time lag of four to six months between question and answer made the matter all the more confusing, especially since neither side seemed to take this lag into account. In a moment of depression and pessimism he could write that only force would solve the problem in Boston, but a few weeks later he would encourage reconciliation through liberal reform and then be unpleasantly surprised by the arrival of a letter informing him of new repressive steps. In the spring of 1771 his writings not only called for severe measures to bring Massachusetts back to line; he also wanted action against Samuel Adams.[30] A law should be passed, he said, making it treason to affirm that an act of Parliament lacks validity, or to deny the authority of Parliament over the colonies. As for Adams, Hutchinson doubted whether there was "a greater incendiary in the King's dominion or a man of greater malignity of heart." Adams had no scruples and would stoop to "any measure ever so criminal to accomplish his purposes." This man, he said, wished "the destruction of every friend to government in America."

Letters from Adams were crossing the ocean alongside those of Hutchinson, and the battle lines were clearly drawn. Adams told Arthur Lee in April that the political affairs of America were in a dangerous state, with a plan afoot to "render ineffectual the democratical part of this government."[31] In a phrase that he liked to use, Adams wrote pointedly, "The tyrants of Rome were the *natives* of Rome." Hutchinson, he said, was power-hungry and possessed an insatiable pride. Perhaps there never was a man in this province more flattered or better pleased with himself, he said, likening Hutchinson to a "miss in her teens, surrounded by dying lovers."[32]

The tensions were growing—some idea of the pressures of conflict in Boston can be gained not only from the breakdowns of Otis and Hutchinson, but also from the exhaustion of young John Adams after a year—his only year—as a representative on the side of the popular party in the General Court. The rough-and-tumble of politics, combined with his work at the trial of Preston and the soldiers, left John Adams thoroughly exhausted, with chest pains, respiratory problems, a general malaise, and a conviction that he needed a long rest. He resolved in March to move back to Braintree, where, incidentally, he would not be able to stand as a representative for Boston, and to "throw off a great part of the load of business both public and private." He took a trip to Worcester and to Stafford Springs, a popular health resort. "I shall certainly become more retired and cautious," he wrote. "I shall certainly mind my own farm and my own office."[33] It was in the grip of these pressures that Samuel Adams doggedly kept on while friends fell away.

The Superior Court opened in Cambridge in early April, showing Hutchinson's court party stronger than it had been since the heyday of Otis and Adams two years earlier; however, after a motion of congratulations to Hutchinson on his commission as governor was staved off by only one vote, Adams managed enough strength to keep the House from any effective business and Hutchinson was forced to dissolve the session on April 26. New elections were in order for May, and with Otis "steady and social and sober as ever and more so,"[34] he became active again and assisted Adams in the drive to seat enough members of the popular party to gain a clear ascendancy in the House. Watching the battle of the newspapers, Hutchinson could see "the black art of Adams" showing through. Of Otis he said, "He happens to be in a lucid interval but really would have been a more fit representative while his lunacy was upon him."[35] When Hancock seemed to be vacillating and unsure of himself, Hutchinson made him a secret offer to take him into the council if Hancock would see to it that Secretary Flucker also was nominated. Although he failed in this move (and therefore vetoed Hancock for the council when his name came up), Hutchinson retained enough influence over the House to force the representatives to compromise their position on refusal to do business in Cambridge. He promised that, if they would give up their insistence on moving to Boston as a *right* and refer to it as a "convenience," he would allow the court to return. Samuel Adams tried to repudiate Hutchinson's offer, but his path was blocked by the now unpredictable Otis, who insisted that a continued refusal to do business was too damaging to the life of the province—and against the desires of the king. In a speech to the House, Otis insisted that the governor had the right to hold the General Court wherever he thought proper and, picking out a small town in a corner of the province, asserted that Hutchinson could carry all of them "to Houssatonick if he saw fit."[36]

Adams was stunned along with the rest of the radicals as the House voted approval of the new wording, and Hutchinson decreed the General Court would move back to Boston. In Hutchinson's mind, Otis had supported the Crown for two reasons—first, he had always disavowed any movement toward a general revolt; second, he acted out of spite. Otis, said Hutchinson, was jealous of the influence which Adams had acquired in his absence, and perhaps now he would be "serviceable" to the government.[37] "The faction in this province against the government is dying," said Hutchinson, "but it dies hard." He knew that the concession had strengthened his position immeasurably. The representatives, he wrote, have "given me more weight in the province than they intended." He saw the return to Boston as a triumph that would open up opportunities for even more concessions.

Otis, with his "Houssatonick" speech, was the talk of the province. In his lucid periods he feared the growing recklessness and belligerence of Adams and wanted to stabilize the House regardless of the price. As one representative bemoaned, "The House voted everything he moved for. Boston people say he is distracted." Otis resumed his law practice, arguing a case on May 15 in which he seemed "the same man he used to be." John Adams, in gratitude to Otis, recommended his old mentor to "fourteen clients in Wrentham and three or four in Boston," some of whom engaged Otis to represent them. "He has come to court and behaved very well," said a happy Adams.

> He is a singular man. It will be amusing to observe his behavior upon his return to active life in the senate and at the Bar, and the influence of his presence upon the public councils of this province. I was an hour with him this morning at his office, and there he was off his guard and reserve with me. I find his sentiments are not altered, and his passions are not eradicated. The fervor of his spirit is not abated, nor the irritability of his nerves lessened.[38]

19

The Committees
of Correspondence

June 1771–January 1773

Vis unita fortior. . . . It is by united councils, a
steady zeal, and a manly fortitude, that this continent
must expect to recover its violated rights and liberties.

SAMUEL ADAMS, September 1771

IN UNION THERE IS STRENGTH. There were stubborn men in Boston, but none more stubborn than Samuel Adams. The movement of the General Court back to Boston under Hutchinson's
conditions was one of the most humiliating disappointments in
his life, and even though the resolution to do so had been passed,
he refused to give in. There was, he insisted, always room for new
motions. He accused Hutchinson of pushing the passage of this
resolve through a thin House, and he warned that an overwhelming majority of representatives "will not go up to the house of
Rimmon or bow the knee to Baal."[1] Writing as Candidus in the
Gazette, he struck hard against the move. It made no difference,
he said, if Hutchinson insisted the king's instructions forbade him
to bring the assembly back to Boston. The location of the assembly was the prerogative of the governor under the province charter, and if instructions from one of the king's ministers could

change a charter right, "may they not control in the exercise of any and every one?" By June, Adams had gathered enough support to repudiate the earlier acquiescence of the House. The representatives, reversing themselves, declared they would not move back to Boston.

Adams followed this victory with another success: he revived the committee of correspondence in the House, which, after its appointment in November of 1770, had accomplished very little. He was determined to bring new life to the committee with the idea of a united confrontation (the new committee included Cushing, Adams, Otis, Hancock, and Heath—nearly the same composition as in the previous session). Adams immediately drafted a letter to Franklin, then the province agent, asserting that the American colonies were "still united in the main principles of constitutional and natural liberty."[2] He then published the "committee's" letter in the *Gazette* without official approval of the General Court, causing Hutchinson to comment that he doubted whether a man with less scruples existed within the empire. "I think I do him no injustice," Hutchinson later said, "when I suppose he wished the destruction of every friend to government in America."[3] Three months later Adams wrote to Arthur Lee that societies should be formed in every province to ward off attacks on the liberty and rights of the colonists. "If conducted with the proper spirit," he asked, "would it not afford reason for the enemies of our common liberty, however great, to tremble?"[4]

With the House now out of session, making it impossible to assemble the committee of correspondence, Adams searched out new material for the *Gazette*. He was attracted into yet another time-wasting and digressive attack when he read a saccharine congratulatory letter presented by a committee of Congregational ministers to Hutchinson on the occasion of his assumption of new duties as governor (John Adams had read the clerics' letter and merely sputtered that "posterity will scarcely find it possible to form a just idea of this gentleman's character"[5]). Samuel Adams ridiculed the clergymen's obsequious address as the kind of flattery that had to be offensive to any sincere man. The truth is, he said, "every man in power will be adulated by some sort of men in every country, because he is a man in power."[6]

For three months Adams carried on a miniature newspaper war with Hutchinson's friends, thrusting and parrying on the question of whether or not the clergy's address was appropriate. It was Adams at his weakest, drawn into battle by his inability to suffer Hutchinson the slightest success, by his self-righteous anger, and by his instinct to respond to the arguments of others rather than to originate the attack himself. It kept up some slight pressure on the governor, but there were many other avenues that would have afforded Adams a greater remuneration for his efforts. By mid-August he finally dropped this endeavor and moved, in a continuing series of articles, to questions of far greater impact.

He revived in print all the irritants of past days—the Stamp Act, and after its repeal, the remaining duty on tea ("a tribute is extorted from us"), the British fleet in Boston Harbor, the branding of Massachusetts as a rebel province, the garrison of troops at Castle William. Our masters have been changed, he wrote, but "we deceive ourselves if we indulge a thought that their hearts are changed."

The tea tax, he insisted, was a symbol of unconstitutional domination by Parliament and a precedent which held the door open for other taxes. He appealed for nonconsumption: "We can easily avoid paying the TRIBUTE by abstaining from the use of those articles."[7]

In mid-September, Adams returned to the idea uppermost in his mind—the union of the colonies. The recognition that his writing might someday be used against him reinforced his natural caution and secrecy, but there are phrases that break through the circumlocution with primal clarity. The circular letter, he said, had effected a "union of the colonies in their common danger, by which they become powerful." It is by "united councils" that the American colonies can expect to recover their rights. The colonies "form one political body, of which each is a member," says Candidus at the conclusion of his letter of September 16, and *the cause of one is the cause of all.*"[8]

In the essay of the following week Adams, well aware of Hutchinson's efforts to catalogue as treasonable the conduct of the radicals, boldly brought up the subject himself. It is true, he said, that there had been acts of treason. There had been attempts to overthrow the constitution. Those who participated in the perversion of the constitution were treasonous, and those who opposed these men were heroes. Time will determine who are the real traitors and what punishment awaits them. This approach, which was a return to the subject of his earliest writings when, in his twenties, he had contributed to *The Public Advertiser,* now was converted into one of the boldest and most determined attacks Adams had made. He followed this thrust with others near the end of September, resurrecting Bernard's letters and accusing him of exaggerating conditions in Boston to convince London to send troops, "journalizing every idle report brought to him and, in short, acting the part of a pimp rather than a *Governor.*"[9] His real aim came out near the end of the essay, when Adams told his readers to beware of the "soothing arts" by which Boston had been lulled into political inactivity. The increase in the severity of his attack came from his realization that only this would attract the interest of blasé readers.

During this extremely active period of Adams' writing, Otis lost further ground in his battle to retain his mental powers. After the disastrous coffeehouse fight in September 1769, Otis had sued Robinson for £3,000. The case finally came up in Suffolk Inferior Court on July 25, 1771, and Otis, with the help of John Adams, was awarded £2,000, which he promptly refused.[10] The case was then placed on the docket for the Superior Court, while Hutchinson grumbled at this "most extravagant" verdict and personally interceded to see that the action was carried over to another term. Though he was upheld in his insistence that Robinson had been the aggressor, this late vindication now did Otis little good; his mind was slipping fast, and nothing could stop that. The progressive mental deterioration now made it impossible for him to control a violent, powder-keg temper that exploded at the slightest spark. He interrupted a quiet coffeehouse meeting of the lawyers of the Boston bar to flail a surprised waiter with curses for not putting enough candles on the table.[11] At home he was a challenge to his manservant, who could never anticipate his wishes. Otis would order his horse saddled and waiting at the door, then leave his servant holding the reins for an hour at a time. John Adams pictured him with "passions all roiled"[12] dashing in one door of his house and out another, and even climbing in and out the windows. Hutchinson said Otis greatly disturbed the neighborhood by his "drunken, distracted frolics every day or two"[13] and added that this actually was no more than he had done for the past half dozen years of "inconsistent publications and confused frantic harangues." But no matter how much trouble Otis caused in his demented periods, a sympathetic Boston suffered him and waited for his recovery. "If Otis should marry his mother," an exasperated Hutchinson wrote, "I am not sure that anybody would be offended whilst he continued to assert the liberties of their country."[14]

Adams now seemed to aim at filling the gap left by Otis, even to the extent of mimicking the kind of florid invective that Otis so often had used on the floor of the House. Candidus informed his readers that Hutchinson had been paid £2,250 by the Crown for his services, describing the governor as "the first American Pensioner," a man tied to the purse strings of the king. The tax money of Americans would soon be paying for the support of "hirelings, pimps, parasites, panderers, prostitutes, and whores" in the retinue of an "abandoned and shameless ministry." In the succeeding issue Candidus elaborated on this point with an essay on tyrants. Using Caesar as his example, he said that no people suffered under tyranny unless they deserved it. "Is it a time for us to sleep," he asked, while the governor and the ministry make changes which erode the Massachusetts charter?[15] To compare Hutchinson with the tyrants of antiquity would not hold good, said Candidus, because "the Tyrant of Rome, to do him justice, had learning, courage, and great abilities." On reading this, Hutchinson wrote Pownall that, with the province apparently moving toward peace and stability, only Samuel Adams continued unabated in virulence and "would push the continent into a rebellion tomorrow if it was in his power."[16]

Hutchinson was right on both counts, including his assessment of the turn toward peace. The later Candidus articles show that Adams, too, realized he was gaining no ground, another reason for the increasingly hard line. At this point Adams had many possible subjects for his ready pen. He could have reopened a discussion of the Otis-Robinson fight, using the court decision as a basis. The committee of correspondence and its importance to the province was another logical source of articles. Nonimportation as an aim needed his support. Twelve Royal Navy men-of-war had sailed into Boston from Halifax, providing additional fuel for the argument that Parliament was substituting intimidation for right reason. Adams, however, chose none of these areas; instead, he resurrected the idea of a plot to destroy the Massachusetts charter rights, producing the heavy-footed argument that Hutchinson and the king were partners in crime. "Kings and Governors," he says, "may be guilty of treason and rebellion."[17] Adams may have been trying to counter the continual rumor that he and Otis were to be arrested and carried to England to stand trial for treason. His argument against those who called him traitor or implied as much was always the same: the treasonous acts lay on the side of those who were attempting to undermine the rights of British citizens. But his return to this subject in the Candidus series indicates the difficulty he was having in finding his way in the absence of Otis.

With the coming of another winter, Otis reached his lowest point. Careful observer John Adams watched him shaking with uncontrollable emotion and correctly predicted he would soon have a relapse. Late in November the Otis family asked the town of Boston to investigate his sanity; they could no longer manage him. To Thomas Hutchinson, as judge of Probate, fell the task of requiring the Boston selectmen to examine Otis. On December 3 the selectmen signed their names to a certificate that James Otis was "a distracted, or lunatic person,"[18] and he was taken off, bound hand and foot, to an isolated farm of his appointed guardian at Nantasket, on the South Shore. Hutchinson summed up his old enemy in a letter to Bernard, using words that the ex-governor would well remember: "He has been as good as his word, set the province in a flame, and perished in the attempt." Hutchinson also sent word of the incident to Gage, expressing his view that, now that "the bundle is broke," the radicals would be easier to manage than when they were together.

Hutchinson had split Hancock away from the faction; only Adams remained as a danger to the provincial government, and the governor had plans for him. "I have taken much pains to procure writers," he said, "to answer the pieces in the newspapers which do so much mischief among the country people." He had two or three writers contributing to Draper's *Massachusetts Gazette,* he said, besides the help of a new press and a young printer "who says he will not be frightened and I hope for some good effect."[19] The Crown writers sallied into print—Chronus, Probus, Benevolus, and Philanthrop—to "blow the coals," as Hutchinson put it.

Candidus was waiting for them. In December, Adams turned his pen against Chronus, who had counseled moderation in complaints against the Crown, pointing out that it would be far more profitable to make "humble and dutiful representation" of the hardship attached to measures emanating from Parliament than to continue to abuse the government and the soldiers in the press. Dismissing the counsels of Chronus as "the barkings of a cur dog," Candidus warned that the province was being lulled to sleep while all the charter rights were taken away.

Chronus was just what Candidus needed, giving Adams a target and a contrary philosophy against which he could build his own case. He charged forward to meet his opponent, armed to the teeth with Locke, Pitt, Camden, Montesquieu—and with his quotations from Hutchinson the historian, a figure that Adams constantly held up as an embarrassing contradiction to Hutchinson the politician. "The constitution of this province, as our own historian informs us, is an epitome of the British constitution"; therefore, curtailing the rights and liberties of the people of Massachusetts must be "subversive" of the constitution. Adams saw unalterably opposed forces at work in Massachusetts, in the other American colonies, and in London. He drew support from the activities of the radical opposition in Parliament and sought ties with Wilkes, Pitt, Barré, and the others.

Through his writings in the *Gazette* and in the House of Representatives, and from the forum of the Boston town meeting, Adams was beginning to succeed in drawing the country towns of the province to his side as he had captured the town of Boston years earlier. He was sure that the large majority of the people, though reluctant or unable to express themselves, supported his views. He sensed their unspoken guidance: "a few of us lead the way as the people follow, and we can go no further than we are backed up by them."[20]

Hutchinson did not, like so many other loyalists, believe that the relationship between England and the colonies would continue unchanged for a long time to come; in fact, he thought it "not likely that the American colonies will remain part of the dominion of Great Britain another century"[21]—the once tiny settlements were growing too powerful and the ocean was too wide. While the tie remained, however, the essentiality of control from London had to be recognized: any compromise with Parliamentary supremacy would lead to chaos.

Adams never ceased his effort to bring good new men into the party and to keep the ones he had. In February he saw to it that John Adams was invited to make the second annual oration on the anniversary of the massacre, in an attempt to revitalize his cousin's commitment to the radicals. He failed: John Adams insisted that he wanted no part of the battle, writing in his diary that he feared the fate of Otis:

> I was solicited to go to the town meetings and harangue there. This I constantly refused. My friend Dr. Warren the most frequently urged me to this. My answer to him always was, "That way madness lies." The symptoms of our great friend Otis, at that time, suggested to Warren a sufficient comment on these words, at which he always smiled and said "it was true."[22]

He was very happy, however, to be associated with Samuel Adams, sensing the turn of the tide in the colony. When former Governor Shirley referred to "this brace of Adamses," John Adams publicized the sobriquet in an essay in which he confirmed the partnership and said the efforts of the Adamses were aimed against Hutchinson. Both men, he said, had been of the same mind on Hutchinson since they first met in 1761. Both were convinced he was out to destroy the liberties of Massachusetts and that the province had more to fear from him than from any man alive. With his characteristic self-concern, John Adams added that, because of their efforts to oppose the governor at every step —even though both members of the brace were not of robust physical constitutions—it might be that the same "art and power which has destroyed a Thacher, a Mayhew, an Otis may destroy the health and the lives of these gentlemen."

The General Court opened on April 8, after one of the longest periods without a session (since July 4, 1771). John Hancock was speaker *pro tempore* in place of the absent Cushing, and was now the principal force behind a motion to petition a move back to Boston for the "convenience" of sitting there, rather than as a right of the House. Although the Whig party seemed sluggish and apathetic, Samuel Adams exercised enough control to defeat Hancock's motion and also to keep the House from doing any business. Again stymied by Adams, Hutchinson dissolved the House after less than three weeks.

When the Boston merchants hired Otis to represent them in 1761, they were aggressive in their desire to fight the imposition of new rules on trade. The decade that followed, however, brought many bitter lessons. Nonimportation, which at first seemed a good answer that would bring quick results, had stifled all trade. Many of the best businessmen were bankrupted by the stagnation of trade in 1765, caused by a tightening customs stranglehold on the port of Boston. The merchants showed their dissatisfaction in a steadfast avoidance of any further affiliation with the radicals of the town: no more nonimportation agreements, they said, no more support for Boston violence, no more attacks on the provincial administration. Hancock, who had inherited the leadership of the Boston merchants, led the way. He broke off his close friendship with Samuel Adams and made his peace with Hutchinson.

As long as Otis had been the dominant figure in Boston opposition to contemporary Parliamentary policy, the merchants were willing to commit themselves to his leadership. He was a radical, yes, but a constructive politician, in background and in philosophy a fellow merchant who might edge near the brink of defiance but whose uppermost concern was the betterment of the empire and consequently of Massachusetts. He was, for the merchants, a force for good—meaning a mutually profitable relationship with the mother country under a very liberal trade policy with increasing power for American colonies without repudiation of the old institutions. Aberrations in his thinking were forgiven him and charged to the pressures of the time. (Otis himself recognized this toleration and used it to extricate himself when trapped by his own inconsistencies.)

Adams had no such inconsistencies, nor did he possess any constructive view of the British Empire as the potential salvation of mankind. He did not seek stability above all—in fact, he was willing to sacrifice a prosperous American trade, at least temporarily, in order to gain other ends. In the eyes of the merchants Adams was far less predictable than Otis; they saw that the end at which he aimed was increasing independence—and perhaps even total independence—of Great Britain. What this would mean no one knew. Additionally, Adams' obstructionism in the House, forcing adherence to the refusal to do business until the governor moved the General Court back to Boston, was beginning to cost too much. Without taxes and legislation, the province could not function, and without good government, commerce suffered. Continued exasperation of the Crown was certain to bring added punishment to Boston. Even the more liberal businessmen began to hope fervently for a return of a healthy Otis to the scene.

Recognizing the reluctance of the merchants to cast their lot with him, Adams had already begun to transfer the basis of political power of the Boston radicals away from the merchants and toward the people. The merchants, he said, had been too long the "unconcerned spectators"[23] on the political scene, who could be depended on only when their close interests were seen by them to be threatened. It was *the body of the people* who must decide the acceptance or rejection of Parliamentary decisions. He would base his fight on them.

Adams thus lost the support of the powerful and influential Merchants' Society, a fact that is discernible in his poor showing in the elections of May 1772. For the past five years he had been reelected by a strong vote (he was high man twice); he now slipped to last place, 30 percent below the other representatives. His refusal to compromise, however, did not cost him his influence over the Sons of Liberty. He had seen to it that the small group, the Loyal Nine of 1766, was expanded into the Sons of Liberty (with 355 members) by 1769. These were the mechanics and small tradesmen of Boston, who now began to dominate the town meeting while the merchants grew ever more fearful of them.

Hutchinson perceived the disaffection of the merchants as an opportunity to reestablish the former ties between Boston's prosperity and the court party. He hoped to cultivate the support of John Hancock, whom he recognized as the emerging leader of the merchants. In May Hancock was elected to the council but decided to remain in the House, where he felt he would be more influential. Hutchinson met privately with Hancock and others of the House as they were preparing an answer to his opening address, letting them know that he would object to any denial of the king's power to instruct the governor. "They encouraged me they would comply with my proposal," he said, "if Mr. Adams did not prevent it, against whose art and insidiousness I cautioned them."[24] The first move of the new coalition, as Hutchinson saw it, would be to bring the House back to Boston under the governor's terms.

The idea appealed to Hancock, who initially supported Hutchinson, but Adams, who never let pride stand in the way of his political goals, sought a reconciliation with his protégé. Hancock, mollified, changed his mind for the time being, joining Adams in insisting that the House would do no business out of Boston and would move back only if Hutchinson conceded it as a right rather than a convenience. Faced with a fourth consecutive year without legislation to run the province, Hutchinson finally admitted defeat and agreed to return the General Court to Boston; Adams had won a lonely uphill battle.

Nothing had changed—the fleet was still in the harbor, the customs men were still inspecting and seizing ships, the tea tax continued, and the salary of the governor was to be paid by the Crown.

Hutchinson, however, was encouraging in his reports to London. He wrote Hillsborough that the friends to government in Massachusetts were on the increase and that the people of the province were "tired of the late disordered state of affairs" and anxious to see government restored and the faction suppressed. Thus he fell into his old error, repeating the up-and-down cycle of optimistic evaluations and discouraging afterthoughts.

At the end of the summer William Legge, Lord Dartmouth, replaced Hillsborough as secretary of state for the colonies. He was a man much respected for strength of character, and Adams professed to regard this as an omen of change for the better. In the

August term of Suffolk Superior Court, James Otis at last won his case against Robinson. He refused to take any payment from his assailant, however, noting that customs man Robinson's money had been squeezed from the town of Boston and was not acceptable. Instead, he forced Robinson to present an apology in open court and to pay all medical and lawyer's fees, amounting to about £200.

Adams had heard the rumors that the provincial judges were soon to be paid their salaries by the Crown, adding to the list of officials in the colonies who were beholden to London, not Boston. Writing in the *Gazette* as "Valerius Poplicola,"[25] Adams speared Hutchinson once again as a pensioner: a state of "infamy, wretchedness and misery" was sure to come "if our judges shall be prevailed upon to be thus degraded to hirelings." At the end of this article he added a request that made clear his faith in the ultimate political wisdom, as well as the power, of the people:

> The next step may be fatal to us. Let us then act like wise men, calmly look around us and consider what is best to be done. Let us converse together upon this most interesting subject and open our minds freely to each other. Let it be the topic of conversation in every social club. Let every town assemble. Let associations and combinations be everywhere set up to consult and recover our just rights.

On October 26, 1772, Adams learned for certain that the provincial judges would be paid out of tax money received from the American customs operations. One of the council members friendly to him whispered that Hutchinson had just received word of this in a letter from Bernard. This was the information Adams had anticipated, a new act of the Crown that would be looked on in the province as yet another step away from the old charter rights. The news had given him the only ingredient he lacked to renew his attack—a clear violation of provincial liberties. He met that day with members of the Caucus and made arrangements to ask for a town meeting to discuss Boston's response to this news, perhaps even to "arouse the continent."

When Adams petitioned the selectmen for a town meeting, he assumed there would be little opposition in Boston. Hancock, however, still saw himself as the leader of the merchants and promoter of political stability. He wanted to quiet the radicalism in Boston, and as a selectman, he was able to influence a rejection of the petition. It was one of the few times that Adams was caught by surprise, but he set to work to gather enough names for a new petition and tried again. In the end, after three weeks of additional work, he arranged for three separate petitions for a meeting, signed by a total of 198 townspeople. This was enough to convince a majority of the selectmen, and over the objections of Hancock the meeting was scheduled.

Otis, in the meantime, searched out John Adams and found him in the printing office of the *Gazette*. There followed a conversation[26] which revealed much about both men:

"You Mr. Edes, you John Gill and you Paul Revere, can you stand there three minutes?" asked Otis, in a conversation which John Adams noted in his diary.

"Yes," they answered.

"Well, do. Brother Adams, go along with me." Leading the way upstairs, Otis locked himself in a small office with John Adams and pummeled him with questions on the possible legal ramifications of a political attack he planned. He was going to concentrate on the improper granting of Crown salaries to provincial judges. What was Adams' opinion? Would this be contempt? The questions poured out, and Adams did his best to answer. When Otis was satisfied, he unlocked the door and thumped downstairs. On the first floor, when Adams, following, brought up a military matter, Otis retorted, "You'll never learn military exercises."

"Ay, why not?"

"That you have a head for it needs no commentary," said Otis, "but not a heart."

"Ay, how do you know—you never searched my heart," argued John Adams, caught by surprise by a conversation that had suddenly penetrated to personal analysis.

"Yes I have," Otis replied, "—tired with one year's service, dancing from Boston to Braintree and from Braintree to Boston, moping about the streets of this town as hipped as Father Flynt at 90, and seemingly regardless of everything but to get money enough to carry you smoothly through this world."

John Adams was deeply hurt. He prided himself in a soldier's fortitude and a talent for things military, and in fact he was to have a lifelong affinity for military organization and leadership.

"This is the rant of Mr. Otis concerning me," he concluded, "and I suppose of 2 thirds of the town." Magnifying the friendly but unnecessarily blunt comments of Otis, he worked himself into a rage. Why did Otis have to say such things, especially in the presence of others? "There is a complication of malice, envy and jealousy in this man, in the present disordered state of his mind, that is quite shocking."

At the town meeting it was decided to write a letter to the governor on the new salary arrangement, and the town approved the appointment of Adams, Otis, and Warren as a committee to petition Hutchinson in order to discover whether the rumors were true. Hutchinson tartly replied that this was no business for the Boston town meeting, but rather a matter for the Crown and the colonial government. An angered Samuel Adams again displayed his conviction that the people supported him: "If each town would declare its sense of these matters I am persuaded our enemies would not have it in their power to divide us."[27]

The town meeting, hearing Hutchinson's answer, voted another committee to petition him for a session of the General Assembly, implying that the representatives could then look into the matter of the Crown-paid salaries. On November 2 the governor's reply was read to the town meeting, now assembled for the third time in a week. Hutchinson said that Boston had no authority to request a session of the legislature, and for him to accede to such a request would establish an undesirable precedent. He would not call an assembly.

Under Samuel Adams' direction, the town voted that the governor's answer was unsatisfactory, and Adams seized the opportunity to move for the creation of a Boston committee of correspondence[28] "to state the rights of the Colonists and of this province in particular, as men, as Christians, and as subjects, to communicate and publish the same to the several towns in this province and to the world as the sense of this town, with the infringements and violations thereof that have been, or from time may be made— also requesting of each town a free communication of their sentiments on this subject." Adams had judged correctly the moment for such a move: the motion passed, and the committee of correspondence was born—though not without some pain. Some of the most influential men of Boston would have nothing to do with such a venture.[29] Of the Boston representatives to the General Court besides Adams, all declined membership on the committee: one by one, Cushing, Hancock, and Phillips insisted that "private business" would not allow their participation. They were followed by the refusals of three selectmen, Austin, Scollay, and Marshall—all merchants who, like Hancock, were tired of paying a heavy price in loss of business for the small political gains they could attribute to the popular party. Otis, however, had agreed to chair the committee, and eventually 21 men were willing to accept nomination. The end result placed the merchants in the minority on the committee, which set out immediately to produce a report to the Massachusetts towns. Adams was to write the "rights" portion of the letter to the towns; Joseph Warren would list the specific violations of the charter; Benjamin Church would compose an introductory letter. Adams, of course, was now fully in charge.

The idea of committees of correspondence was not new. It had long been customary in Europe and America for legislative bodies to employ committees to correspond with other governments or individual officials. Adams may have considered the idea several years earlier, in 1764, when he mentioned to James Warren in Plymouth his feeling that such a committee might serve as a basis for displaying a unity within the province that would cause the Crown to pay more attention to the welfare and the aspirations of Massachusetts colonials. In Virginia, Richard Henry Lee had suggested in 1768 that the House of Burgesses form a committee to open a continuous and systematic communication with the other colonies. Nevertheless, it was in Boston that the idea became a powerful political weapon for revolutionary action.

A town meeting was convened on November 20 to approve the letters. In what was to be his last significant political act, James Otis read the report of the committee of correspondence to the assembly.[30] His own contribution to the writing had been negligible, but he gave the effort his full support.

The paper he read was the statement by Adams on the rights of the colonists, a 6,000-word argument that is Adams at his persuasive best.[31] He began by lifting the argument to the highest philosophical planes, invoking Locke and the rights to life, liberty, and property as branches of the first Law of Nature. His paper is buttressed by footnoted references to Locke, to specific English laws, to the Massachusetts charter, and to Coke, Blackstone, Vattel, and the New Testament. His ability to project a religious conservatism and correctness was a powerful influence in his favor. He classified the colonists in three categories: they were men, they were Christians, and they were subjects of the king. As men, they possessed every natural right which they had not specifically ceded to society. As Christians, they had the right to free practice of religion for "all whose doctrines are not subversive of society" (eliminating thus all Catholics, since they put the Pope ahead of king). As subjects, the men of Massachusetts had a right to personal security, personal liberty, and private property. It is the relationship of the ruler to his subjects that Adams judged to be the most important of all, and here he made his philosophy clear:

> —the legislative authority may be *arbitrary* but it cannot be absolute. The law must be just, therefore a greater law must govern.
> —judges must be independent of the Prince and People, or justice cannot be dispensed.
> —no man can be taxed unless he is represented in the legislative decision-making. Since the province sends no members to Parliament, London has no more right to tax Massachusetts than it has "to choose an Emperor of China."

Self-government was dying in Massachusetts, he said, and with it would die a bustling trade, a healthy farm economy, a comfortable way of life, and a constitutional freedom that all Englishmen had earned the right to enjoy.

Many of the provincial towns were still dominated by loyalists and suspicious of the big city of Boston and its liberal ideas. Adams knew this and had built a message that was calculated to overwhelm any opposition that might be present in the meeting-houses where it would be read. The mind of Adams can be seen at work in the decision to give to the towns a careful list of almost undeniable "grievances" and to couch them in terms of timeless philosophy, sending the town meetings soaring out of their normal run of backwoods business. Even the use of a committee, rather than a single leader, lent an aura of consensus and did not seem overly authoritarian.

Adams ended his essay with a prediction: "The inhabitants of this country," he wrote, "in all probability in a few years will be more numerous than those of Great Britain and Ireland together," yet they are governed by indifferent and uninformed men 3,000 miles away. If those men will take our money in taxes, he warned, they will soon also become our landlords, "who will ride at ease, while we are trodden in the dirt." The final words were ominous: "How long such treatment will, or ought to be borne is submitted."

To this letter was appended Joseph Warren's list of specific violations of the rights of the colonists by the succession of acts of Parliament. Here Warren laid out with a lawyer's careful delineation the dozen actions that had troubled the provincials over the preceding decade: taxes, new and oppressive customs laws and commissioners, the presence of a military force, transferral of the General Court out of Boston, Crown salaries for provincial judges, the surrender of Castle William to the Regulars, the extension of the power of Vice-Admiralty Courts, restraints on local manufacture, the loss of the right of trial by jury. To these documents were added the exchange of correspondence between the town of Boston and Governor Hutchinson on the question of Crown salaries ("Thus gentlemen it is evident his excellency declines giving the least satisfaction as to the matter in request"). The introductory letter, written by Church and corrected in draft by Adams, served as a précis of the grievances.

The accompanying request did not ask for direct action and its attendant risks; it stated that people in England had been led to believe that the colonists were undisturbed by the late measures taken by the Crown and were told that any uneasiness was the work of the few designing radicals. The letter asked for "a free communication of your sentiments to this town, of our common danger." The towns, for full response, needed only to agree that the grievances were in fact legitimate. Adams knew that he was tapping a strong potential: there existed in Massachusetts a long tradition of intertown cooperation, especially in time of danger from Indian uprisings, ever since the beginning of the colony.

The town voted to accept the letter and have it sent to every other town and "elsewhere, as the Committee of Correspondence directs." Six hundred copies were printed. At first the loyalists laughed at the "foolish scheme" that was certain to make the radicals look ridiculous. Hutchinson commented, "You may judge of this committee by their chairman, who is but just now discharged from his guardian and is still once in a few days as mad as ever—the effect of strong drink." The court-party writers in Draper's *Gazette* insisted that the approval of the letter had been voted in a thin house in which "there was not twenty men present besides the gentlemen selectmen and some of the committee." Adams returned to the newspapers as Candidus, insisting that more than 300 were present for the approval and that the House thinned out only after that vote,[32] leaving to the remaining members the less significant discussion of the best method of sending the letter. Nevertheless there were misgivings among the radicals, many of whom felt they were risking their political futures on a cause that might well fail disastrously.

Responses to Adams' message to the towns began to trickle in, written in the plain and awkward prose of the old clerks, the words of simple men of the back towns who were to find themselves thrust into the limelight by the genius of Adams and elevated by his example. As replies of towns arrived, they were published in the *Gazette*. The town of Petersham called the payment of judges by the Crown a contribution fostering "a system of bondage equal to any ever before fabricated by the combined efforts of the ingenuity, malice, fraud, and wickedness of man." Marlborough prepared to defend itself "and regain, support, and secure our lives, properties, liberties, and privileges, civil and sacred; and that without any further delay." Gorham said, "It is better to risk our lives and fortunes in the defense of our rights, civil and religious, than to die, by piecemeal, in slavery." Roxbury noted the independence of the judges "a *most* dangerous innovation." By the middle of December, 80 of the 260 towns had replied.[33]

Adams remained the guiding hand. James Warren at one point wrote from Plymouth that he was trying to arrange for town meetings in his area, but that he feared most towns would refuse. *"Nil Desperandum,"* Adams told him. "That is a motto for you and for me."[34] A few days later Plymouth responded with a letter to Boston, announcing that, as in all times of difficulty and danger, "the worthy inhabitants [are] ready to assert the natural religious and civil rights . . . of all colonists in general and of this . . . united province in particular."

As the movement grew, the loyalists began to recognize the danger and change their tune. In January, Daniel Leonard wrote, "This is the foulest, subtlest, and most venomous serpent ever issued from the egg of sedition. I saw the small seed when it was implanted; it was a grain of mustard. I have watched the plant until it has become a great tree."[35] The violent response indicated how well the conservatives recognized that the provincial town committees of correspondence were serving their purpose. Adams had organized a network of associations and as it grew influential, it became the focal point of the radical effort, supplying a cohesion that had never been present in the other organizations from which it had grown—the solemn league, the Sons of Liberty, the Boston Caucus Club, and the Society of Merchants. The incoming letters from the towns opened a public dialogue in which the committee led the way, and the dialogue allowed the committee to bring in new points, keeping the pot boiling.

The town of Boston had become a battleground of words and even of violent acts, and the atmosphere of tension and hostility took its toll. John Adams after a single year in the House had retired to the country, convinced that his health could not withstand the continual stress. Hutchinson suffered a minor stroke and a nervous attack which he attributed at least in part to the pressures of his position. Otis, too, had driven himself hard and the strain showed. Although his powerful physique was able to withstand the punishment of a decade of battle in the law courts, legislature, town meetings, newspaper offices, and streets of Boston, his mind was failing.

Gray-headed and shaking, Adams was the opposite of Otis; his body weakened but his mind and will grew stronger. He looked a generation older than Otis although they were contemporaries.

The palsy that ran in his family had increasingly taken over control of his muscular system so that his head nodded constantly and the continual trembling of his hands made it difficult for him to write. When he saw a failing of the old power in Otis, he tried to fill the void with contributions of his own, but he was quick to recognize, as in the case of the Massachusetts Convention, that he still did not possess the charismatic influence of Otis in the House, in town meetings, or anywhere except in his writings. Then, with the abrupt decline of Otis after the Robinson fight, Adams found himself thrust into sole leadership of the Boston radicals.

PART IV

The Struggle Becomes War

20

Parliament and the Charter

January–May 1773

If I am wrong in my principles of government or in the inferences which I have drawn from them, I wish to be convinced of my error. Independence I may not allow myself to think that you can possibly have in contemplation. If you can conceive of any other constitutional dependence than what I have mentioned, if you are of opinion that upon any other principles our connection with the state from which we sprang can be continued, communicate your sentiments to me with the same freedom and unreservedness as I have communicated mine to you.

HUTCHINSON to the General Court, January 6, 1773

SEEING THE OVERWHELMING RESPONSE of the towns to Adams' *Rights of the Colonies,* Hutchinson realized that the conservatives of the backcountry towns were losing the control which for many years had allowed them to dominate the town meetings. Even during the times when the popular party had gained great strength, as in the land-bank problems of 1745 and the hard-money issue of 1747, when its representatives increased in the House, town government was little affected. But the times had changed, and the selectmen, instead of ignoring the letter from

Boston or pigeonholing it as Hutchinson expected, surprised him by calling for immediate town meetings to discuss the contents.

The responses from the towns gave the governor a chilling confirmation of the inroads that Adams' campaign of words had caused. In the published letters he could see a growing belief that Parliament had acted in an unconstitutional manner to steal the liberties of the province, and a conviction that the Massachusetts charter rights were beyond the power—and even the purview—of Parliament. This was what could happen, Hutchinson thought, when unlettered townsmen of no political experience fell under the influence of an unprincipled charlatan. In their ignorance they had been carried off by Adams and his theories. Well, they could be carried back again by the same tactic; he would explain to them in detail the law and the truth. He resolved to make a strong public response to Adams, a reply that would rally the province and reunite the towns under the banner of loyalty to the king and recognition of the supremacy of Parliament. In the fading weeks of 1772 he put his pen to paper, intending to present Parliament in its correct light and to show the good people of the province how they had been led astray by Adams and his committee of correspondence. Searching out his sources in the documents he had so carefully collected and published, he began to write and revise a refutation that would become his opening speech to the January session of the General Court.

He knew, of course, that his words would find their way to the press. Among his papers Hutchinson had his own accumulated writings, the anonymous tracts marking the occasions in earlier days when he had turned to the pen to fight back against opposition in the land-bank controversy, the hard-money issue, the writs of assistance, the fight over his seat in the council, and his efforts to moderate the impact of the whole series of Parliamentary acts bearing on the colonies and to enlighten the London view on questions of American trade, government, and politics. He had not won every battle, but his pen had served him well in all of them. Often his opposition had been Adams or, before him, Otis, and it was natural for him now to meet Adams on the familiar battleground of the newspaper columns. This time he sensed an opportunity to achieve a significant victory by taking the side of the constitution and rallying the people of the province to him. For once, he could turn the tables and put Adams in the wrong, forcing him to oppose the British constitution or be quiet.

Stopping the erosion of rural conservatism was only one of the reasons that led Hutchinson to build his opening speech of 1773 on the question of Parliamentary supremacy. He knew that he needed some new accomplishment—perhaps a successful campaign against the radicals—that would raise him in the eyes of the ministry in London and insure that his governorship would not be just an interim before the appointment of a man of rank from England. He had not sought this post all his life only to have Adams destroy it before his eyes. There was a hint of desperation in his decision, however; a failure in this effort would leave him no recourse—after the events just past, his back was to the wall, and his overconscientious mind was tormented by the thought that he had not done enough to merit the approbation of his superiors or even to support their policies in America. He had reached the point where he could no longer bear reading the Boston newspapers with all their extravagances. He was resolved to educate the people of the province—to "show them what their constitution was."[1] He would turn again to the activity which had brought him so much success in the past; he would sum up his side of the greatest controversy of his lifetime and lay it before the people of Massachusetts. Actually, for several months he had been mulling over in his mind the idea of a public statement in opposition to the trend and had given an indication of this in his speech proroguing the General Court in the summer of 1772.

Now he set the tenor of his approach to the question as one of reluctance to be drawn into a discussion of matters that ought to be clear to all, writing to England that it was much against his inclination to be so engaged.[2] Hutchinson's pen described the state of the province as disturbed and disordered by the machinations of dangerous men. He could not find, he said, in the annals of the past, any time that the supremacy of Parliament had ever been called in question, except for the anarchy and confusion preceding the restoration of the monarchy under Charles II. In the past seven or eight years, however, there had been a change, and the practices of a hundred years were under an attack that grew day by day in intensity. What was first whispered was now printed: the authority of Parliament was denied by many. It is now impossible, he said, to conceal what he wished might have never been made public. Those who repudiate the supreme authority of Parliament are "repugnant to the principles of the constitution" and have alienated the affections of the people from their sovereign—which makes them guilty of high treason.

The Massachusetts charter, Hutchinson wrote, assures the rights of the colonists as Englishmen, but by their voluntary removal from England they have relinquished certain rights, such as direct representation in legislative bodies. To object to this as too restrictive is equivalent to rejecting the idea of government. There cannot be two legislatures of equal power; this in effect would make two separate governments, as in the case of Scotland and England before the union. To carry such thinking to the absurdity of its extremes, this would make Massachusetts Bay a free and independent state, with the consequent loss of the protection that England had always provided. The province, isolated and vulnerable, would fall prey to one of the European nations. "Is there anything which we have more reason to dread," he asked, "than independence?"

Hutchinson ended with a reaffirmation of his conviction that there could be no exception to the power of Parliament. To allow weight to contrary interpretations of the law would destroy the government, he warned. Such problems as laws may sometimes create in their application can be dealt with through conventional means for redress. Then Hutchinson brought his argument to a close with a terse paragraph. When government is weakened, he wrote, those entrusted with power should omit nothing which will tend to strengthen it. The specific meaning of this would be something for his audience to contemplate. If I am wrong, Hutchinson wrote, "I wish to be convinced of my error." But if not, he said, there is much ordinary business to be done and these confusing and debilitating attacks against the constitution should be forgotten.[3]

The governor spoke these words to a full assembly on Wednesday, January 6, 1773, and then sat back to await the reply which he knew would be the first business of the council and the House.

In his judgment, the speech had gone well, a vindication "to all the world" of the primacy of Parliament. He had laid out in plain terms the authority of Parliament, and his countrymen now had the opportunity to see the issues clearly, to declare their loyalty to the Crown, and to prove that the Massachusetts radicals, however vocal, were confined to a small group of discontented Bostonians.

Hutchinson's speech, certainly the most significant of his political lifetime, would not be easy to counter. Adams not surprisingly was appointed to head a committee to produce a reply for the House. He gave the responsibility for a rapid first draft to Joseph Warren and searched beyond the committee for whatever other help he could enlist. His full use of available talent was so obvious that it led to mistaken rumors that Pennsylvania's John Dickinson of the *Farmer's Letters* received word by express rider that his pen was needed.

When Warren presented his draft, Joseph Hawley recommended that John Adams be consulted on improvements that might be made,[4] even though Adams was not a member of the House. Samuel Adams agreed, and gave the draft to his cousin, who pronounced it entirely too rhetorical, too flowery, and too full of vague democratic political theory. He constructed a solid array of hard reasoning backed by legal and constitutional authorities to replace the errant phrases,[5] and the committee approved his changes. For two weeks Samuel Adams and his committee wrote and edited the draft response, presenting it to the House on Friday morning, January 22. A reading of the paper was postponed until that afternoon so that more of the representatives could attend, and then Adams read it aloud, paragraph by paragraph.[6]

If the people were uneasy, as the governor said, it was because of their justifiable alarm over the recent acts of Parliament and the debates surrounding these acts. What the province wanted was the right to make its own laws as long as they were not repugnant to the laws of England. It was not the sense of the charter that Massachusetts would be subject to Parliamentary control.

The reply then turned to historical aspects of the question which had been addressed by the governor. Adams had read every word of the two volumes of the *History of the Province of Massa-chusetts-Bay* and he knew that Hutchinson the historian had been far more liberal, objective, and candid than Hutchinson the politician. He now concentrated on refuting the governor as he had done so often before, simply turning Hutchinson's own words back on him, holding up to the public his inconsistencies.[7] The *History* made clear, he said, that the founders of the colony had been assured "they were to be governed by laws made by themselves" and not by Parliament, and that the agreement specified that "no tax, tallage, assessment, custom, loan, benevolence, or imposition whatever shall be laid, assessed, imposed, or levied" on them. In the *History* jurisdiction of Parliament under the first charter was, said Adams, "very different from that which your Excellency in your speech apprehends it to have been."

Hutchinson the governor tells us, Adams said, that there is no line to be drawn between the supreme authority of Parliament and the total independence of the colonies. In that case, either the colonies are the vassals of the Parliament or they are totally independent. Since it could hardly have been the intention of the colonies to reduce themselves to a state of slavery, the logical conclusion is obvious. Since Hutchinson has stated it is impossible to have two independent legislatures in the same state, "May we not then further conclude that it was their sense that the colonies were, by their charters, made distinct states from the mother country?" Hutchinson had asked the rhetorical question, "Is there anything which we have more reason to dread than independence?" Adams answered *yes:* "There is more reason to dread the consequences of absolute uncontrolled power, whether of a nation or a monarch, than those of total independence."[8] He added that the governor seemed to want to draw a line of distinction between the supreme authority of Parliament and the total independence of the colonies. The General Court would not make such a broad proposal, so important to all the other colonies, "without their consent in congress." In making this statement Adams advanced the suggestion of a continental congress, its first appearance in an official document.

Adams had quoted Charles I, who had signed the original charter, and James I as his sources. Some members of the House asked for more detail on his research, and he agreed to provide more notes. On Tuesday, January 26, his paper was read again and unanimously approved. Adams printed it a week later in the *Gazette*, where he knew it would provide fuel for discussion throughout the winter. Most of the points Adams made were those he had been stressing for years, but never before had he been given such an important occasion, or such a foil, for the display of his convictions.

Hutchinson would have preferred to let his own speech stand, but the challenge of the House reply was too strong to be overlooked. He had to answer, and for three weeks he did little but sit again at his desk, working out a rebuttal.[9]

He began with a schoolmasterish warning that the House had built the logic of its argument on a foundation "that shall fail . . . in every part of it." He refused to accept the picture of British history set forward by Adams, making no reference to the support that Adams had found in the Hutchinson volumes. Instead, he chose other historical examples, pointing out that royal grants of colonial charters to men such as Ferdinando Gorges were afterwards repudiated by Parliament as monopolies. He accused the House of being "incautious" in their definition of terms, applying the word "realm" to mean "kingdom," when actually the ancient territorial realm meant only England, excluding Ireland, Wales, Calais, Guernsey, Jersey, Alderney, and the colonies. In this manner, he said, they had drawn false conclusions on a crucial point—the relationship of the plantations to the rest. True, they were not a part of the realm, but they were definitely part of the kingdom. This they "might easily have discovered" if they had looked in the statute books.

He then turned to the quotations that had been lifted from his history and arrayed against him. While this did honor to the book, he said, it did little justice to the author. He himself could have found passages more appropriate to the points in question that would have reconciled his present speech and his judgments on the past history of the colony. "My principles in government are still the same," he assured the House, "nor am I conscious that by any part of my conduct I have given cause to suggest the contrary."

Hutchinson presented his rebuttal to the assembly on February 16, and again Adams was picked by the House to prepare a new reply. The governor had accused the House of incautious expressions and poor research, indicating that Adams had misconstrued the passages used to support his key arguments. Samuel Adams knew he needed the support of lawyer John Adams, whom he now pressed back into service. In a hasty note to John he admitted that the possible incaution in the use of the word "realm" was his own, but based on research done by his cousin. "The assertion is *mine*," he said, "upon *your* authority. . . . Pray give me your aid in that as briefly as you please."

John Adams proved again that he could not be outmatched in his research, and when Samuel Adams presented a draft reply[10] to the House two weeks later, he could quote from "the Judges of England" to support his use of "realm": "If a King go out of England with a company of his servants, allegiance remaineth among his subjects and servants, although he be out of his realm, whereto his laws are confined." In this case, "realm" and "kingdom" were the same, and the words did not mean Old England. He again took up the attack against Hutchinson by quoting more instances of irreconcilable differences between Hutchinson's historical and political views. He had made large extracts already, he told Hutchinson, which showed the incongruous nature of some of the governor's current thinking. "We pray you again to turn to those quotations, and our observations upon them," he wrote, "and we wish to have your Excellency's judicious remarks." Following this with more excerpts from the books, Adams noted that Hutchinson apparently had changed his mind on several critical issues. The governor has explained away the legislative body of Massachusetts as a mere phantom, subject to the will of Parliament:

> Is this the constitution which so charmed our ancestors that, as your Excellency has informed us, they kept a day of solemn Thanksgiving to Almighty God when they received it?[11]

The exchange broke off at this point; Hutchinson dissolved the General Court four days after he received the response of the House, writing to Dartmouth that he did not intend to call the assembly together again.[12] He continued to insist that his opening speech had not suffered at all; that the replies left his words unchallenged. Stubbornly refusing to believe that the Massachusetts House could ever meet him on even terms in matters of political analysis, he asserted that many of the unpolished country members approved the words of Samuel Adams without a glimmer of understanding as to what was at stake. "I could not find any of them," he told his old friend Israel Williams, "who could give any account of the messages after they had voted them."[13] He said he was convinced that, all in all, his words had given new strength to the sagging court party.[14]

Hutchinson appeared to sense, however, that all had not gone well. Immediately after his second speech he wrote at least three letters within four days—to Mauduit, Gambier, and Montague—expressing in almost identical phraseology his rationale for having entered the controversy in the first place (he had to teach the people of the province the meaning of their own constitution). He seemed to be anticipating criticism from London for airing the problem of Parliamentary power in such an inflammatory situation. If he had done nothing in the face of Adams' concerted assault on Parliament, he said, his silence might have been construed as tacit approval of the anarchy and chaos in the General Court. John Adams, ever a careful watcher of Hutchinson, was amazed that the governor would challenge the Massachusetts House with these speeches supporting Parliamentary supremacy, adding to the fiery controversy already then raging. "His ruin and destruction must spring out of it either from the ministry and Parliament on one hand or from his countrymen on the other."[15] Whether he fully realized it or not, Hutchinson had no support in the inland towns beyond a few staunch loyalists who fought a grim battle for survival and who were of little use to him in any case. As an aristocrat who made no attempt to hide his conviction that the General Court already had too many representatives, as a politician who had been successful in blocking the creation of new towns solely in order to avoid the problem of new representatives, as the strongest proponent of hard money, he had become more a target than a leader.

Samuel Adams published the full exchange between the House

and the governor and sent it to the committees of correspondence of all the towns, asking for their "sentiments" on the subject. As for the messages of the House, Adams told the towns that their representatives had "thought it prudent to enter into the subject, but with caution, rather supporting the opinion of our ancestors, which appeared to us to be opposite to the sentiments of the Governor . . . than explicitly declaring our own." He would rely on his neighbors' judgments as to how well the representatives had acquitted themselves. Hutchinson read the pamphlet and passed it on to England. The published document, he insisted, showed that the responses of the House and council were "nonsensical" and did him no damage. In general, his defense of Parliament's power over the colony had settled the General Court and stopped the "contagion."[16]

But it was untrue. He had failed to convince the General Court; he had failed to stop the committees of correspondence and in fact had given strength to the movement; he had lost the most important debate of all. The defeat of Hutchinson marked the beginning of his sharp decline in influence and abruptly left Adams as the only political power in Massachusetts. The provincial committees of correspondence were solidly established and functioning—and responsive to Adams. For all his anonymity in the past, Adams—with Otis gone—was now the most well-known political writer in America. He had captured the spirit of revolution and he was the man most prepared to exploit it. In early May he wrote to Arthur Lee that America was ready to challenge England as never before. "I believe it will be hardly in the power even of that powerful nation," he said, "to hold so inquisitive and increasing a people long in a state of slavery." Adams had achieved the greatest victory of his political career. He returned to his work with the committees of correspondence, elated that there was "now a fairer prospect than ever of union."[17]

21

The Whately Letters

June–September 1773

He was, for nearly 20 years, a writer against government in the public newspapers; at first, but an indifferent one: long practice caused him to arrive at great perfection, and to acquire a talent of artfully and fallaciously insinuating into the minds of his readers a prejudice against the characters of all whom he attacked, beyond any other man I ever knew. This talent he employed in the messages, remonstrances, and resolves of the house of representatives, most of which were of his composition, and he made more converts to his cause by culminating governors, and other servants of the crown, than by strength of reasoning. The benefit to the town, from his defense of their liberties, he supposed an equivalent to his arrears as their collector; and the prevailing principle of the party that the end justified the means, probably quieted the remorse he must have felt, from robbing men of their characters, and injuring them more than if he had robbed them of their estates.

HUTCHINSON on Samuel Adams, February 19, 1773

IN EARLY 1773 Thomas Cushing received a package from Benjamin Franklin in London, and when he opened it, he knew that Hutchinson would not be governor of Massachusetts for very much longer. A number of Hutchinson's letters over the years—his thoughts on the state of the province and his recommendations for improvements—had been addressed to Thomas Whately, his friend and a member of Parliament; Hutchinson knew that by writing to Whately he would have an indirect influence on Grenville and possibly other members of the ministry since Whately, with appropriate discretion, would circulate the letters. He could thus write without his usual inhibitions and formality, and yet make his thoughts known in the inner circles.

By 1772, however, both Grenville and Whately were dead and the letters were in the possession of Sir John Temple. This staunch Whig showed the letters to Benjamin Franklin, who persuaded him to allow them to be sent to America for the perusal of a certain few influential figures in Boston. Hutchinson's correspondence, along with letters by Andrew Oliver and several other Boston conservatives, thus reached Cushing, who immediately showed them to Samuel Adams, John Adams, and several others. (Franklin paid for his actions; he lost his job as American postmaster general and suffered a famous and blistering denunciation in the Privy Council.)

For Samuel Adams it was the shock of confirmation of an old suspicion. Hutchinson's desire to limit American freedoms—his participation, as Adams saw it, in the plot to destroy the rights of the colonists—was at last documented.

The response of Adams was slow to develop. At first he merely complained that the agreement with Franklin made it impossible to release the letters to the public. It is a pity, he said, that "the most important intelligence is communicated with such restrictions as that it serves rather to gratify the curiosity of a few than to promote the public good."[1] John Adams responded to the letters in the same way, pouring forth on Hutchinson and the others a catalogue of adjectives ("cool, thinking, deliberate . . . malicious and vindictive as well as ambitious and avaricious"[2]) and lamenting, as did his cousin, that under the injunctions to secrecy the letters were of little advantage. He did, however, copy them out in his own hand, and he passed the word into the rumor mills by telling several of his associates and even a talkative aunt. He did not consider making the letters public, and when he heard the secret was leaking out through loyalist channels, he wrote in his diary, "I am glad it is not to be charged upon any of us—to whom it has been committed in confidence."

But Hutchinson's letters were too revealing, too damaging, too useful to stay long hidden. Although most of the passages were simply frank repetitions of the public views long expressed by the governor, there were other comments that he might well wish had never returned to Boston. Perhaps the most potentially inflammatory of all was an excerpt that became famous as his "abridgement passage."

> I never think of the measures necessary for the peace and good order of the colonies without pain: there must be an abridgement of what are called English liberties: I relieve myself by considering, that, in a remove from the state of nature to the most perfect state of government, there must be a great restraint of natural liberty: I doubt whether it is possible to project a system of government, in which a colony, 3000 miles distant, shall enjoy the liberty of the parent state: I am certain I have never yet seen the projection.[3]

Reading this, Samuel Adams must have been spurred to action, but he remained quiet on the letters throughout March and April, waiting for the upcoming session of the General Court. In the meantime he occupied himself with other concerns. On March 12 the Virginia House of Burgesses had approved a standing committee of 11 to correspond with the other colonies on the doings of Parliament. The measure was the work of Thomas Jefferson and his brother-in-law, Dabney Carr, along with Patrick Henry and Adams' friend, Richard Henry Lee. This news reached Boston April 10 and Adams wrote Lee that the committee of correspondence of the Massachusetts House, at a special meeting, voted to print enough copies of the Virginia letter for every town in the province.

The May elections were predictable, returning Adams, Cushing, Hancock, and Phillips from Boston to a House that, knowing little or nothing of the letters, was already overwhelmingly in opposition to the governor and determined to stop all incursions against the Massachusetts charter. Hutchinson, ever the fighter, was ready for the new assembly. When John Adams, who had not run for representative, was nominated by the House to fill a seat in the council, Hutchinson rejected him, recognizing that Adams was too articulate and now too radical to serve any purpose but obstruction of the king's administration. (When a friend commiserated with John Adams for having received this "check," Adams replied that it was not a check but a *boost*.)[4]

Hutchinson then tried to direct the House to the usual business of the day, but the representatives had other matters in mind. With copies of the Virginia letter spread throughout the province, they turned immediately to that subject and passed a motion resolving, "Whereas this House is fully sensible of the necessity and importance of the union of the several colonies in America," it would reappoint a standing committee of correspondence to communicate with the other colonies. Among its first acts, this committee wrote the assemblies of all the American provinces to say Massachusetts would "readily and cheerfully comply with the wise and salutary resolves of the House of Burgesses in Virginia." Adams now had created two levels of committees of correspondence—a network among the Massachusetts provincial towns and another connecting Massachusetts with the rest of the colonial assemblies. To Hutchinson the move was equal to an avowal of the independence of the colonies.[5]

As if this were not enough, Hutchinson later wrote, "There was another affair, which had a more direct tendency to alarm the people and which was managed with great art, and succeeded beyond all expectation."[6] Samuel Adams, in the weeks after the arrival of the Whately letters, had conceived a way to put them before the public. As more and more information concerning the letters spread through the town by word of mouth, he spurred the already enormous interest by continuing to insist on secrecy. Since the letters, if favorable to the province, would require no protection, the elaborate and mysterious treatment heightened the interpretation of them as essentially destructive. "They have buzzed about for three or four months a story of something that would amaze everybody,"[7] said Hutchinson; Adams was telling everyone he had 17 letters which subverted the constitution. Remembering how Bernard's letters had been used to discredit him,

Hutchinson was apprehensive when he heard that Adams intended to discuss the letters in the House, but he made no attempt to block consideration of them. To do so only would have increased their importance, making him appear afraid the letters would be damaging. Better to remain silent, he said, than to play into the hands of "the masters of the puppet show in the Council and House."[8]

His words were appropriate. On June 2, Adams took the floor and announced that, under heavy restrictions, the letters would be communicated to all the assembled representatives. The House galleries were cleared and the door locked. All the members were sworn to secrecy. Then, in a hushed and tense room Adams read excerpts from Hutchinson's words, carefully emphasizing the passages that called for limitations of the charter rights and stricter government in Massachusetts.

The result was devastating to Hutchinson. The House sent a message to him requesting that he comment on the authenticity of the letters and provide information about other writings. He refused to submit additional correspondence and denied that his letters were intended to be damaging to the province; on the contrary, he said, he had ever sought ways to better the relationship between the colony and the Crown. Regardless of his protestations, the reading of the letters and the subsequent new surge of rumors had the effect that Adams wanted: the pressure on Cushing to make the letters public was increased to the point that the Speaker had no other choice.

A way was found. Hancock, who was angered by comments made against him in the letters, proved to be amenable to a plan in which he would assert that he had been handed a copy of the letters while walking on the Common—thus indicating that the letters were already out on the streets. Then on June 10 all barriers fell. Hawley notified the House that Samuel Adams had conversed with the gentleman from whom he received the letters (Cushing) and could inform the House that "the said gentleman consents (as he finds that copies of said letters are already abroad, and have been publicly read) that the House should be fully possessed of them to print, copy, or make what other use of them they please." The House voted 101 to 5 that the letters tended to "subvert the constitution of the government and to introduce arbitrary power into the province" and that they should be sent to the press. Adams, not yet satisfied, moved for a statement from the House recognizing that for some time a plot had existed to destroy the charter. On June 16 he succeeded. The House resolved that

> it is manifest that there has been, for many years past, measures contemplated, and a plan formed, by a set of men, born and educated among us, to raise their own fortunes, and advance themselves to posts of honor and profit, not only to the destruction of the charter and constitution of this province, but at the expense of the rights and liberties of the American colonies.[9]

The "plot" was now an official fact. Adams at once moved for a petition to the king to remove Hutchinson and Oliver from office. The draft he wrote accused the governor and lieutenant governor of participating in "a combination of evil men" who sought personal gain at the expense of the colony. Both men, he said, also have attempted to alienate the affections of the king from the province (a charge that he knew had been leveled against himself and other radicals). He then outlined the list of grievances[10] that had become standard, concluding with the accusation that Hutchinson and Oliver were responsible for the bloodshed of the 1770 massacre. It would matter little that the petition would be rejected by Parliament and the king; Adams knew it would create a doubt in the minds of the Ministry concerning the continuing ability of Hutchinson and Oliver to be of service in carrying out Crown policy. The House approved the petition to the king 82–12, then voted to adjourn for three days. Adams sent a copy to Benjamin Franklin.

In a letter to Lord Dartmouth on June 26, Hutchinson described his difficult position and requested permission to take six to nine months' leave of absence, if necessary, to get out of Massachusetts and to defend himself in London. "I am almost worn out with four years' hard service," he told Bernard. "I was therefore meditating a retreat."[11] Adams, he said, was the "chief conductor" responsible for creating an issue on the basis of the letters. His guiding principle seemed to be that in politics his idea of the public good came before all other considerations "and every rule of morality when in competition with that may very well be dispensed with."[12] The end justified the means—that was Adams' way, said Hutchinson.

22

Tea

September–December 1773

While the Governor and other servants of the Crown were endeavoring to quiet the minds of the people, by removing whatever they had been brought to consider as a grievance, a plan was projecting in England, for raising greater disturbances in the colonies in general, to begin in Massachusetts-Bay, than had ever been known before.

THOMAS HUTCHINSON, writing in England after 1775

IT WOULD SEEM IMPOSSIBLE, after the setbacks of the salary fights, the debate on Parliament, and the publication of his letters, that Hutchinson still could believe that there were reasons for optimism—impossible if one did not know something of the Hutchinson mind. In the fall of 1773, after the buffeting he had taken, the indomitable governor looked for good signs and found them; he thought he could see the end of a phase in the political temper of the province. As he rode through the towns of Worcester County to complete his Supreme Court circuit, he was charmed and refreshed by the pastoral Massachusetts backcountry and everything came to look much better; in fact, he was "surprised to find the flame, which had spread so universally, so soon and so generally extinguished."[1] How could such a rapid change have

260

come about? Only through a general recognition of the falsity and extravagance of Adams and the radicals rather than any change in the minds of his countrymen. The fallacies of Adams' reasoning had destroyed Whig credibility, Hutchinson thought, reading the encouraging and sympathetic letters he had received "from the principal persons in this province as well as from gentlemen of the first character in other colonies" who had written to express their "detestation" of the actions of the Massachusetts assembly. The best American minds had made cool and considered assessments of the latest activity of Samuel Adams, and in their judgments the flash of radical political activity was dying out.

There was in fact some reason to be optimistic about the state of affairs. From the time of the massacre, nearly four years had passed with no major event to disturb the tranquility of the province. London had made no more of the earlier drastic mistakes; there had been no more repressive legislation. Barring the recent problems, which after all were now past, this had been the longest trouble-free period since 1760. A good indication of a growing impotence in the ranks of the radicals, Hutchinson thought, was the failure three weeks earlier of an attempt to stir up trouble on the anniversary of the Stamp Act riot of 1765.[2] Adams and John Hancock harangued the usual gathering of the Boston rabble, but the mob was small and the rest of the radical leadership was noticeably absent. These signs of declining strength told Hutchinson he had weathered yet another series of attacks. Perhaps, after all, the worst was over.

Adams, on the contrary, saw the period not as a backsliding of the popular party but as a time of waiting. He had made the most of Hutchinson's mistakes, with the result that the committees of correspondence were in being, uniting the province behind Boston's leadership. He was free of the Boston merchants; the power and backing once supplied by them had been replaced—and magnified a hundredfold—by the network of town committees and its intercolonial parallel. The petition for the removal of Hutchinson and Oliver was on its way to the king, with copies out to the whole Atlantic coast, along with the now infamous letters of Hutchinson to Whately. Adams was ready to put the potential for

united action to a test, and his aim was to drive Massachusetts—
and hopefully the rest of America—beyond the turning point in
the confrontation with London. To do this he needed a new rallying point, one which would convince even the most reluctant
patriot that there were only two roads—one to independence, the
other to slavery.

From their opposite points of view both Adams and Hutchinson turned all their efforts to the same question, the path for
Massachusetts in the immediate weeks ahead. Hutchinson resolved to make new efforts to ameliorate the sore spots concerning
trading restrictions and taxes. He tried to explain to Dartmouth
that conciliation had to be the watchword, not realizing that—to
a certain extent as a result of his own letters and reports—harsh
decisions had been made in England that would destroy all his
efforts to calm the province.

In London a problem that had been growing for several years
finally came to full fruition. The East India Tea Company was
about to collapse.[3] This vast enterprise, in which the British
government was deeply involved, had a surplus of tea which
poor management had allowed to grow to 8,500 tons, some of
which had been stored in English warehouses for as long as seven
years. The company's American market was suffering badly because of large-scale smuggling, which even the drastically increased customs activities had not been able to stop. The only
solution was to find a way to undersell even the smugglers—and
this was what the company now suggested.

Under the existing system, the East India Company sold tea
at auction to London merchants, who then sold part of it to
American merchants—who sold to the American retail shopkeepers. The company wanted to eliminate the British and American
middlemen by taking over the role of shipping and wholesaling
the tea for America. The savings in profit-taking could then provide for a price low enough to undersell any competitor, legal or
illegal. On May 10, 1773, Parliament capitulated to business
pressures and passed the Tea Act, allowing the East India Company to export tea directly to America. The three-penny-per-
pound tax on tea, however, would remain. With the new low
cost—half the price which a Londoner had to pay for his tea—the
Americans were not expected to complain.

The merchants on both sides of the water were to bear the losses under this arrangement. In Boston, tea was the top seller of all imported commodities, with an average of 130,000 pounds of dutied tea a year unloaded officially at the docks, in addition to a large but unknown amount that was smuggled into the town. The merchants realized that the impact on their businesses would be catastrophic. The most obvious point was that they would lose all profits of the tea trade, but that was only the beginning. The new legislation created a monopoly which would give the East India Company control of the merchandising and allow it to set whatever price it wished. If the company could retail tea, it could also be expected to bring pressure on Parliament to allow it to retail silks, drugs, and other commodities, items which the "tea" company had been selling for years. And if the East India Company could take over American merchants' roles, then other British companies would covet the same kind of operation, and soon American merchants would be out of business.

At this point the merchants, who had seen no reason for continuing nonimportation or for supporting Adams in his fight against Hutchinson, found themselves in need of help, a situation which Adams was not the last to see. Where appeals to abstract ideals had failed time and again, he now noted that simple economics could drive them back into his camp. He responded with all his energies to their appeal and took them in; the price he exacted would become apparent only later. The Adams machine —for now it could be described as such—went to work. The provincial and intercolonial committees of correspondence considered the tea issue. The radical *Gazette* writers began their articles. Preparations were made to bring the matter to the General Court. Adams reached out with letters to his correspondents in the other colonies and in England. The Sons of Liberty made their plans. A Boston town meeting was called to discuss the new development.

Loyalist writers tried to point out that the American merchants were dredging up every argument but the real one, which was that they would be cut out of a lucrative enterprise. This fact was overwhelmed by scores of articles playing on the fear that the East India Company, once established as the sole vendor of tea, would raise prices; that the example would bring pressure on Parliament from other British merchants for more of these projects; that such manipulation would result in an economic depression; that the company would grow to dominate American port operations; that its record of inefficiency, mismanagement, and duplicity in India would be repeated with even graver consequences in America. ("They have levied wars, excited rebellions, dethroned princes.")[4] Other arguments conjured up Americans as a new race of slavish "hewers of wood and drawers of water" under the company, which would come to control all manufacture, as it did in India, leaving only menial tasks for the "natives." Even the rumor that tea was an unnatural and unhealthy drink now came into the catalogue of reasons to reject this new move of Parliament.

What did *not* come up was the argument that the new arrangement was another assault on the colonials' right to tax themselves. At first it was not understood that the tea was to bear a tax; in fact, it was assumed there would be no tax. The opposition was based on the monopoly issue; even without the question of a tax, the events that followed in America probably would have taken place. It is attributable to the genius of Adams that he was later able to create and sustain the myth that the battle over tea was a battle over taxes.

Hutchinson's response to the growing crisis was complicated and weakened by his direct personal involvement in the merchandising of tea. Although he had turned his import-export business over to his sons, Thomas and Elisha, he kept abreast of the market and knew this trade very well, as his letters attest. Now his two sons had been named agents and consignees of the East India Company, along with his nephew, Richard Clarke. Parliament had strengthened Sam Adams' hand: the chosen few were heavily loyalist and the name Hutchinson was at the forefront.

At two o'clock in the morning of November 2, there was a pounding at the door of Hutchinson's mansion on Garden Court Street. Hutchinson's son, Thomas, awakened, came down to find a note from the Sons of Liberty requiring him to be at the Liberty Tree at noon of that day in order to repudiate his tea commission. As day broke there were printed handbills "at almost every corner" calling for a meeting of all freemen of the port and the neighboring towns under the Liberty Tree at noon, to hear and accept the resignations of the tea consignees.

The town was alive with anticipation of another spectacle but the crowd that gathered found that neither the Hutchinsons nor any of the other tea merchants were available. A committee was appointed to visit the recalcitrants and impress them with the need to be present on the following day, and on that afternoon the handbills announcing the news of a new meeting for the next day ended with the words, "Show me the man that dare take this down."[5]

The second meeting also fizzled, and the disappointed mob could only vent its anger on the house and shop of Richard Clarke, breaking windows and inflicting minor damages. The courage of the Hutchinsons had triumphed, and the radical cause suffered an embarrassment. Hutchinson knew, however, that there would be more to come. In a letter to Dartmouth he attributed the worsening situation to the work of Adams, who frustrated every conciliatory move. The art and skill of this one man, he said, prevents any good effect of government, "sometimes by exercising his talents in the newspapers . . . at other times by an open opposition . . . in the House, where he has defeated every attempt as often as any has been made."[6]

In the meantime, Boston was looking far more timid than the other colonies. The Sons of Liberty in New York and Philadelphia sent letters to Boston in late October, enclosing resolves that called the new duties on tea a tax imposed without consent, aimed at producing revenue which would support the extra Crown officials in America. The letter warned that anyone who helped unload tea was an enemy to America. Goaded by these reports, Adams and the Sons of Liberty called for a town meeting and this time there was no objection by the merchant-selectmen. The meeting was held on November 4 and 6, with Hancock moderating. It adopted the Philadelphia resolutions and voted that no tea would be imported into Boston—while on the other side of the Atlantic merchant ships of the East India Company prepared to sail from England for Boston, New York, Philadelphia, and Charleston, carrying a total of 600,000 pounds of tea.

In the meantime, Adams kept the pressure on. There was an

ominous move on November 17 after a ship arrived with word
that it had observed the merchantman *Dartmouth*, loaded with
tea and anchored at London, ready to sail for Boston. The tea
ship could not be far behind. The news was hurried through the
town, and that night for the second time in two weeks a mob
surrounded Hutchinson's mansion, demanding the appearance
of son Thomas and threatening to wreck the house.[7] A servant
announced that he had gone to his father's home in Milton
(which was true) and the mob dispersed, leaving the Hutchinson
family thoroughly frightened by the grim reminder of other
days. That same night, tea merchant Richard Clarke was not so
lucky. His house again received the brunt of the attack, suffering
damage from flying bricks and cobblestones. He and some of the
other tea consignees moved to Castle William to avoid further
attacks, and the wait began for the arrival of the first tea ships.

British maritime law required any ship entering port with
cargo destined for that port to pay duties on its cargo within 20
days or face confiscation; in other words, once the tea ships entered Boston Harbor, they would be committed to unload the
tea. This was a problem Hutchinson hoped to avoid. He therefore told Admiral Montague to stop the first tea ships down in the
harbor, well off from the docks, until the issue of acceptance of
the tea was settled. On November 27, ten days after the warning
of its arrival, the *Dartmouth*, first of the four tea ships which
had left London destined for Boston, anchored as directed by
Admiral Montague well down the harbor. Adams saw the meaning of this maneuver and did not intend to allow it to succeed.
Placards appeared, announcing a joint meeting of the towns of
Boston, Dorchester, Roxbury, Brookline, and Cambridge, to
"arouse all the towns" over the coming of the tea, and on the
29th Boston blossomed with posters announcing a meeting in
Faneuil Hall to plan a united resistance to "the detested tea
. . . the last, worst and most destructive measure of administration." At that meeting the town voted to order Francis Rotch,
the *Dartmouth*'s owner, to have his ship tie up to Griffin's Wharf,
where it would be guarded by 25 armed men to see that it was
not unloaded. Hutchinson told Rotch to comply. The ship was
then registered with customs in order to unload other goods

which it carried in addition to the tea, thus beginning the 20-day period allowed for compliance with the law. Hutchinson saw this as an opportunity to force the issue. The ship would have to be unloaded or delayed beyond the 20-day limit, in which case he would have the Regulars unload the cargo—then it could be sent to its proper destination, the consignees. Either way, Adams would lose. The ship was at the dock and the line was drawn, and violence could be averted only if Adams or Hutchinson backed down.

As the days passed with no move to unload the ship, Hutchinson could see the showdown coming. On December 2 he wrote Lord Dartmouth that the Sons of Liberty ought to be called the "Sons of Violence,"[8] and a week later he told William Palmer, "A fatality seems to attend the tea concern."[9] He felt that without this new problem of the tea he could have weathered very well the matter of the Whately letters, which he now saw as creating the opposite effect that Sam Adams had intended. Indeed, he said, there were some who thought he might become a popular governor. But now two other tea ships arrived, the *Eleanor* and the *Beaver*. These also were tied up at Griffin's Wharf, the total cargo of tea amounting to 342 chests, valued at £18,000 sterling. Since the *Dartmouth* had arrived first, the question would hinge on that ship. Hutchinson had made his decision and he was determined not to let the *Dartmouth* sail without unloading her cargo. On December 14 he ordered Colonel Leslie, now commander of Castle William, to insure that the cannon were loaded and aimed to cover the narrow slot through which any ship would have to pass to reach the open sea. Also at Hutchinson's request, Admiral Montague ordered his warships the *Active* and the *Kingfisher*, which had been laid up for winter, to "fall down to guard the passages out of the harbor."[10] No ship would put to sea without written permission of Thomas Hutchinson. Then on Thursday, December 16—the nineteenth day for the *Dartmouth* —the governor retired to his Milton home, a gesture which he hoped would show Adams that he did not intend to negotiate. Hutchinson was confident that, in the last resort, the tea was safe: the town merchants, as men of property, would not allow it to be damaged.

In the late afternoon of Thursday, December 16, tension in the town was near the breaking point as 8,000 people crowded around the Old South Church in a cold, drizzling rain to hear whether or not the governor would allow the tea ships to leave Boston. Francis Rotch was called forward once again and asked whether he planned to unload the tea or—as the people desired —clear his ship out of the harbor. Rotch said he wanted the ship to leave, but he dared not try to run the castle and take the risk of being blown out of the water by Leslie's guns. He agreed to go to see the governor and make one last attempt to get permission to sail.

While the swelling crowd waited for Rotch to return from Milton, Josiah Quincy took to the podium and in a burst of rhetoric predicted an oncoming war: "I see the clouds which now rise thick and fast upon our horizon, the thunder roll, and the lightning play, and to that God who rides the whirlwind and directs the storm I commit my country." It was to this kind of atmosphere that Rotch returned just after sunset to tell the crowd that Hutchinson had refused to grant him permission to leave. By prearrangement, Samuel Adams made the comment the mob was waiting for: "This meeting can do nothing more to save the country." Moments later the captain of the *Dartmouth* watched stoically as the mob, in hasty Indian disguises, surged down Griffin's Wharf to his gangplank. The leaders clambered up and demanded lanterns and keys to his holds. Without a word he complied, as did the captains of the other two ships; resistance would have been useless. The crews stood by helplessly as chest after chest was hauled up and emptied over the side. In the darkness 500 yards away, British warships rode quietly at anchor.

Among the "redskins" on that night were at least 15 of the town's principal merchants—men who a few weeks earlier were determined not to become involved in any more of Adams' Boston mobbishness. The price of Adams' support against the East India Company was now clear—many merchants who had been fence-sitting were now physically as well as morally committed along with the rest of the province to a course that could lead only to a major confrontation with Parliament. The incident created an unprecedented spirit of defiance in Boston and in effect turned the province over to the control of Adams. As if to indicate the shift of power, all the justices who before had staunchly insisted they would accept salaries from the king now changed their minds and publicly refused to take the money. "Adams," said Hutchinson sadly, "never was in greater glory."[11]

23

The Port Bill

January–July 1774

> You cannot imagine the height of joy that sparkles in the eyes and animates the countenances as well as the hearts of all we meet on this occasion, excepting the disappointed, disconcerted Hutchinson and his tools.

SAMUEL ADAMS, 1774

SAMUEL ADAMS COULD AFFORD to gloat over his success in stopping the tea, foiling Hutchinson, defying London, and moving the colonies along the road to union and independence. He had based his effort to create the committees of correspondence on his belief that the people of Massachusetts, if given the opportunity, would overwhelmingly reject the court party and the course that Parliament had taken. And in this the towns were beginning to prove him right. From Plymouth on the South Shore, from Marblehead and Newburyport along the North Shore, from the close-in towns of Cambridge and Charlestown, and from Worcester County in the west replies poured in until nearly every Massachusetts town was represented.

Now that he had made a decisive move in destroying the tea, Adams knew that he could not simply sit still and await the reaction of London. He first had to make sure that those who were calling for reimbursement to England for the tea were silenced and that the province—and especially Boston—presented a unified stand on the issue.

The committees of correspondence were perfectly suited for Adams, fitting his political view that the people needed only a forum to show how displeased they were with the existing situation. As an organization the committees were calculated to avoid the image of leadership from the top down (Adams carefully kept his name in the background and allowed no other personalities to stand out in the movement) and to give credence to the "grass-roots" nature of the effort. Tactically the committees were complementary to his method of operation, which emphasized the written and recorded word over oratory and concentrated on backstage negotiation and careful planning for all "spontaneous" action. Psychologically the organization allowed him to use his knowledge of people and his remarkable sense of the aspirations of the provincial townsmen and Boston mechanics. The committees, like Adams himself, were essentially reactionary: they responded to particular, concrete events and their prime concern was the preservation of traditional political arrangements against the inroads of change. This basically conservative element accepted Adams now, having rejected him ten years earlier, because the times—not Adams—had changed: these country townsmen, now educated by him, could see their privileges and prosperity slipping away, and they were determined to preserve their "charter rights." Whether their stand would lead to revolution was not yet a question to them, though the more perceptive of them realized that Adams had already turned that corner.

In many ways, the committees finally made up for the loss of Otis, providing Adams with an exchange of ideas and information within the province and, in fact, throughout the other colonies as he moved from reform toward revolution. His extensive correspondence with Richard Lee, John Dickinson, Elbridge Gerry, Silas Deane, Joseph Hawley, and Arthur Lee gave him sounding boards for his philosophy.

In London, Lord Dartmouth did what Adams could have

hoped he would do. This statesman who enjoyed a reputation for objectivity and coolness, a man well liked in the colonies, now became the implacable vigilante. He proposed a drastic response to the destruction of the tea, recommending the port of Boston be closed to all traffic until the tea was paid for. His arbitrary and extralegal display of naked power satisfied London's need for revenge but showed how the lack of men of stature was affecting colonial relations. In a government controlled by mercantile interests, the Dartmouth solution was quickly accepted.

The king was infuriated, and in his anger he had more agreement in Parliament than ever before. Early in the year the first of several retaliatory bills was drawn up, beginning with the Boston Port Act, which closed the port to all shipping effective June 1. The bill transferred Boston customs activities to Marblehead and moved the government administration to Salem, which became temporarily the province capital. The port would be reopened when the East India Company, the customs officers, and others who had suffered damages from mob action were reimbursed, and when trade and customs could be carried on correctly. Even then only a few wharves would be permitted to accept cargo. Boston was to be killed as a commercial center.

The Sons of Liberty responded to news of the bill by attacking the nearest representative of the Crown, who was, of course, Thomas Hutchinson. In early February the *Gazette* published a vicious assault against him, covering nearly the whole front page of the newspaper and calling him the most malignant and insatiable enemy of his country. Hutchinson had done more mischief, the writer declared, and had "committed greater public crimes than his *life* can repair or his *death* satisfy."[1]

The moderating influence was gone. Otis remained in Boston under the eye of his brother, Samuel. He was not so troublesome of late, Samuel wrote to Joseph Otis in Barnstable, and behaving decently enough in town, but there were signs. Then in a quick confession Samuel blurted out, "I know not what to do with him," telling Joseph in a groping sentence that James really needed to be "kept."[2]

Samuel Adams, who never tried to establish with any other radical figure the partnership he had known with Otis, and who continued alone as the leader of Boston's resistance, now searched for new ways to maintain the momentum he had created with the committees of correspondence, the Sons of Liberty, and the popular party. He had engineered the petition requesting the removal of Hutchinson and Oliver, but he knew that, aside from the propaganda value of the petition, nothing would be gained. He needed something new, and he quickly accepted an idea from John Adams. Since a few recalcitrant justices within the province still stubbornly planned to take their salaries from the king, regardless of the conflict with the province charter, the only recourse, said John Adams, was to impeach them all in the General Court. Intrigued, Samuel Adams asked the advice of Joseph Hawley, who said that the idea had possibilities. Hawley then spent a weekend with Judge Trowbridge, the only Supreme Court justice who had refused the Crown salary. Trowbridge reluctantly agreed that, legally, an impeachment was possible under the charter. Samuel Adams decided to go ahead, making Chief Justice Peter Oliver the prime target.

A committee of the House, led by Hawley, began to prepare the articles of impeachment. John Adams, though not a member of the House, continued to be instrumental in arranging the legal details and providing appropriate sources, working with Hawley and other members, who met evenings at his office to discuss the legal ramifications. At one point during this series of meetings Benjamin Gridley met John Adams on the street. "Brother Adams," he said, "you keep late hours at your house: as I passed it last night long after midnight, I saw your street door vomit forth a crowd of senators."[3]

Discussion of the articles of impeachment was completed in the assembly by February 28, and the House quickly voted 92–8 to impeach Oliver. Hutchinson, knowing that his presence was required in order for the council to pass on the impeachment, refused to attend the session. When Samuel Adams, as clerk of the House, began to read the motion of the House to "your Excellency and Honorable Council," a council member interrupted to point out that the governor was absent. Adams answered that the governor was the head of the council and could be "presumed" to be present whenever the council met.[4] He continued to read, and later entered into the record that the impeachment was read "before the Governor and Council." The council refused to act on the impeachment, but that was almost immaterial. Adams had what he wanted—another document that could be placed in the machinery of the committees of correspondence and also sent on its way to England. Though Hutchinson did all he could to stop it, the impeachment vote "remained on the journals of the House, was printed in the newspapers, and went abroad to the world."

Samuel Adams tried to keep the talents of his valuable cousin at work, but John Adams in those days was a hard man to pin down. When Samuel tried again to get him to speak at the annual massacre oration, John repeated his earlier refusals. One reason, and a strong one, was that John Adams disbelieved in this kind of crude political show, which was far removed from the sober style of the massacre trials. But the main reason for his elusiveness was that he still did not know in which direction he ought to aim his energies. Although Samuel Adams could sometimes enlist his aid in the political activities of the province, especially if there were interesting legal questions, John Adams was not yet a committed man, for all his acerbic commentary on Hutchinson; he was still searching for the best way to employ his talents. At one point he thought seriously of preparing a history of the conflict between England and America. "Let me ask my own heart. Have I patience and industry enough?" he wrote in his diary in March.[5] Industry and patience he certainly had, and he expended it all that winter on painstaking research into the legal bases under which the province claimed "lands to the westward of New York" (now Vermont). This study became a lengthy manuscript which John Adams later in life insisted was lost by Samuel, who had borrowed it to read.

Thomas Hutchinson now wanted to go to England, to leave the province, if not for good, at least until times changed. But with Lieutenant Governor Andrew Oliver ailing, he had no one who could take his place. Then, early in March, Oliver died. He had been considered one of the leading proponents of a stronger control over the provincial government and was believed by many to be a member of the "cabal" which planned to ruin the province for personal gain. He was a solid, singleminded loyalist whose disdain for the mobbish Bostonians had long been evident, and his enemies crowded in on him to have the last word. His funeral turned into a disgraceful affair which marked the seamy side of the popular movement. A mob followed the cortege, hooting Oliver to his grave and even giving three cheers as, in the presence of a grieving family, his body was lowered into the ground.

Andrew Oliver's surviving brother, Peter, now ran into more trouble. His impeachment as chief justice had been rejected, but since the House had approved the motion, Adams insisted Oliver had no right to try cases in Superior Court. Under pressure from the Sons of Liberty, juries of the province refused to sit while Oliver presided, thus closing down the court.

April ended with no word from England on the tea. "Still! Silent as midnight!" John Adams wrote,[6] while all waited for the next ship from England. On May 10 it came, and the shocking news was to Samuel Adams a clear example of "Hutchinsonian vengeance." The merchant ship *Harmony* brought the Port Bill and the word that Gage would become acting governor while Hutchinson went to England "to report on the state of affairs."[7] No ship would be allowed to enter the harbor after June 1. Those merchantmen still in port on that date would be given two weeks to depart. Three days later, as General Gage's ship dropped anchor in the harbor, a Boston town meeting decided to act for Massachusetts. With the concurrence of eight adjoining towns, Boston ordered its committee to send a circular letter to the other colonies, giving details of the port closure and asking the questions, Do you consider Boston as now suffering in the common cause of America? May Boston count on your suspending trade with Great Britain?[8]

The extraordinary appeal of this letter shows the ability and sensitivity of Samuel Adams. The bombastic, emotional prose of the newspapers and the angry recriminations of the House of Representatives gave way to an understated, simple Massachusetts homespun: "The more thinking part of those who have hitherto been in favor of the measures of the British government look upon it as not to have been expected, even from a barbarous state." Gage conferred with Hutchinson and the members of his council at Castle William on Saturday, May 14; meanwhile, the committee of correspondence met all day at the request of Samuel Adams in the Representatives' Room of the Town House to prepare copies of the letter, the town's resolutions, and the legislation from Parliament.[9] Paul Revere was commissioned to ride down the coast to New York and Philadelphia with the papers.

Samuel Adams had carefully nurtured his connections in the towns of Marblehead and Salem, and his effort now paid dividends. Both towns, although they stood to benefit greatly by receiving all the commercial activity formerly centered on Boston, emphasized their support for the provincial capital. Marblehead's merchants signed a letter inviting the merchants of Boston to use their docks and warehouses free of charge.

Tuesday, May 17, was a wet, gray New England day. All arrangements to receive the new governor had been made, however, and Gage stepped ashore at Long Wharf. The ships' cannon salutes were muffled in the rain-swept harbor as the Boston Cadet Regiment, John Hancock commanding, escorted the general past an honor guard of Regulars formed along King Street below the Town House. Gage had unequivocal permission from Dartmouth to employ his troops "with effect" in the event of further disturbances, and he also carried orders to find the persons guilty of destroying the tea and to punish them.

The annual elections came in the middle of this activity and the Caucus Club met to vote that the "same representatives as last year" should be chosen at the upcoming town meeting. With this backing, the Boston slate of Samuel Adams, Cushing, Hancock, and Philips received almost unanimous approval. In what had become a ritual, John Adams was elected by the House to the council on May 26, only to be vetoed by Gage. The new governor rejected a total of 13 names proposed by the House, but accepted James Otis, Sr., who, he felt, would be pliable enough because of the old man's evident willingness to compromise in order to keep his political power. Two days later he ordered the session closed, announcing it would reopen on June 7 in Salem.

Replies to the Massachusetts committee of correspondence began to arrive from the cities to the south, but they proved less encouraging than expected. In New York the merchant faction took charge immediately and resolved to "postpone active measures"[10] to some later date. Word of the New York position arrived in Boston in the last week of May, along with the news from Philadelphia that discussion of the matter would be deferred to the Pennsylvania provincial convention in late July. New Jersey's message was equally noncommittal. At this point, the merchants began to fear that they had gone too far with Samuel Adams. They tried to influence the town meeting of May 30 to consider payment for the tea, and they followed this with a letter to Hutchinson offering compensation. Then, when in June it became evident that the other American port cities were not prepared to stop importation, the Boston merchants reneged and broke the boycott.

British Navy ships had been arriving in Boston almost every day during the latter part of May, and the siege aspect of the harbor became quite evident. Admiral Montague's flagship, the *Captain*, dropped anchor just off Hancock's Wharf, while the gunships *St. John* and *Canceau* blocked the harbor and the Charlestown ferry way. The *Tartar*, the *Lively*, the *Magdalen*, and the *Tamur* rode in the channel from Castle William toward the open sea, and the *Mercury* and the *Halifax* watched the north and south flanks of the outer harbor.[11] The port closed on the first day of June; the 500 ships that entered Boston each year would now have to find dockage in Salem or Marblehead. The last ship to leave, the merchantman *Rose*, threaded her way past the men-of-war and into the channel, carrying Thomas Hutchinson and his family to England. He had remained in Milton to the very last moment, unwilling to leave his beloved hilltop home for the long journey into an unknown future. For 37 years to the day, he had been a part of the Massachusetts political scene. He had fought on alone at the end, in an impossible situation, powerless, blocked at every turn, but constant in his belief in eventual success and vindication. He had weathered the storm of James Otis, but Samuel Adams had destroyed him.

Adams in his moment of victory faced the combined pressure of the British men-of-war in the harbor and the clamor of the Boston merchants for capitulation. He chose to fight, pitting the

committees of correspondence against the merchants, asking
the people of Massachusetts to support a *Solemn League and Covenant.* Echoing in its title the Cromwell days, the covenant was
conceived by Adams in the Boston committee but made to appear as a spontaneous act of the country towns. Adams circulated
the draft quietly to the provincial town committees in early June,
requesting signatures on an agreement to refrain from the purchase and use of British goods after the first of October, four
months away.

While the town committees read his letter, Adams turned his
attention to the upcoming Continental Congress in Philadelphia.
He worked carefully, realizing that Gage would dissolve the
House immediately if it made any move toward electing representatives for the congress. He first had himself elected chairman
of a nine-man committee to prepare a message on the state of the
colony. Taking care to isolate loyalist sympathizers such as Daniel Leonard, he worked behind the scenes to gather support until
he was sure of a good majority. The court party, in the midst of
an effort to put a motion on the floor advocating payment for
the tea, did not notice the nightly meetings in which Adams constructed the support for a vote for the delegates. On June 17,
Adams came out in the open. Locking the doors of the House to
keep out Secretary Thomas Flucker, who had been sent by Gage
with orders to close the session, Adams presented a slate: John
Adams, James Bowdoin, Robert Treat Paine, Thomas Cushing,
and himself as the men who would go to the Philadelphia congress to consult upon wise and proper measures to be recommended to all the colonies for "reclaiming their rights and liberties." The five delegates were approved by a vote of 117–12,
and Adams then gave up the key to the main door, allowing
Gage's messenger to dissolve the assembly.

By June 27 the merchants had learned enough about the covenant then circulating in the towns to try to vote for its censure in
the Boston town meeting. Adams was ready for the showdown,
however. He gave up his seat as moderator to step down on the
floor as the primary speaker in defense of the committee. In two
days of debate he staved off all attempts to throttle the new action. In the end, Adams triumphed by a large majority and the

covenant received, instead of a censure, a vote of confidence. The merchants could do no more than send around a protest displaying 129 signatures. Town after town approved the covenant, with the Worcester town meeting even voting a change which would make nonimportation effective two months early—in August rather than October. This caught on and quickened the pace; the new boycott grew popular enough to be approved by the Massachusetts Provincial Congress when it assembled in the fall.

Adams had defeated the merchants in their attempt to regain the position they had enjoyed a few years earlier. The closing of the port destroyed the political power of the old Merchants' Society, and it is symbolic that its last significant effort was an assault on the committees of correspondence, the new power that had replaced it. Adams had used the merchants in a way that Otis never did, cajoling some and intimidating others. He had taken the town meeting away from them; to get what he wanted he was not adverse to building up the old antagonisms between the Boston merchants and the countryside which James Otis in the early 1760s had torn down. The merchants had tried to control Adams, but they were not willing to pay the price. This was a mistake: Adams by now had made sure he was not tied to the merchants as Otis had been; he knew they wanted only liberalization of the trade laws, while he wanted economic warfare. When they finally saw his aims and balked at nonimportation, he by then had other options; he deserted them and sought power elsewhere, to their detriment.

Gage considered seizing Adams, but he saw the possibility of a violent reaction within the province. He also did not want to make Adams a martyr and a *cause célèbre* around which the American colonies might rally. He, therefore, in the early days of his tenure as governor, apparently tried to bribe Adams into ceasing his efforts against the administration.[12] Persistent rumor at the time indicated Gage sent one of the colonels under his command to offer Adams certain "benefits as would be satisfactory" to stay out of the way for a while. Gage knew very little of Adams beyond the views of Boston loyalists, and he may have been willing to make a tentative move to test his opponent, even if the odds against success were long. An old story concludes with

Adams' warning Gage not to "insult the feelings of an exasperated people."

The ship carrying Hutchinson docked at London on Friday, July 1, and he hurried to see Lord Dartmouth. After an hour's discussion, Dartmouth insisted that Hutchinson come immediately to speak with the king, who otherwise would not be available for several days. This was the last thing on earth that Hutchinson wished to do. A man who had all his life taken an intense interest in his own personal appearance, who was always especially concerned that his clothing conformed with the current London style, now found himeslf being asked to see the king without time to change from his simple New England traveling clothes. He had a respect and admiration for the English court nobility that perhaps only an outsider can acquire, and now he was to see them all again and to talk to the king privately for the first time—but in street wear.

He was ushered into the king's private rooms, there to meet George III, who in a friendly manner for two hours asked him questions about the life and times of Massachusetts Bay, revealing in the process an abysmal lack of even the most rudimentary knowledge of his distant dominion. "What," asked the king, "gives Samuel Adams his importance?" "A great pretended zeal for liberty," Hutchinson replied, "and a most inflexible natural temper. He was the first that publicly asserted the independency of the colonies upon the kingdom."[13] They talked on, the old ex-governor and the young king, and an awed Hutchinson could not bring himself to explain what he knew to be true—that there was no hope of reconciliation in Boston. When he left, George III told Lord North, "I have seen Mr. Hutchinson, late Governor of Massachusetts, and am now well convinced they will soon submit. He owns the Boston Port Bill has been the only wise and effectual method."[14]

24

The Continental Congress

August–December 1774

It is an indispensable duty which we owe to
God, our country, ourselves and posterity, by all lawful ways and means in our power to maintain, defend
and preserve those civil and religious rights and liberties, for which many of our fathers fought, bled and
died, and to hand them down entire to future generations.

THE SUFFOLK RESOLVES, 1774

SAMUEL ADAMS WAS ABOUT TO MAKE THE LONGEST JOURNEY of his
life—300 miles south to Philadelphia for the Continental Congress—and it was with many misgivings that he prepared for his
departure. He could not refuse the appointment as a delegate, yet
he disliked leaving Boston during what he felt was a critical period. Gage would have an opportunity to rally the loyalists within
the court party, who, though scattered and demoralized, still
represented a significant potential force. They were not strong
enough to prevent a vote in the House refusing to pay for the
tea, but they had given in only after a hard battle. The merchants, defeated in the last series of town meetings, would be certain to continue their attempts to eliminate the committee of correspondence and the covenant, which they insisted would result

in the strangulation of the province. Adams was already discouraged with the poor response to nonimportation. To him the covenant was more important than the congress—and this short-sightedness was the first indication that, as Adams ranged out beyond the challenges of Massachusetts Bay politics, there was something lacking in his perspective. The congress, he thought, would be ineffectual. The delegates would talk when it was already too late for talk—and while they wasted their time, what would happen in Boston?

Adams was the key member of the newly organized Committee of Safety, the coordinating group for revolutionary operations in Massachusetts. He was also the chairman of the Donation Committee, which controlled the distribution of gifts received from sympathizers all along the Atlantic coast, giving him a powerful influence over the poor and the unemployed in Boston. At Coolidge's Tavern in Watertown on August 10 he assembled the members of these committees and many other Sons of Liberty—50 of the most radical leaders in the province—to lay out instructions for activities during his absence.[1] Most important of the plans he made was the arrangement to have Joseph Warren lead the upcoming Suffolk County convention into voting for a set of resolves defying the repressive acts and calling for a provincial congress. When approved, this document was to be sent immediately to Philadelphia for presentation to the Continental Congress.

The journey would be a period of learning and broadening. With John Adams and Thomas Cushing, Adams set out southward down the Post Road. Bowdoin, who wanted to stay by the bedside of his ailing wife, would join them later.

Adams was well aware that the delegates to the congress would represent a wide variety of views; many would be limited by the specific instructions of their colonial legislatures, and doubtless many would have ideas not entirely in consonance with his own. In fact, some had spoken of the congress as a good opportunity to effect a conciliation with the mother country—possibly through an offer to pay the damages of the "tea party," or at least by a public rejection of the lawlessness that had been a part of it. Others hoped to see an abandonment of efforts to stop importa-

tion from Britain. Many simply abhorred the thought of civil
war or violence and wanted to use the congress to open transatlantic communications and restore good relations.

Gage, confident he could measure feelings in New York and
other colonies, mirrored the thoughts of Adams when he predicted that Boston would get "little more than fair words"[2] out
of the congress. Hawley had advised John Adams to walk softly,
because of the fear in many of the other colonies that the Boston
faction would try to run things. This tactic was the one that Samuel Adams also adopted, but it did not change the very simple
and powerful point of view which he took to the congress. He
was determined to effect the union and independence of the colonies, while John Adams at this time still said that Americans
would not seek independence unless the British continued their
oppression.

The road took the delegates first to Hartford, then to Middle-
town, New Haven, and New York. At big towns and villages the
local Sons of Liberty turned out to meet the men from Massachusetts and encourage their venture, while provincial political
figures dined with the delegates and lent their advice. In these
conversations Samuel Adams discerned the differing opinions on
the value of boycotting British goods and—especially—the fear of
possible violence. There was a strong desire to protect American
rights, but little support for outright revolutionary talk. He resolved to be careful, to moderate his language, to bide his time
at the convention.

Across the ocean in England, Thomas Hutchinson at this time
was much sought after as a fresh returnee from the troubled area.
An active man who found himself deposited in an unfamiliar
place with nothing to do, he wrote of his homesickness and the
hopes he cherished of eventually returning, even if only to lay his
bones in New England. "I consider myself," he said, "only upon
an excursion from home."[3] But he was on call as the local expert
on Massachusetts—the source of the latest news—and he had audi-
ences with North, Hillsborough, Barrington, Townshend, and
his old boss, Pownall. In his conversations he proved himself still
an American, bridling at a suggestion by Lord Mansfield over

dinner that the persons causing trouble in Boston ought to be brought over to London for trial. Things would never be right, said Mansfield, until England made a few examples of these radicals. Thomas Hutchinson replied that he "wished to see examples made of British offenders in like situations first."[4] But while he defended his fellow Americans, they were not inclined to reciprocate. Accusations against him multiplied in a relentless chain. Samuel Adams' wife wrote:

> We see by the papers that the infamous Hutchinson got home safe and was well received . . . and would insult this people by endeavoring to make them believe he is now soliciting in their favor: —when at the same time I believe that the most rancorous envy and venom swell the contaminated veins of the fell tyrant.[5]

Adams was correct in his assumption that Gage would try to move in his absence. Acting under the new laws, Gage appointed Thomas Oliver lieutenant governor. (Peter Oliver, no relation, remained chief justice.) Thomas Hutchinson's two sons were made judges and Harrison Gray was continued as treasurer of the province. All of the council, formerly elected by the House, were now appointed by Gage. These changes were to Adams a confirmation that his suspicion of a plot had been correct and that, although Hutchinson was gone, there was still a tribe of people in Massachusetts that the radicals would have to fight. Adams' subordinates, however, were more capable of carrying on without him than he had assumed. The Massachusetts Superior Court opened on August 29, with Peter Oliver presiding. As soon as the room was called to business, the chairman of the grand jury announced the unanimous refusal of the 22 jurors to serve.[6] All the jurors then filed out of the court and gathered at the Exchange Tavern, where they put together a statement for the newspapers announcing that their service on a jury over which Peter Oliver presided as judge would be "betraying the just and sacred rights of our native land."

At Carpenter's Hall in Philadelphia, Adams found that he had correctly anticipated the divergencies in the congress. It was difficult even to reach informal agreement on the nature of the problem that brought them all together. When it appeared that there might be difficulty in selecting the proper clergyman to give the opening prayer, Congregationalist Adams surprised the assembly by suggesting that the Anglican Reverend Jacob Duché might read to the Congress. Duché was acceptable to all, and on September 7, amid rumors that the town of Boston was under bombardment from the cannon of British ships in the harbor, the minister read the Psalm 35.

One of the early motions of the congress was the appointment of a committee to state the rights of the colonies in general and to name the instances in which those rights had been violated. Samuel and John Adams were the Massachusetts members of this group. As they began their deliberations, Paul Revere arrived in Philadelphia, having ridden hard all the way from Boston with the piece of paper Samuel Adams was waiting for—a copy of the Suffolk Resolves. Warren had been true to his word: they were bold and forthright, calling for the establishment of provincial congresses, for holding back the collection of provincial tax money until these assemblies could be constituted, and advocating nonimportation from Great Britain and the West Indies. Over the objections of Pennsylvania's Galloway the congress adopted *in toto* the Suffolk Resolves, thus taking the first irrevocable step in the direction that Adams wanted to go. Although the movement toward independence would be hesitant and slow (nonimportation, for example, would be delayed until September 1775), the die was cast, and John Adams wrote, "This day convinced me that America will support the Massachusetts [sic], or perish with her."[7] The Suffolk Resolves arrived at just the right moment.

It was not until September 28 that Galloway was ready to present his own plan to the congress. He then, with strong and influential backing, introduced a conciliatory motion which would provide for a "Grand Council" of the colonies, an American parliament in a sense, which would serve as a subordinate legislature for American matters. The plan met with a wide initial acceptance in the hall, frightening Adams. If it passed it would stifle all impetus toward independence.

The most important contribution Samuel Adams made in

Philadelphia was his response to Galloway—his organization of a large enough group to defeat the conservative plan by one vote, opening the way to a more radical solution. Adams had won again. The course of the congress, he said, had gone as if he alone had directed it,[8] while at the same time he had been able to stay in the background.

The congress now needed a set of resolves of its own. A committee of five, including Cushing of Massachusetts and Samuel Adams' friend Richard Henry Lee of Virginia, drafted 14 articles and presented them to the assembly on October 12. The agreement called for nonimportation, nonconsumption, and nonexportation until the repeal of all the repressive American trade laws made since 1763. It also demanded the repeal of the acts closing the port of Boston. The implementation date was December 1, 1774, for cessation of imports and September 10, 1775 for exports. A revision of this document, called the Continental Association, was approved on October 20.

While this agreement was under discussion in Philadelphia, there was a new turn of events in Boston that proved the strength of the political organization Samuel Adams had created by uniting the committees of correspondence. The General Court, due to open in Salem on October 5, was canceled by General Gage at the last minute. The representatives, however, defied Gage and met on schedule in Salem, where they voted to form a provincial congress and adjourned to Concord. Adams, *in absentia*, was voted secretary of state of this congress.

In Philadelphia the Continental Congress dissolved itself, its business being done, on October 26, after resolving to meet again on May 10, 1775, "if the rights and liberties of America have not been fully restored." Many of the representatives, unable to imagine an all-out war, believed that the second congress would not be necessary. Adams knew it would be.

On his return to Boston, Adams found that his fears were justified—the Provincial Congress, meeting in Cambridge, was in the doldrums; there seemed to be nothing to talk about, and in fact the main activity was absenteeism, which Adams quickly cured by threatening to publish attendance lists in the press. He then gave the congress a sense of direction and movement by focusing on training and preparation of the Massachusetts militia and minutemen. His workers in this effort were the members of the new Committee of Safety, which in effect provided a general staff for coordination of the not so small army that would grow to 47 regiments of militia and minute men, totalling over 14,000 Massachusetts men under arms prior to April 19.[9]

In freezing weather in early February the Provincial Congress, shivering in the unheated Cambridge meetinghouse, first voted to allow wearing of hats for warmth during the session and then proceeded to elect five general officers for the army and to approve a message to the citizens of Massachusetts calling on them to "nobly defend those rights which Heaven gave and no man ought to take from us."[10] Though Hancock was president, Samuel Adams was the driving force in the Provincial Congress, amid rumors that Parliament had ordered him to be seized and carried in irons to London for trial. According to letters from Britons who were in a position to know, Otis was also to be taken—though certified insane by Hutchinson himself and under care of a guardian for more than two years—a sign of the ignorance of American affairs that existed in Parliament and the vacuum in which decisions were made.

General Gage was at first unimpressed with what he considered the rather pitiful attempts of the Massachusetts towns to improve their militia companies. "They have been training men in several townships," he said, "as they could get them in the humor to assemble."[11]

He changed his mind, however, when a number of cannon showed up at Concord and it became clear the local militias were forming a battery of horse-drawn field pieces. He was also receiving reports on the Committee of Safety, which talked of war and had turned virtually the whole town of Concord into a supply base. He was confident his Regulars could make short work of the militia bands, but he knew that artillery could not be brushed aside so easily. He had sent his columns out to investigate rumors of cannon in other places; now, under pressure from London and from the loyalists in Boston, he resolved to smash the war preparations by destroying the cannon and supplies at Concord.

The Provincial Congress adjourned at Concord on April 15, having made no attempt at reconciliation with the Crown; Gage then drew up his order for the march. Adams and Hancock, aware that Boston might be unsafe for them, had decided to wait at Lexington for a few days before departing for the May session of the Continental Congress in Philadelphia. On the following day, however, Paul Revere rode to Lexington to warn the two men that the Regulars were planning a march, possibly through Cambridge and Lexington to Concord.

Revere's information was correct; he was out on the road again on the night of April 18, only a few miles in front of the Regulars. Adams and Hancock hurried from Lexington just ahead of the British, who skirmished with the town militia, killing several, and marched on to Concord. The war of the American Revolution had begun; Samuel Adams' "glorious morning" had arrived.

Adams went on to Philadelphia for the opening of the Continental Congress on May 10. His star was then as high as ever it had been; as the leader of the Massachusetts delegation, he was the key revolutionary figure in a congress that would approve of armed resistance, would "adopt" the militia surrounding Boston and send Washington as a general to command it, and would order Massachusetts to establish its own civil government. But this was not enough for Samuel Adams, who wanted an immediate declaration of independence. "America is a great, unwieldy body," he wrote[12] after his unsuccessful campaign to convince his fellow delegates. John Adams and Elbridge Gerry were on his side, and his old friend Richard Henry Lee agreed with him. He found support from Thomas Jefferson, Patrick Henry, and others less well known, but he lacked the deep knowledge of the characters of the men around him, knowledge that had been his forte in Boston politics, and he was trying to move too fast for a group of men who also listened to John Dickenson's plan for resistance but eventual reconciliation.

In the end Samuel Adams would win the great battle that for years had consumed his every effort: not this congress, but the next, would declare American independence along the unequivocal lines that he never ceased to demand. But the uphill struggle to arrive at that point was to him a period of grim and deadly infighting, dominated by specters of fear and hatred and characterized by intrigue. The final step to independence was a vote in the congress on July 3, 1776. By the time that vote was taken, Samuel Adams had burned out all his early prestige and promise in the Congress and was a lesser figure than the Massachusetts firebrand of early May 1775. His was an unwitting but inevitable self-sacrifice, caused by his long-gathered momentum toward independence that—for all his desire to proceed with caution—propelled him like a cannonball into the sedate assembly. His precipitous manner was combined with a fanatic suspicion of the motives of any who disagreed with him, a tendency to see cabals of opposition mushrooming around him, and consequently a preference to achieve his ends by backstage manipulation—and indeed intrigue—rather than by open confrontation in the conference hall.

25

Conclusion

WHERE IN UNITED STATES POLITICAL HISTORY had there ever been times like these? Where had there ever been such a jostling of events? Many have seen the 15 years leading up to the clash of arms in Massachusetts as a kaleidoscopic jumble of individual happenings, each existing within its own vignette, isolated from the rest, each a curiosity in itself. The path to revolution was bedecked with a fantastic array of these episodes:

Otis, a "flame of fire," defies Hutchinson and Parliament over writs of assistance, as all the lawyers of Boston look on.

Thomas Hutchinson stands outside the ruins of his beautiful town house, thumbing through the muddy mass of papers that had been the manuscript of his *History of Massachusetts*.

Samuel Adams, after years of menial political jobs, rides the Stamp Act into the House of Representatives and immediately seizes the influential position as clerk of the House.

Otis paces the floor of the House, beside himself with rage over the "monkeys, pimps, and panderers" in Parliament who have demanded the circular letter be rescinded.

Adams and Otis, working far into the night, set up the columns of invective for the press of Benjamin Edes.

Otis stalks through the door of the British Coffee House, swinging his cane and looking through the dim light for the face of Robinson.

On a snowy night a line of Redcoats, hemmed in against the custom house by a violent mob, opens fire.

An exhausted Hutchinson, in the council chamber, hears Samuel Adams say, "If you can remove one regiment, then you can remove them both."

Stumbling and smelling of wine, Otis visits Hutchinson to blubber, "I meant well."

In a hushed House Adams reads a letter in which Hutchinson has called for an abridgement of English liberties.

Otis, having struggled back from insanity, reads Adams' report aloud to the town meeting and calls for a committee of correspondence.

In the South Meeting House on a rainy night Adams silences a roaring crowd only long enough to tell them, "This meeting can do nothing more."

Hutchinson for the last time looks northeastward from his hilltop home in Milton across the darkening town of Boston and the harbor's islands, knowing he will sail for England in the morning.

Given such a welter of images seemingly carried along irresistibly like flotsam spread over some great wave of historical change, it is difficult to see the importance of individual personalities, and harder still to imagine them as controlling the events. It all seems as if, even without the theory of Otis, the activism of Adams, and the unwitting complicity of Hutchinson, the confrontation with an unyielding Parliament would have happened pretty much the same anyway; the road would have led to Lexington and Concord no matter what. Such a vision, however, is deceptive. War came to the colonies—or rather they came to war —as the deadly result of a great blossoming in size, in economy, and in a spirit of unity. *But why war?* Could not the vast adjustments, the balancing, have occurred in other ways? Part of the answer lies in Boston.

In this matrix city existed the tremendous potential of several coinciding forces: the unshakeable commitment to the old Massachusetts charter, which could be interpreted to leave the colony free of any control of London; the "town meeting" style of government, which severely limited executive action of the selectmen and put all decision making on the floor of the meetinghouse; the growth of the parapolitical merchants' and mechanics' societies and the Sons of Liberty; and the rise of fledgling political parties, one "loyal" and reactionary, the other radical. These forces contributed to the drift toward Lexington, but, taken together, they were still not enough to bring war to Boston. The true catalyst, the sparkling powder train leading to the keg, can be followed in the chemistry of the interrelationship between Hutchinson and his opponents, Otis and Adams, over the span of 15 years.

When Otis mounted a brilliant attack against Crown incursions on the Massachusetts charter rights, he established the theoretical support for Boston radicalism and opened the way for the man who must be ceded undisputed first place among American political activists. Samuel Adams might have followed his father's footsteps through the Boston Caucus Club and into the House of Representatives, but he would not have had the backing of the country towns—or perhaps even of Boston—without the political philosophy that established an environment in which he was acceptable. That philosophy was created by Otis in his attack on the writs of assistance ("a law contrary to the constitution is void") and in his *Vindication* ("Kings were, and plantation governors should be, made for the good of the people"). Otis brought together the provincial towns and the capital in a loose alliance that gave him power in the House, but it was Adams who provided definitive direction to Otis' theoretical mind, using the Caucus Club and the Boston town meeting to influence the Massachusetts House and "working the political machine."

In a rough way, each had what the other lacked. Otis was an orator, a trained lawyer, a member of a trading family; Adams, who was none of these, possessed a hard-won knowledge of Boston workingmen, an entrée into the Caucus Club, and an obsession with a single idea, American independence. Otis was an idealist and a conservative who for a long time tried to maintain the supremacy of Parliament and the English constitution but who always upheld the Massachusetts charter; Adams was a pragmatic realist and a fighter who knew what changes he wanted and was willing to sacrifice whatever necessary in order to get those changes. Where Otis was creative and adaptive, Adams remained to the end of his days dogmatic and inflexible. Otis was repelled by what he saw in Adams as a willingness to bow to expediency; Adams saw Otis as a powerful theoretician but an unsteady politician who constantly required propping up.

As they grew and developed in the Boston matrix, their interaction was strong. Otis was in many ways responsible for the creation of Adams the political thinker; Adams brought Otis to the world of political manipulation. Through Adams, Otis saw the value of what now might be called "ward politics," and at the same time he showed Adams the way toward domination of the country towns. From Otis, Adams learned to couch his persuasive letters, columns, and essays in the conservative terms that were acceptable to Massachusetts farmers, but he was never the apprentice or amanuensis of Otis. From the time that Otis moved to Boston in 1750, where Adams was already writing anonymous political essays for the newspapers, a loose partnership gradually grew, expanding from town-meeting work into cooperation in the caucuses, the Merchants' Society, and the Sons of Liberty, and then into the cooperation in the General Court and the writings for the *Gazette*. The two were thrown together often and early enough to recognize each other's capacities, and a partnership of opportunity—and, to a great extent, a friendship—simply happened by degrees.

It took a long time for Samuel Adams to come to the surface of Boston politics, even though his father was a powerful figure in the caucuses and the General Court. One reason for the delayed "arrival" is that Adams is almost alone in history as a man who sincerely desired anonymity. His major writings were signed not "Adams" but "Determinatus," "Candidus," "Vindex," "Populus," "Alfred," "Valerius Poplicola," "T.Z.," "Shippen," "a Bostonian," "a Tory," "E.A.," "a Layman," "an Impartialist," "a chatterer"—even later, when he could have gained great credit by acknowledging his full opus, he would not take the trouble. The writings had done their work; that was what he wanted. He often ended his letters with the command "Burn this," and he took his own advice by consigning nearly all of his correspondence files to the flames, leaving behind a relatively small amount in the hands of others or in public print. He called no attention to himself, and although he had an undeniable instinct for power, he sought it for the furtherance of a cause. He was always willing

to let others have center stage, always humble enough to accept
help from anyone expert enough to provide it, always ready to
help young politicians on the way up (and furnish them with a
direction). He was also secretive, an intriguer who liked the de-
vious route, who hated more passionately than he loved, who saw
a black-and-white world.

Otis without Adams might have been a different man, more
ready to follow in the line of his father, accommodating to political realities, generally supporting the establishment. He was not
an intriguer, not a man attracted to factions. He was too independent to have shifted from his belief in Crown and empire,
his conservative support for the status quo, to embrace the radical cause without the influence of Samuel Adams. The two men
were much alike. Each found at Harvard a fascination for John
Locke's works; each had a father influential in Massachusetts
politics; each was a prolific writer with a deep interest in the uses
and misuses of power. And each hated Thomas Hutchinson.

Hutchinson, for all his intellect, courage, and quick wit, was
a perfect foil; it was easy to make him the star villain of the Boston melodrama. After waiting for two frustrating decades, he arrived in the governor's chair in July of 1769, three years too late
to change the course of events in Massachusetts. He can be excused if all did not go well from then on; nevertheless, there was
much he could have accomplished prior to that time that might
have given him a better chance of success. He was a man ridden
hard by inhibition. His ideas on the changing relationship of
England and America—and how both sides could adjust without
upheaval—constituted some of the most objective and constructive thinking on the subject, but he could not bring himself to
put the full weight of his name behind his convictions. It was
not appropriate, he said, for a servant of the Crown to be a part
of the affray. Thus the strength of his broad historical knowledge
of Massachusetts politics and his long practical experience in
helping to run the colony were kept out of the fight in the crucial
early period. Though he knew what was wrong, he seemed psychologically unable to convey his very accurate judgment to the
administration in England, and when he had the opportunity to
go as an embassy to London on the Sugar Act, he let the chance
escape in a Hamlet-like sequence of confrontations with Bernard.

Although he was the informal head of the court party, he did not see the need for political organization until he was already overwhelmed by the growing unity of Otis' popular party. There were opportunities to organize the Boston merchants and the conservative backcountry farmers to his side even under the pressures of the Stamp Act, but he allowed them to slip away, and when he finally brought himself to appeal to the people of Massachusetts with his addresses on the supremacy of Parliament, the province by then was only 26 months away from armed rebellion.

He never managed to deal directly with the accusation that he and the other principal members of the court party were part of a cabal that was willing to sacrifice the Massachusetts charter to further their own personal fortunes and satisfy a lust for power. Hutchinson's takeover of the post of chief justice in 1761 was seen not only as a further expansion of his long list of offices, but also as the seizure of a pivotal position for enforcing execution of the old Molasses Act; thus, when even tighter strictures came along soon after, his complicity seemed obvious. His most significant contributions to the well-being of the province, including his persuasive efforts as early as the 1740s to balance the economy and provide a solid currency, were dredged up as proof of his callous disregard for the hard-pressed common man. Unfortunately, his usual response to such accusations was to ignore them with an elitist's lofty disdain, which in the eyes of many was an indication of his inability to answer the charges.

He was the kind of conservative who believes so strongly in the governing institution that, whatever the strength of the threat to it may be, he cannot imagine a radical change; he tended to feel that, though the ship might not be on an even keel, it would right itself without help ere long. He refused to worry, and for far too long maintained an extremely superficial understanding of the activities and influence of Otis and Adams: in his view the two men were not focal points of unrest but merely dangerous incendiaries whose removal from the scene would quiet the province. When after 1765 he did begin to see the threat, he was never able to explain it to London. He was not helped by the lack of continuity occasioned by the rapid turnover of ministries, but for the most part the problem was of his own making: his alternating letters, expressing optimism one day and a foreboding pessimism the next, imposed an additional source of confusion on a Parliament already hopelessly muddled in its understanding of the American economic and political situation.

Still, without Otis and Adams, the years would have been very different for Hutchinson. There were no other radical leaders of the stature necessary to oppose him. Oxenbridge Thacher, brilliant and fiery, might have been another Otis, but he was dying of tuberculosis. Josiah Quincy, certainly eloquent and possibly equal to Thatcher in asperity and intelligence, also died young. Joseph Warren, for all his heroics, lacked stability and maturity. Benjamin Church was a fence-sitter, ready to follow the winning side. John Adams was only then beginning to blossom, and John Hancock was a lightweight, out of his class. Gridley was too old and conservative, Pratt, too loyal, Hawley, too far from Boston—there were no stand-ins waiting in the wings to give focus and direction to the fight against London.

From the perspective of the interrelationship of Otis, Adams, and Hutchinson, the turning points in the march of events from loyalty to revolution are not the crises usually mentioned (Stamp Act, Townshend Acts, "massacre," tea party, Port Bill). The first clear turn down the road to revolution was Otis' attack against the writs of assistance in 1761. When he followed this with his *Vindication* in 1762 he established the first popular doctrinal basis for the defense of the province charter and the repudiation of Parliament. Otis' early challenges set the tone of response to the Stamp Act and created the environment that brought radical Samuel Adams into the House of Representatives in 1765. The united efforts of Otis and Adams through the period of the Townshend Acts (1767–69) resulted in the destruction of the popular party on the issue of whether or not the circular letter would be rescinded. Then, with Otis gone, Adams organized the provincial committees of correspondence, which became the backbone of the resistance in Massachusetts and later in the other colonies. Adams was unable to move until the times made it possible—but to a great degree the profound shift of loyalties from the king to the provincial charter came about through the work of Otis.

Afterword

IN FEBRUARY 1775, just before the outbreak of war, Hutchinson had written to his son, Thomas, in Boston on two subjects that never were far from his mind—speculations on his eventual return to Massachusetts, and the memory of his wife, Margaret, by that time dead more than 20 years. He was still confident that, come what may, regardless of the fires of furious resentment against him that he saw sweeping through his native province, he somehow would be able to go home to live out his last years in Massachusetts. His driving ambitions were now a thing of the past; he was sixty-four; his one remaining vision, one that quieted his soul, was the prospect of returning after this period of strife to a peaceful retirement in Milton and, in the end, finding a resting place beside his wife in a family tomb there. He gave directions to his son to remove her remains from a Boston cemetery to a new tomb to be constructed in Milton.[1] The plan, he said, would be to make sure he was buried alongside the woman whose spirit had never left his side.

But these were idle dreams. It was already too late for Hutchinson to think of ever returning to Boston. The port was under siege and, when the British finally sailed away, the last loyalists would go with them. His Milton house had been seized as a barracks for militia, and the furnishings that were not carried off by looters eventually were sold at auction. His carriage was presented to George Washington for his use as commander of the army around Boston. His Garden Court Street mansion in Boston was sold, along with 18 other pieces of real estate that he owned in New England, to bolster the provincial treasuries. He was effectively erased as a figure in the political life of the new state; the only references to his name were vilifications.

John Adams later provided a view of Hutchinson's arrival in England, as seen by Bostonians. "They laughed at his manners at the levee," he said, "at his perpetual quotation of his brother Foster, searching his pockets for letters to read to the King, and the King turning away from him with his head up, etc."[2] Actually he was respected in England, and he had moments when he could feel that his efforts for the Crown had not been entirely forgotten, as when Oxford University honored him for his career as a Massachusetts judge, presenting him with the degree of Doctor Civilis Juris[3] at a formal ceremony in the presence of 2,000 interested onlookers, but the event was memorable to him primarily because of its sharp contrast with the rest of his lonely days. Ironically, the date selected for the ceremony was July 4, 1776.

Although he knew he could not go home, he still refused to see himself as an exile. He was unable to find a new life in England, where only those things which stirred memories of home seemed good to him. Little by little, however, reading newspapers and letters from Boston, talking to friends, following the course of the war, he came to realize that to think of returning to Massachusetts was futile. When the Provincial Congress published the names of the more than 300 loyalists to be banished forever from Massachusetts, his name headed the list. "The prospect of returning to America," he wrote, "is less than it has ever been. God grant me a composed mind, submissive to His will."

His daughter, Peggy, his wife's namesake, died in 1779 after a long illness, probably from tuberculosis. Her death seemed to hasten his own decline, and within a year he, too, was dead of an apparent heart attack. He was buried, according to his wishes, alongside his daughter at the church in Croydon, near London. Death spared him a final humiliation: in 1781, only a year later, his Milton house was purchased by James and Mercy Otis Warren, and thus James Otis' sister became the lady of the house that had been planned and built so lovingly for Margaret Hutchinson.[4]

The political life of James Otis was short by any standards; he arrived on the scene with the battle over the writs of assistance in 1761, and by 1769 his growing mental instability cut off his career just as he reached his peak. In that eight-year period his total published production consisted of four essays and several articles, more than half of them anonymous. Nevertheless, his words established a political doctrine with force enough to provide a large part of the ideological basis of the Revolution. He was volatile and inconsistent to the degree that he confused his own radical followers, who at times accused him of "wavering in his opinions," but his deviations were in fact insignificant. At the height of his powers he possessed a force and a magnetism that allowed him to assume a lofty disdain for mere verbal consistency for its own sake when the fate of the empire was in the balance.

After his failing mind eclipsed his career, he lived on, sometimes unaware of events around him, sometimes watching the progress of the war with interest. On his lucid days his visitors found conversation with him as challenging, stimulating, and far-ranging as it always had been, but there were also other days. His wandering mind suffered another hard blow when his only son, James, was taken prisoner by the British and died in captivity in 1777, and he seemed to slip further into a world that he alone knew and that others could divine only in part from his absent murmurings. His face grew puffy; indolence weakened his powerful frame and made him flabby.[5] His nosebleeds continued, sometimes occurring daily over long periods, but all his troubles could not keep him down; occasionally he could summon enough strength to achieve temporary recoveries. In 1778 he appeared at a Boston town meeting, spoke brilliantly, and found himself elected moderator by ecstatic fellow townsmen who never could believe that Otis would not resume his old form. It was only a short few days, however, before his goblins closed in on him again.

In the spring of 1783 he returned again to Boston, where he paid a call on John Hancock, then governor, in the council chamber where both men had seen moments that neither could ever forget. Otis chatted rationally and happily for a while, at ease, reminiscing, but then suddenly grew nervous and upset. He left, and by the time he was hurried to his brother's house across town, it was obvious that he would have to go back to the Andover farm. A week later his life ended. He was in the house of his guardians, talking calmly as an afternoon thunderstorm raged outside. There was a loud explosion as a lightning bolt struck the chimney and tore through the frame of the house to a door-post against which Otis had leaned for a moment. He fell dead without a mark on his body. Several of his friends recalled he had argued that, if one had a choice, the best way to die was to be struck by lightning.

With Hutchinson and Otis dead, Adams lived on for another two decades. He returned to the Continental Congress, where his narrow views began to be all too evident and where his tireless fanaticism, in contrast to earlier days, now served little purpose. He had been respected and feared for his abilities as a manipulator; he had been a man of action who put other men's theories to work for one overriding idea—independence. His singlemindedness made him valuable in the congress, helping to prosecute the war, and for a while he was in his element, on the attack, relentless. He bristled at the suggestion of conciliation with Britain and would not hear of the return of any of the loyalist exiles. He roasted lackadaisical army leaders with fiery criticism, not sparing even Washington, whom he supported. As victory approached, however, his limitations became less tolerable to his contemporaries in the congress and even to his fellow townsmen. It appeared that the long fight against Hutchinson and "the cabal" had rendered him useless for anything but righteous anger. He was set, inflexible. Committees had worked well to unite the Massachusetts towns against Hutchinson, and committees, rather than secretaries, he said, should control the departments of the federal government. But there was little room in the congress for his caucus-style infighting, and by 1781 he himself could see that his contribution was of little consequence. He left, not unhappy with the knowledge that his departure caused hardly a ripple. He would return to Boston, he thought, and "be useful . . . in a narrow sphere."

But even there he miscalculated. When he did begin to assert himself again in Massachusetts, it was not with that accurate sensing of the pulse of the province that had helped and guided him in earlier days. He had become an awkward obstacle, an anachronism thrust into the mainstream by his prestigious past, someone to be got around. In 1783 he ran for governor and lost; he no longer had the support of rural Massachusetts. The province he had led into the American union now did not understand him; it rejected him, thought him unimportant. He marched on, however; he had a long life yet to live and he wanted to put it to service for Massachusetts. His simple desire to serve a cause kept him going, but predictably, his inflexibility showed at every turn. He had no sympathy for the leaders of Shays' rebellion: "The man who dares rebel against the laws of a republic ought to suffer death." This was the same man who in the 1760s quoted Vattel to caution the people of Massachusetts against naming men as rebels simply because they *"do not hold out their hands to chains"* and refuse *"tamely* to suffer the strokes of arbitrary power."

His puritanism held sway as he grew older, more conservative, and increasingly religious. He began to wonder whether the people of Boston were worth saving, when the loss of virtue was obvious to him everywhere.

Voted to the post of lieutenant governor in 1789, he gained enough political strength to be elected governor the year after John Hancock died, in 1793. He served for four years as governor—longer by a few months than Thomas Hutchinson had held the position—but too much had changed. Massachusetts was now a complex and bustling commercial state and Adams, who admitted ruefully that he "never understood" the intricacies of trade, was out of his element. Politically he continued to oppose consolidation of power in a central government, a course that led him into controversies over the ratification of the Constitution; he also opposed the 1796 candidacy of John Adams for president, convinced that his cousin wanted to weaken the states in order to establish a too-powerful federal government.

After leaving the governorship in 1797, he ceased to have any further influence on local or national events, retiring to his ramshackle Boston house to live out his final years in nearly complete obscurity. He still wore the wig, buckle shoes, and cloak in the plain style of his great days of the 1770s, and to all he was a curiosity, a man of an earlier time. For nearly a decade his palsied shaking had not allowed him to write in his own hand, but he still dictated a few letters, helped by his old companion and member of the Loyal Nine, John Avery. His last days were lightened by the successes of another close friend, Thomas Jefferson, who was for Adams the symbol of all that he had aimed for in the new America. "How much I lament that time has deprived me of your aid!" wrote Jefferson in 1801 as he assumed the presidency. "It would have been a day of glory which should have called you to the first office of my administration." Whether Adams believed those words or not, they must have been a great comfort to him.

On a Sunday morning in the fall of 1803 he died. He was eighty-two, and John Adams said he had been a "weeping, helpless object of compassion for years." He died at home, trying to whisper something to his wife, some few words that she could not make out. A friend, William Bentley, tried to sum him up that day in an entry in his diary. "He was feared by his enemies," Bentley wrote, "but too secret to be loved by his friends."[6] He went on:

> He could see far into men, but not into opinions. He could be sure of himself on all occasions, and he did more by what men thought of him, than what he discovered to them. His religion and manner were from our ancestors. His politics from two maxims, rulers should have little, the people much.

Sources

Manuscript letters and writings:

Principal sources:

Adams, Samuel: New York Public Library. Most of his correspondence and essays are in *Writings of Samuel Adams* (4 vols.), ed. H. A. Cushing. New York: G. P. Putnam, 1904–1908.

Bernard, Francis: Houghton Library, Harvard College. Copies he retained of outgoing letters.

Hutchinson, Thomas: Originals in Massachusetts Archives, State House, Boston, primarily consisting of copies he retained. Typescript (by Catherine Mayo) at Massachusetts Historical Society. His later writing is collected in *Diary and Letters of Thomas Hutchinson* (2 vols.), ed. Peter O. Hutchinson. London: 1883–1886. The Egerton Manuscripts in the British Museum contain the main body of his writings, including his annotated almanac for 1770.

Otis, James: Massachusetts Historical Society and Butler Library, Columbia University. His major writings were published by Charles F. Mullett in "Some Political Writings of James Otis," *University of Missouri Studies*, Vol. IV, No. 4, 1929.

Newspapers:

Primary sources were the *Boston Gazette* and *Boston Evening Post*, both collected in the Boston Public Library, along with the *Massachusetts Spy*, *Boston News-Letter*, *Boston Post-Boy*, and *Boston Chronicle*. In the Harbottle Dorr files, Massachusetts Historical Society, Dorr has annotated and cross-referenced his contemporary collection of the *Gazette* and *Evening Post*.

Books:

Only those referred to in the notes are listed.

Adams, John. *The Works of John Adams.* 10 vols. Edited by Charles E. Adams. Boston: 1850–56.

————. *Diary and Autobiography of John Adams.* 4 vols. Edited by L. H. Butterfield. Cambridge: Harvard University Press, 1961.

Brown, Abram E. *John Hancock His Book.* Boston: Lee & Shephard, 1898.

Dickerson, Oliver M., ed. *Boston Under Military Rule, 1768–1769;* as revealed in *A Journal of the Times.* Boston: Chapman and Grimes, 1936.

Forbes, Esther. *Paul Revere and the World He Lived In.* Boston: Houghton Mifflin, 1942.

Freiberg, Malcom. *Thomas Hutchinson of Milton.* Milton: Milton Historical Society, 1971.

Frothingham, Richard. *The Life and Times of Joseph Warren.* Boston: Little, Brown, 1865.

Gage, Thomas. *Correspondence of General Thomas Gage with the Secretaries of State . . . 1763–1775.* 2 vols. Edited by Clarence E. Carter. New Haven, 1931–33.

Galvin, John R. *The Minute Men.* New York: Hawthorn, 1967.

Gordon, William. *The History of the Rise, Progress and Establishment of the Independence of the United States of America. . . .* Vol. I, 3d American edition. New York: Samuel Campbell, 1801.

Harlow, Ralph Volney. *Samuel Adams: Promoter of the American Revolution; A Study in Psychology and Politics.* New York: H. Holt, 1923.

Hosmer, James K. *Samuel Adams.* Boston: Houghton Mifflin, 1891.

————. *The Life of Thomas Hutchinson.* Boston: Houghton Mifflin, 1896.

Hutchinson, Thomas. *The History of the Colony and Province of Massachusetts Bay.* 3 vols. Edited by Lawrence S. Mayo. Cambridge: Harvard, 1936.

Jensen, Merrill. *The Founding of a Nation: A History of the American Revolution 1763–1776.* New York: Oxford University Press, 1968.

Jensen, Merrill, ed. *Tracts of the American Revolution 1763–1776.* New York: Bobbs-Merrill, 1967.

Journals of the House of Representatives of Massachusetts 1760–1761. Boston: Massachusetts Historical Society.

Lincoln, William, ed. *Journals of Each Provincial Congress of Massachusetts 1774–1775 and of the Committee of Safety.* Boston: Dutton & Wentworth, 1838.

Miller, John C. *Sam Adams: Pioneer in Propaganda.* Boston: Little, Brown, 1936.

Morgan, Edmund S. and Helen M. *The Stamp Act Crisis.* Chapel Hill: University of North Carolina Press, 1953.

Oliver, Peter. *Peter Oliver's Origin and Progress of the American Rebellion: A Tory View.* Edited by Douglas Adair and John A. Schutz. San Marino, California: Huntington Library, 1961.

Quincy, Josiah. *Reports of Cases Argued and Adjudged in the Superior Court of Judicature of the Province of Massachusetts Bay Between 1761–1772.* Edited by Samuel M. Quincy. Boston: Little, Brown, 1865.

Rowe, John. *Letters & Diary of John Rowe, Merchant 1759–1762, 1764–1779.* Edited by Anne Rowe Cunningham. Boston: Harvard University Press, 1903.

Schlesinger, Arthur M. *The Colonial Merchants and the American Revolution, 1763–1776.* New York: Columbia University Press, 1918.

Shaw, Charles, Esq. *A Topographical and Historical Description of Boston. . . .* Boston: Oliver Spear, 1871.

Shipton, Clifford K. "James Otis." In *Sibley's Harvard Graduates.* Vol. 11, pp. 247–287. Boston: 1960.

Town Records. *A Report of the Record Commissioners of the City of Boston, Containing the Boston Town Records, 1770 Through 1777.* Boston: Rockwell and Churchill, 1887.

Tudor, Thomas. *The Life of James Otis.* Boston: 1823.

Waters, John. *The Otis Family in Provincial and Revolutionary Massachusetts.* Chapel Hill: University of North Carolina Press, 1968.

Wells, William. *The Life and Public Services of Samuel Adams.* 3 vols. Boston: 1880.

Zobel, Hiller B. *The Boston Massacre.* New York: Norton, 1970.

Notes

Abbreviations: B: Bernard; JA: John Adams; JO: James Otis; SA: Samuel Adams; TH: Thomas Hutchinson; *BG: Boston Gazette; BEP: Boston Evening Post.* A question mark indicates recipient of a letter is unknown.

Introduction

1. TH, *Diary*, I: 46.
2. Oliver, p. 36.
3. JA, *Diary*, II: 351.

Chapter 1

1. Shaw, pp. 78, 119.
2. Bernard papers, 18 Mar. 60.
3. He was transferred to South Carolina, but he gave up that post without occupying it and returned to England.
4. Frothingham, *Warren*, p. 29.
5. JA, *Works*, II: 67.
6. JA, *Works*, X: 263, 275.
7. Sibley's, XI: 249.
8. Waters, *passim.*
9. *BG*, 4 Apr. 65.
10. Memo by Colonel James Otis in the Otis family mss., noted in Waters, p. 105.
11. JA, *Works*, X: 286.
12. TH, *Diary*, I: 65.
13. *BG*, 11 Apr. 63.
14. B to Parrington, 28 Aug. 61.

15. B to Halifax, 29 Sep. 60. Bernard promised to explain in a follow-
    ing letter his reasons for appointing TH, but apparently never
    wrote that letter.
16. B to Shelburne, 22 Dec. 66; TH, *Diary*, p. 165.
17. B to Shelburne, 22 Dec. 66; *BG*, 4 Apr. 63.

Chapter 2

1. TH, *Hist.*, III: 65.
2. Quincy, *Reports*, p. 556.
3. JA, *Works*, II: 522; *Mass. Spy*, 29 Apr. 73; JA, *Diary*, I: 83; *Mass.
   Civil List*, p. 70.
4. JA, *Diary*, I: 83.
5. JA, *Works*, X: 246.
6. TH to Conway, 1 Oct. 65.
7. TH, *Hist.*, III: 120n.

Chapter 3

1. TH, *Hist.*, III: 120.
2. B to Pownall, 20 Aug. 61.
3. Quincy, *Reports*, p. 57.
4. *Ibid.*, p. 56.
5. *House Journal*, 28 Nov. 61.
6. TH to ?, 14 Dec. 60.
7. *BEP*, 4 & 11 Jan. 62; TH, *Hist.*, III: 72.
8. TH, *Hist.*, III: 72; B to Lords of Trade, 12 Apr. 62.
9. B to Lords of Trade, 8 Apr. 63.
10. *House Journal*, 6 Mar. 62.
11. TH to Bollan, 6 Mar. 62.

Chapter 4

1. JA, *Diary*, VI: 226n.
2. Col. Otis to Joseph Otis, 30 May 62.
3. *House Journal*, 8 Sep. 62.
4. Otis, *Vindication, passim* (in Mullett); TH, *Hist.*, III: 71.
5. Shipton, pp. 257–58, notes that to the ordinary reader "*Vindication* came as a religious revelation."

Chapter 5

1. *BG*, 11 Jan. 62.
2. B to Jackson, 1 Feb., 21 Feb. 63.

3. *BG,* 31 Jan. 63.
4. TH to ?, 14 Feb. 63.
5. *BG,* 21 Feb. 63.
6. *BG,* 28 Feb. 63.
7. *BEP,* 7 Mar. 63.
8. Samuel Otis to Joseph Warren, 8 Mar. 63.
9. *BEP,* 21 Mar. 63.
10. *BG* and *BEP,* 21 Mar. 63; *BEP,* 4 Apr. 63.
11. *BEP,* 4 Apr. 63.
12. *BG,* 11 Apr. 63.
13. Schlesinger, pp. 59-60.
14. TH to Stiles, 4 Jul. 64.

Chapter 6

1. *BEP,* 20 Jun. 63.
2. B to Jackson, 8 Jun. 63.
3. *Ibid.*
4. *BG,* 11 Jul. 63.
5. *BG,* 15 Aug. 63.
6. TH to Jackson, 3 Aug. 63.
7. *Town Records,* p. 8.
8. *Town Records,* p. 92; *BEP,* 11 Jul., 12 Sep. 63; *BG,* 11, 19 Jul. 63.
9. B to Jackson, 7 Jan. 64.
10. *House Journal,* 1 Feb. 64; B to Jackson, 2 Feb. 64.
11. TH to Halifax, 3 Feb. 64; TH to Lords of Trade, 8 Feb. 64.
12. JA, *Works,* X: 295–96.
13. Morgan, p. 26; Jensen, p. 48.
14. *Rights, passim* (in Mullett).
15. *Town Records,* pp. 120–22.
16. B to Lords of Trade, 29 Jun. 64.
17. B to Pownall, 2 Aug. 64.
18. TH to Jackson, 23 Jul. 64.

Chapter 7

1. *House Journal,* 18 Oct. 64.
2. TH to Bollan, 7 Nov. 64.
3. TH to Jackson, 5 Nov. 64; TH to Bollan, 4 Mar. 65; TH to Cheseborough, 16 Mar. 65.
4. Dorr, *BEP,* 11 Mar. 65.
5. TH to Jackson, Nov. 64.

6. JO to Col. Otis, Dec. 64.
7. Schlesinger, p. 57.
8. Quincy, *Reports,* p. 102.
9. *House Journal,* 1 Feb., 8 Mar. 65.
10. JA, *Works,* X: 296.
11. *BG,* 6 May 65.
12. JA, *Works,* X: 296.

Chapter 8

1. TH to ?, 9 Apr. 65.
2. Gordon, I: 119–20.
3. TH to Loudoun, 10 Nov. 65.
4. TH, *Hist.,* III: 119n; JA, *Works,* X: 286.
5. JO, *Considerations, passim* (in Mullett).

Chapter 9

1. TH, *Hist.,* III: 87.
2. TH to ?, 16 Aug. 65.
3. Rowe, p. 89; JA, *Diary,* I: 259–61.
4. TH to ?, 16 Aug. 65.
5. JA, *Diary,* I: 259–60.
6. TH, *Hist.,* III: 88.
7. TH to ?, 16 and 26 Aug. 65.
8. B to Pownall, 18 Aug. 65.
9. B to Jackson, 24 Aug. 65.
10. The accounts of the riot are taken from B to Gage, 27 Aug. 65; TH, *Diary,* II: 359; TH to Jackson, 29 Aug. 65; TH to Pownall, 31 Aug. 65; B. to Halifax, 31 Aug. 65.
11. TH, *Diary,* II: 359.
12. Quincy, *Reports,* p. 170.
13. Gordon, I: 123–25.
14. TH to Conway, 1 Oct. 65.
15. TH to Bernard, 6 Aug. 71.
16. Oliver, p. 52.

Chapter 10

1. TH to ?, 12 Sep. 65.
2. B to Jackson, 10 Sep. 65.

3. *Town Records,* p. 156.
4. B to Conway, 25 Nov. 65.
5. TH, *Hist.,* III: 335.
6. B to Jackson, 27 Sep. 65.
7. Morgan, p. 106.
8. Gordon, I: 121.
9. *BG,* 4 Nov. 65.
10. B to Pownall, 19 Oct. 65.
11. B to Pownall, 5 Nov. 65.
12. TH to Franklin, 27 Oct. 65.
13. TH to Franklin, 18 Nov. 65.
14. TH, *Hist.,* III: 341.
15. SA, *Writings,* I: 23.
16. *BEP,* 4 Nov. 65.
17. TH, *Hist.,* III: 96.
18. Morgan, pp. 135ff.
19. JA, *Diary,* I: 267; Quincy, *Reports,* pp. 202–09.
20. *Town Records,* p. 160.
21. JA, *Diary,* I: 272.

Chapter 11

1. *BG,* 16 Dec. 65.
2. *BG,* 30 Dec. 65.
3. SA to DeBerdt, 21 Dec. 65.
4. *BG,* 30 Dec. 65.
5. TH to Franklin, 1 Jan. 66.
6. Col. Otis to Joseph Otis, 4 Feb. 66.
7. B to Conway, 25 Feb. 66.
8. TH to ?, 27 Feb. 66.
9. JO to Col. Otis, 8 Jan. 66.
10. B to Conway, 25 Jan. 66.
11. *BG,* 20 Jan. 66.
12. *BG,* 12 Jan. 66.
13. Morgan, p. 142.
14. *BG,* 27 Jan. 66.
15. TH to ?, 27 Feb. 66; TH to Pownall, 8 Mar. 66; B to Lords of Trade, 10 Mar. 66.
16. TH to Bollan (not sent) about 25 Dec. 65.
17. Quincy, *Reports,* p. 213.
18. JA, *Diary,* I: 305.
19. TH to ?, 26 Mar. 66.

20. *Ibid.*
21. JO to Mercy Warren, MHSC LXXII: 2, quoted in Shipton, p. 267.
22. TH to TH Jr, 29 May 66.
23. *BG,* 31 Mar. 66; *BEP,* 31 Mar. 66.
24. TH to TH Jr, 14 Apr. 66.
25. Rowe, 13 Apr. 66.
26. TH to Jackson, 21 Apr. 66.
27. *Town Records,* pp. 175–76.
28. *BG,* 19 May 66.
29. *BEP,* 26 May 66.

Chapter 12

1. *BEP,* 28 Apr., 5 May 66.
2. *BEP,* 31 Mar. 66.
3. *BEP,* 19 May 66.
4. TH to TH Jr, 29 May 66.
5. SA, *Writings,* I: 84–85.
6. *Ibid.,* p. 88.
7. *BEP,* 9 Jun. 66.
8. Samuel Otis to Joseph Otis, 17 Jun. 66.
9. *BEP,* 23 Jun. 66.
10. *BEP,* 17 Nov. 66.
11. TH to Pownall, 8 Dec. 66.
12. P. Oliver to TH, 8 Dec. 66.
13. TH to ?, 7 Nov. 66.
14. SA, *Writings,* I: 109.
15. *House Journal,* 10 Feb. 66.
16. B to Jackson, 9 May 67.
17. TH to Mauduit, 6 Jun. 67; TH to Bollan, 2 Jun. 67.
18. B to Shelburne, 30 May 67.
19. B to Jackson, 30 Jun. 67.

Chapter 13

1. *BG,* 10 Sep. 67.
2. Hancock, *His Book,* p. 142.
3. *BEP,* 23 Nov. 67; *BG,* 30 Nov. 67.
4. B to Shelburne, 21 Nov. 67.
5. B to Barrington, 20 Feb. 68.
6. B to Barrington, 20 Feb. 68.

7. TH to Pownall, 23 Feb. 68.
8. B to Jackson, 20 Feb. 68.
9. TH to ?, 17 Feb. 68.
10. *BG,* 29 Feb. 68 (Dorr marked his copy "Dr Warren"); Frothingham, *Warren,* pp. 40–41.
11. B to Shelburne, 5 Mar. 68.
12. TH to Nathaniel Rogers, 26 Mar. 68.
13. B to Hillsborough, 4 Mar. 68.
14. Frothingham, *Warren,* p. 54.
15. TH to ?, 4 Jun. 68; B to Pownall, 30 May 68.
16. TH to ?, 26 May 68; TH to Nathaniel Rogers, 31 May 68; TH to ?, 4 Jun. 68; TH to Pownall, 7 Jun. 68.

Chapter 14

1. TH to Richard Jackson, 16 Jun. 68; Frothingham, *Warren,* pp. 59–60; B to Hillsborough, 11 Jun. 68.
2. *Court Records,* p. 254; TH, *Hist.,* III: 139n.
3. B to Hillsborough, 16 Jun. 68.
4. SA, *Works,* I: 421.
5. TH to Richard Jackson, 16 Jun. 68 and 14 Jul. 68.
6. Rowe, p. 166.
7. *Town Records,* pp. 258–59.

Chapter 15

1. *BG,* 20 Jun. 68.
2. B to Hillsborough, 9 Sep. 68.
3. B to Hillsborough, 25 Jun. 68.
4. B to Hillsborough, 1 Jul. 68.
5. *BG,* 18 Jul. 68.
6. *BG,* 4 Jul. 68.
7. B to ?, 9 Jul. 68.
8. B to Hillsborough, 9 Sep. 68.
9. TH to Bollan, 14 Jul. 68.
10. TH to Grant, 27 Jul. 68.
11. TH to ?, 27 Jul. 68.
12. B to Hillsborough, 30 Jul. 68.
13. Frothingham, *Warren,* p. 73.
14. *BG,* 8 Aug. 68.
15. Rowe, p. 171.

16. *BG,* 5 Sep. 68.
17. B to Hillsborough, 16 Sep. 68.
18. *Ibid.*
19. Frothingham, *Warren,* p. 83.
20. *BG,* 19 Sep. 68.
21. B to Hillsborough, 16 Sep. 68.
22. Frothingham, *Warren,* p. 93; Gordon, I: 165; B to Hillsborough, 27 Sep. 68.
23. B to Hillsborough, 26 Sep. 68.
24. TH to Bollan, 1 Nov. 68.
25. B to Lawrence Monk, 23 Dec. 68.
26. JO to Arthur Jones, Nov. 68 (Tudor, p. 35).
27. Dickerson, *passim.*
28. TH to Mauduit, 5 Dec. 68.
29. *BG,* 12 Dec. 68.
30. TH to ?, 8 Dec. 68.

Chapter 16

1. TH to Whately, 20 Jan. 69.
2. "Shippen" in *BG,* 30 Jan. 69.
3. SA, Petition to the town, 13 Mar. 69 (SA Papers, NYPL).
4. *Town Records,* p. 202.
5. *Ibid.,* p. 272.
6. SA, *Writings,* I: 336.
7. Tudor, p. 356.
8. *BG,* 3 Jul. 69.
9. *BG,* 17 Jul. 69.
10. B to Hillsborough, 25 Jul. 69.
11. TH, *Hist.,* III: 171; *BG,* 4 Sep. 69.
12. *BG,* 10 Jul. 69.
13. *BG,* 7 Aug. 69.
14. TH to B, 8 Aug. 69.
15. TH to B, 26 Aug. 69.
16. *Boston Chronicle,* 11 Sep. 69.
17. *BG,* 4 Sep. 69.
18. JA, *Diary,* VI: 342.
19. TH to B, 5 Sep. 69.
20. *BG,* 4 Sep. 69.
21. Morgan, p. 134.
22. JA, *Diary,* VI: 343.

23. Rowe, p. 191.
24. TH to MacKay, 11 Sep. 69.
25. SA, *Writings*, I: 381–82.
26. *Ibid.*, p. 386.
27. TH to Pownall, 26 Sep. 69.
28. TH to B, 20 Sep. 69.
29. SA, *Writings*, I: 424.
30. TH to B, 5 Oct. 69.
31. TH to B, Nov. 69.
32. JA, *Diary*, I: 348.

Chapter 17

1. *BG*, 8 Jan. 70.
2. TH to B, 10 Jan. 70.
3. TH to ?, 9 Jan. 70.
4. TH to B, 18 Feb. 70.
5. *Boston News-Letter*, 12 Dec. 70.
6. *BG*, 24 Sep. 70.
7. *BG*, 12 Mar. 70.
8. JA, *Works*, X: 251.
9. TH, *Hist.*, III: 199.
10. *BG*, 24 Sep. 70.
11. TH to Hillsborough, Mar. 70.
12. *BG*, 29 Sep. 70.
13. *BG*, 12 Mar. 70.
14. *BG*, 24 Sep. 70.
15. Frothingham, *Warren*, p. 145.
16. TH, Fragment of a letter, 1770.
17. TH to B, 25 Mar. 70.
18. Jensen, *Tracts*, p. 219.
19. Hillsborough to TH, 9 Nov. 68.
20. TH to B, 18, 22, 25 Mar. 70.

Chapter 18

1. TH, *Hist.*, III: 210.
2. *BG*, 21 May 70.
3. TH to B, 11 May 70.
4. TH to B, 22 May 70.
5. TH to R. Wilson, 11 May 70.

6. *BG,* 4 Jun. 70.

7. TH to B, 1 Jun. 70.

8. *BG,* 25 Jun. 70.

9. TH to B, 26 Jul. 70.

10. TH to Pownall, 8 Jun. 70.

11. TH to MacKay, 24 Jul. 70.

12. TH, *Almanac,* 11 Aug. 70.

13. TH to Parker, 26 Aug. 70.

14. TH to B, 28 Sep. 70.

15. TH to B, 15 Sep. 70.

16. SA to Sayre, 16 Nov. 70.

17. TH to B, 30 Nov. 70.

18. Miller, p. 223.

19. SA, *Writings,* II: 58.

20. TH to Jackson, 27 Dec. 70.

21. TH to B, 26 Dec. 70.

22. TH to Hillsborough, Dec. 70.

23. TH to Mauduit, 19 Dec. 70.

24. Paine papers, 2 Dec. 70. Quoted in Zobel, p. 281.

25. Rowe, p. 212.

26. TH to Hillsborough, 22 Jan. 71.

27. *Ibid.*

28. TH to MacKay, 3 Feb. 71.

29. *BG,* 11 Mar. 71.

30. TH to B, 23 Apr. 71; TH to Pownall, 18 Apr. 71.

31. SA to A. Lee, 19 Apr. 71.

32. SA to A. Lee, 31 Jul. 71.

33. JA, *Diary,* II: 11.

34. *Ibid.,* p. 8.

35. TH to B, 10 May 71.

36. TH, *Hist.,* III: 243–44; TH to ?, 5 Jun. 71.

37. TH to Whately, 24 May 71.

38. JA, *Diary,* II: 14.

Chapter 19

1. *BG,* 10 Jun. 71.

2. SA to Franklin, 29 Jun. 71.

3. TH to Pownall, Jul. 71. At this time, unknown to Adams, Dabney Carr of the Virginia House of Burgesses also suggested a union of American colonies by means of committees of correspondence.

4. SA to A. Lee, 27 Sep. 71.

5. JA, *Diary,* II: 34–35.

6. SA, *Writings,* II: 197.

7. *Ibid.,* p. 211.

8. *Ibid.,* p. 221.

9. *BG,* 30 Sep. 71.

10. TH to Pownall, 23 Sep. 71.

11. JA, *Diary,* II: 49.

12. JA, *Diary,* II: 50.

13. TH to Pownall, 20 Sep. 71.

14. TH to B, 12 Nov. 71.

15. *BG,* 14 Oct. 71.

16. TH to Pownall, 17 Oct. 71.

17. *BG,* 11 Nov. 71.

18. TH, *Hist.,* III: 249. JA, Legal Papers I, 160.

19. TH to B, 3 Dec. 71. It was Ezekial Russell, editor of *The Censor,* which ran until May 1772.

20. Miller, p. 126.

21. TH to J. Hutchinson, 14 Feb. 72.

22. JA, *Diary,* III: 290–91.

23. SA, *Writings,* II: 332–37.

24. TH to ?, 27 May 72.

25. *BG,* 5 Oct. 72.

26. JA, *Diary,* II: 64–66.

27. SA, *Writings,* II: 341.

28. SA, *Writings,* II: 348n.

29. Schlesinger, p. 257.

30. Frothingham, *Warren,* p. 206.

31. SA, *Writings,* II: 351–59.

32. *BG,* 14 Dec. 72.

33. TH, *Hist.,* III: 265n; *BG,* Feb. 73; Galvin, 49–51.

34. Frothingham, *Warren,* p. 212.

35. Hosmer, *Hutchinson,* p. 238.

Chapter 20

1. TH to Gambier, 19 Feb. 73.

2. TH to Montague, 22 Feb. 73.

3. *BG,* 11 Jan. 73.

4. Frothingham, *Warren,* pp. 222–23.

5. *Ibid.;* TH, *Hist.,* III: 269.

6. SA, *Writings,* II: 401–26.
7. *Ibid.,* p. 420.
8. *Ibid.,* p. 425.
9. *BG,* 22 Feb. 73.
10. SA, *Writings,* II: 431–54.
11. *Ibid.,* p. 454.
12. TH to Dartmouth, 6 Mar. 73.
13. Wells, II: 30.
14. TH to Gage, 7 Mar. 73.
15. JA, *Diary,* 4 Mar. 73.
16. TH to B, 10 Mar. 73.
17. SA to A. Lee, 9 Apr. 73.

Chapter 21

1. SA to A. Lee, quoted in Wells, II: 74.
2. JA, *Diary,* II: 79–80.
3. TH to Whately, 20 Jan. 69; TH, *Hist.,* III: 293. See opening of Chapter 16, above.
4. JA, *Diary,* III: 315.
5. TH, *Hist.,* III: 397.
6. TH, *Hist.,* III: 282.
7. TH to B, 29 Jun. 73.
8. TH to Smith, 28 Jun. 73.
9. Hosmer, *Hutchinson,* p. 440.
10. SA, *Writings,* III: 45–48.
11. TH to B, 29 Jun. 73.
12. Hosmer, *Hutchinson,* p. 290.

Chapter 22

1. TH to Dartmouth, 6 Sep. 73.
2. TH to J. Pownall, 8 Sep. 73.
3. Schlesinger, p. 264.
4. *Ibid.,* p. 275.
5. Rowe, pp. 252–53.
6. TH to Dartmouth, 9 Oct. 73.
7. TH to Aryon, 21 Nov. 73.
8. TH to Dartmouth, 2 Dec. 73.
9. TH to Palmer, 9 Dec. 73.
10. TH to Dartmouth, 14 Dec. 73.
11. TH to Mauduit, Dec. 73.

Chapter 23

1. *BG*, 7 Feb. 74.
2. Samuel Otis to Joseph Otis, 4 Jun. 74.
3. JA, *Works*, X: 240.
4. TH, *Hist.*, III: 446.
5. JA, *Diary*, II: 95.
6. Frothingham, *Warren*, p. 295 (JA, *Works*, IX: 337).
7. Rowe, p. 269.
8. SA, *Writings*, III: 109.
9. Rowe, p. 270.
10. Schlesinger, pp. 327ff.
11. Rowe, pp. 272–73.
12. Wells, II: 193.
13. TH, *Diary*, I: 157ff.
14. Hosmer, p. 326n.

Chapter 24

1. JA, *Diary*, II: 97.
2. Schlesinger, p. 395.
3. TH, *Diary*, I: 231.
4. *Ibid.*, p. 29.
5. Elizabeth to SA, 12 Sep. 74.
6. *BG*, 5 Sep. 74.
7. Wells, I: 212.
8. Lovell to Quincy, 28 Oct. 74; in Wells, II: 245.
9. Galvin, pp. 141–43.
10. *Journals of Prov. Congress*, p. 93.
11. Gage, *Corresp.*, I: 392.
12. SA to Elizabeth, 17 and 18 Jun. 1775.

Afterword

1. TH to TH Jr., 22 Feb. 75.
2. JA, *Works*, X: 262.
3. Hosmer, pp. 337–38.
4. Freiberg, p. 17.
5. Sibley's, p. 286.
6. Bentley's diary, 3 Oct. 1803, in Harlow, p. 356.

INDEX